Twisting Throttle Australia

Mike Hyde

HarperCollins*Publishers*

National Library of New Zealand Cataloguing-in-Publication Data

Hyde, Mike, 1956-
Twisting throttle Australia / Mike Hyde.
ISBN 978-1-8695-0660-5
1. Hyde, Mike, 1956—Travel—Australia. 2. Motorcycle
touring—Australia. 3. Australia—Description and travel. I. Title.
919.404—dc 22

First published 2007
HarperCollins*Publishers (New Zealand) Limited*
P.O. Box 1, Auckland

ISBN (10-digit): 1 86950 660 X
ISBN (13-digit): 978 1 86950 660 5
Cover design by Matt Stanton
Cover photograph by Mike Hyde
Internal text design and typesetting by Springfield West
Printed by Griffin Press, Australia.

79gsm Bulky Paperback used by HarperCollins*Publishers*, is a natural, recyclable product
made from wood grown in a combination of sustainable plantation and regrowth forests.
It also contains up to a 20% portion of recycled fibre. The manufacturing processes
confrom to the environmental regulations in Tasmania the place of manufacture.

Dedication

For John 'Hutch' Hutcheon.

Hutch passed away in July 2006. He was a stalwart
of the Dust Devils motorcycle club and loved his
biking. During his last weeks he received the daily
logs and photos off my website. His wife Dorothy
reckons that he would have been, in spirit, along for
the ride too. It was his sort of adventure.

Contents

Preface

THE CABIN LIGHTS are dimmed as most passengers around me are dozing. I'm annoying my neighbour — whom I only know anonymously as 28B and whose head is lolling closer to my shoulder by the minute — by having my reading light on as I tap away on the laptop. It's 6.30 a.m. and we're two hours away from landing in Sydney where it is 4.30 a.m. Aircraft passenger protocol says I should unselfishly switch off my light, snuggle down into my economy seat and pretend to snooze. There is every chance I would emerge from such half-slumber feeling more grotty, more tired and, uppermost in my mind right now, closer than I really want to be to 28B. Besides, I'm too excited to sleep. This is a big day.

What is it about aircraft seats? You are imprisoned so close to your fellow passengers that your normal personal space shrinks beyond society's norms. If this were a bus, seat 28B's head wouldn't be lolling on my shoulder as it is now. All I know about my companion is she's Asian and travelling on her own. I know that last fact because 28A — the prized window seat and presumably where any partner would be sitting — is empty. For the flight to Sydney that makes us as good as married.

I was the last person to board the plane an hour ago, and here I am in seat 28C having just wound the clock back two hours and reliving 4.30 a.m. again. The cabin attendant, with not a lot on his hands, is a Virago motorcycle rider, so I'm looking forward to some special attention. I haven't been upgraded to First Class yet, but I should be in line to hand around the sweets closer to landing. I'm racking my brain as to what a Virago is. I suspect it's a Yamaha, but that's the thing about bike riders shooting the breeze with each other: you're expected to know the specs of every motorcycle ever invented. It goes with the territory and your ego cannot yield to any hint that you have no idea what a Breva 750, a Tuono 1000 or a Rocket III Classic is — or even which company makes it. The cabin guy, Simon, noticed my Suzuki wallpaper on the laptop, squatted down by my aisle seat and we're chatting about Viragos. I throw out questions about torque, heated grips, V-twins and raked-out forks. He slips me two Cokes free of charge. It is like a mile-high club of bike riders and this is the first of countless conversations I will have in Australia where I will carry off my contribution having no idea what is being talked about. I ultimately come to appreciate this as a unique social skill.

The rest of the morning is a whirlwind of airport processing. Plane lands. People get off. Line up for Customs. I'm asked, 'So where are you spending your first night, sir?' 'Don't know.' 'Why is that, sir?' 'I'm travelling around on a motorbike.' 'Welcome to Australia, Mr Throttle.'

This is a story about my motorcycle ride around the edge of Australia. It took five weeks and I rode 17,350 kilometres before I found myself starting the second lap. My companions were my Suzuki V-Strom 1000-cc bike, an iPod with 492 songs that I eventually came to detest, a GPS that kept me pointing anti-clockwise, and my laptop. Each night I was — and I lapse into Australian jargon here — stuffed. That means I was very tired, but, before I lapsed into unconsciousness,

I tapped out my day's log while the events were still fresh in my mind. This book is a reproduction of those logs. You may not learn much about Australia, its history, attractions or geography. (*Lonely Planet* is good for that.) My story is of a journey and what happened on that journey. I was, at times, hot, cold, bored, excited, tired, fresh, happy, miserable, lucky and unfortunate. But I made it around, although not without incident. At one point in Northern Territory I chatted to a fly which rode in my helmet for 95 kilometres. This is a story of solitude in a very, very big place.

Chapter 1

The map shows a route around Australia with the following labelled locations: Darwin, Katherine, Mataranka, Turkey Creek, Croydon, Cairns, Broome, Threeways, Mt Isa, Mackay, Karratha, Overlander, Gold Coast, Kalgoorlie, Ceduna, Walcha, Perth, Port Wakefield, Madura, Goulburn, Sydney, Jerramungup, Mt Gambier, Cann River, Melbourne, St Helens, Hobart.

Sydney–Walcha

Day's ride: 416 kilometres.
Journey to date: 416 kilometres.

AND SO THE journey began. I went outside the terminal at Sydney Airport and turned right towards the taxi stand. In doing so, I travelled the first 10 of 17 million metres, or 17,000 kilometres; that is the distance around the edge of Australia.

I nudged up to the head of the queue at the taxi rank. An Indian guy got out of his car and put my bag into the boot. 'Where to mate?' he asked in an Aussie twang, and I was stumped by the juxtaposition of skin colour and slang. I gave him the address of the freight depot where the bike was ready to be picked up. The depot is in the wider airport complex and a few kilometres away. Of all the fares the taxi guy could have got, he had drawn the shortest taxi ride possible from the airport. With a family to clothe and feed, he could only answer me one way. 'P*** off, mate. I'm not doin' that.'

'Didn't think you blokes could refuse a fare.' This was me slipping in some Aussie jargon hoping for some empathetic cooperation.

'Sorry, mate, try walkin' it.' He unloaded my bag onto the pavement and drove off with the next in the line. I found myself wishing his fare was seat 28B and that her head was now lolling on his shoulder.

The exact starting point of my ride was outside Luna Park, under the shadow of Sydney Harbour Bridge. When I came back in five weeks' time, all I would have to do would be to ride over the bridge and the two ends of the dotted line would join up. The slight flaw with my starting-line selection was that it was a tourist trap. Joggers, families out for a Saturday-morning stroll along the waterfront, Luna Park visitors and customers of a nearby outdoor café swarmed around the patch of pavement where I was illegally parked. I set up my tripod, clicked the time-delay shutter and sprinted back, in full riding gear, to the bike on its stand. I had to clamber up, balance on the pegs and wave in time for the photo to be taken. I then clambered down, walked back to the camera and tripod and checked the photo's quality. I had to do this repeatedly, because that's when I would notice what had moved into the background of the shot. A couple with a pram, two teenagers roller-blading, a dog defecating against my tyre. The iconic photo had to be perfect, empty of other people, so I tried and tried again. It was like attempting a pigeon-free shot in Trafalgar Square. It kept the café customers amused, no doubt, and I all but heard a muted cheer go up from them when finally I had a window of 12 seconds to myself. With a satisfying click the photo was taken.

And so I stood there under the Harbour Bridge, sweaty, flushed and wondering which direction to go. By that I don't mean how to find the on-ramp to the freeway; rather which way to ride around Australia. It's a fair enough question. Clockwise or anti-clockwise? Did it matter? One way I'd be leaning the bike over to the left a lot more, and vice versa if I headed the other way. To the south lay Victoria, Tasmania, fan heaters, hot chocolate, rain, black ice and logging trucks. To the north lay Queensland, warmth, watermelon, no gloves, sunshine and quiet roads. I pointed my wheel to the north, kicked it into gear and twisted throttle.

For my first day's ride I was joined by two mates from Sydney, Steve and Pete. These two rode BMWs and knew the best route out of Sydney. They also knew the best pie shop in New South Wales. It was worth tagging along with them. We mounted up and rode onto the freeway, which surges up the coast as far as Newcastle where it turns into the Pacific Highway thereafter, all the way to Brisbane. 'The Pacific? Nah, mate,' my guides scoffed, 'That's for tourists. We'll take you the back way.' I tail-gated the two Sydneysiders as the freeway sliced its way through the suburbs of North Sydney. It was impossible to determine where the city finished as the miles rolled by and my hypertension at finally being on the road evaporated. I say hyper-tension because earlier that morning, as I methodically packed up the bike, I was racked by a sense of negativity. Bizarrely, the same feeling would crop up again on the final day of the journey. I can only put it down to nerves. I was convinced that my first puncture would happen 50 kilometres out of Sydney; that I'd skid on diesel at my first refuelling stop; that I'd get food poisoning from my first chicken burger. But that irrationality switched off like a light as I sped past the Gosford freeway exit, and I can only put its disappearance down to a heart-warming interaction with my first Australian fellow motorist. This is what happened.

A white Holden Commodore and I had been paralleling each other for miles as he sat in the fast lane at 115 km/h, and I occupied the neighbouring middle lane doing exactly the same speed. I felt a bond growing and can, even today, recall his personalised number plate that was something pithy like FCKØFF. I felt we were friends, and apart from a few lane-swapping manoeuvres to get around slow trucks, we covered at least 75 kilometres seemingly joined at the hip. My iPod was blasting out Bruce Springsteen through my helmet speakers and I almost regretted I wasn't riding a Harley, such was the moment. The looming problem was that he wanted to exit to Gosford. One option for him was to speed up, get ahead of me, cross over four lanes and get off the freeway. Alternatively, he could slow down and get across behind me. As I maintained a constant speed in my lane I saw the growing frustration as he obviously thought I was blocking him. The exit rapidly approached and I can only think that the slowing-down option was too much for his machismo to handle. His main problem was that he had run out of time to speed up and hope to cross over to the exit. He braked. I saw him, in my mirrors, careen over two lanes and speed up to be parallel with me, still at 115 km/h, only this time he was on my left. In a display of gentlemanly affection he showed me that he wasn't wearing a ring on his middle finger and I last saw him braking hard to avoid over-running the off-ramp. The single-fingered salute warmed my heart. He clearly wanted to communicate to me that he had enjoyed the camaraderie of the three-quarters of an hour we had spent together, car and bike, as one on the fast freeway to Newcastle. And that is why my earlier tension had now evaporated. Australia, in the form of FCKØFF and his Holden Commodore, had welcomed me into their bosom. I was blooded.

Steve and Pete's tail lights were visible far ahead. At the end of the freeway at Beresfield they coasted a few more kilometres into a town called Raymond Terrace. The bikes enjoyed a fuel top-up and the riders descended on New South Wales's best pie shop, called Heatherbrae's Pies. This was to be a visit to gourmet pie heaven and you found yourself thinking 'only in Australia'. Sated after a 'pie combo', namely a steak-and-cheese pie followed by dessert — a custard pie — I burped lightly but repeatedly as the three bikes headed out onto the Pacific Highway for the short burst to the turn-off to Bucketts Way. Instantly I felt as though we had passed through a gateway into the rural back blocks. I tailed a ute for several miles. It had a bumper sticker which said 'Save The Trees — Wipe Your Arse With An Owl'. Road signs pointed down narrow farm roads to distant places with names like Dungog, Coolongolook, Cooplacurripa and Ghin-Doo-Ee National Park.

Small rural towns and villages came and went. Booral, Stroud Road, Stratford and finally the sizeable Gloucester. This was where I met Kane. As I fussed around checking my oil and tyres while the Gloucester Caltex's fuel tank emptied into mine, a small boy with a cap on backwards sauntered around trying not to show interest. 'How's it going, son?' 'Yip.' 'You live here?' 'Yip.' 'What's your name?' 'Kane.' (or he might have been saying 'OK' or 'King' or local slang for 'Mind your own business mister'). 'Want to look at the bike?' 'Yip.' He came over and looked at the bike. 'Can you ride a motorbike?' 'Yip.' 'Reckon you could ride this one?' 'Yip.' I held out the keys and he ran off never to be seen again. Kane and I had communicated on a basic level, but I believe we were both richer for the experience.

Bucketts Way turns into Thunderbolts Way as it leaves Gloucester. Thunderbolts Way is named after Australia's 'gentleman' bushranger Fred Ward, also known as Captain Thunderbolt. Whatever his notoriety, I liked him immediately. Any criminal horse-thief who lent his name to a road such as this one could rob banks and steal chickens with my full blessing. I'm waxing lyrical here because a motorcyclist inherently likes corners. The best corners are those where you don't have to change gear or slow down. You simply lean with the bike and centrifugal forces right you again on the other side. The more corners there are in quick succession, the more fun you have. On the Thunderbolts Way we were having fun. It was clear the two Aussies wanted to get going and were all but salivating at what lay ahead. This was, after all, their backyard. I soon realized why they had jumped at the chance to escort me out of Sydney, although we had cleared Sydney's outer limits 250 kilometres back.

And that chance-jumping was all because of the Great Dividing Range, up which we were now wending our way. This range, also known as the Great Divide or Eastern Highlands, stretches almost the length of eastern Australia and encompasses iconic ranges such as the Blue Mountains and Snowy Mountains, both further south. At Barrington, the road transformed into an endless series of hairpins and tight corners as it traversed gullies, sped across small valleys and wound its way up and down bush-covered escarpments. The three of us lost sight of each other for about an hour as we were plunged into solo riding through this forested landscape.

At a remote lookout, at what seemed like the highest point, we regrouped and gazed out over the Great Divide. The highlands of the

Nowendoc National Park stretched for as far as the eye could see. While we were there, a sports bike roared up in a shower of gravel. The rider was dressed in black and the bike was red. I felt like a badly-dressed wallflower in comparison. We kicked each other's tyres, made some polite noises about how great each other's bikes were, conversed about scuffing foot pegs on the tight corners, moaned about the price of petrol and enjoyed the brief, friendly encounter. Then the Ducati rider mounted up, kicked it into first, crouched over the tank and careened off in a second shower of gravel. It was an excellent display of one-upmanship and I paid him the compliment of watching him lean his bike over to a 45-degree angle on the corner before he vanished into the forest canopy.

There was a further stretch of 80 kilometres to go as Thunderbolts Way descended from the summit onto the flat khaki-coloured grasslands surrounding Walcha, our intended overnight stop. The road became a motorcycling dream again. It was as if someone had taken a 40-kilometre-long roller coaster and stretched it out to double its length. Dusk was creating shadows across the road and the last rays of the sun lit up the stands of gum trees till they glowed like beacons. I saw a dead wombat on the side of the road and learned later that they are like bricks to run over. Like turning a light-switch dimmer, our speeds slowly crept up to 160 km/h as we sliced through the countryside, leaning into the gentle bends and enjoying the warm evening air through our open visors. Had I known any poetry I would have started to recite it out loud, it was that sort of 'at one with nature' experience. Instead a song about Slim Shady came on the iPod and the moment was lost.

At the cracking pace at which we were motoring, the small town of Walcha soon materialized nestled in a smoky haze of wood fires and evening mist in the valley. After a steak and accompanying beers in the Walcha pub, I ambled back down the darkened main street, belly full and at peace with the world, reflecting on the first day of Twisting Throttle's journey. It had been a highly satisfactory start and many cobwebs had been duly swept away. The bike had enjoyed its first big run after a month in a crate, and I felt grateful for being allowed some time in sixth-gear overdrive. But more importantly, I had immersed myself in Australian culture and, I'd have to modestly say, felt some connection. There were the pies in Raymond Terrace, the bonding with young Kane in Gloucester, and steak and beer just now in Walcha. But transcending all this, on a sheer emotional plane, was my freeway relationship with FCKØFF and his farewell gesture of kinship. If you're reading this book, my friend, and you recognize your plate number, I return your salute and, yes, I WAS blocking you. That'll be the day a clapped-out rust-bucket like yours passes a 1000-cc motorcycle. Get over it.

BIKE'S FUEL FOR DAY: 31 L, costing $45.
RIDER'S FUEL FOR DAY: Weetbix at Steve's place, two coffees, steak-and-cheese pie, custard pie, four beers, steak and chips at Walcha.

Chapter 2

Map of Australia showing route with locations: Darwin, Katherine, Mataranka, Turkey Creek, Croydon, Cairns, Broome, Threeways, Mt Isa, Mackay, Karratha, Overlander, Kalgoorlie, Ceduna, Gold Coast, Perth, Madura, Port Wakefield, Walcha, Jerramungup, Goulburn, Sydney, Mt Gambier, Cann River, Melbourne, St Helens, Hobart.

Walcha–Gold Coast

DAY'S RIDE: 592 kilometres.
JOURNEY TO DATE: 1,008 kilometres.

THE GOLD COAST. It's after nightfall and I'm here in Australia's playground and holiday mecca experiencing two things. First, a sense of achievement at having racked up my first 1,000 kilometres, and, second, throwing up. Why the latter? It's because I'm experiencing the after-effects of an evening encounter, my first of many as it would turn out, with Australian wildlife. Stay with me as I recount today's ride through two states and end the day giving new meaning to the phrases 'swallowing (on) one's ride' and 'eating humble fly'.

We accelerated out of Walcha at 9.00 a.m. in a light fog and on a moist road surface. Twenty kilometres after we had climbed up to a plateau, the fog burned off and the landscape revealed itself as something I can only describe as majestic. It is hard to set down in writing, but if you can imagine the grounds of an English stately home minus the peacocks, substitute gum trees for oaks and recolour the whole landscape in ochres and pastel greens, then you might be close to understanding the Zen-type exhilaration I felt. I was the lead bike in this 40-kilometre sprint to Uralla. I frantically surfed the iPod for some Enya to capture the inspiration of the ride.

At Uralla we tanked up with fuel. I'm referring, of course, to the riders — and the fuel was labelled 'The Drover's Big Breakfast' on the café's menu board. There is something about an early-morning start and an initial period on the bike during which your senses are twanging. Such a ride simply makes you hungry beyond belief. This breakfast was to be recalled 10,000 kilometres later in Western Australia when I had nothing else to do but compare the differences between east- and west-coast styles of big breakfast presentation. Here's my point. I sat with Steve and Pete in the little café in the deserted main street of Uralla on a sunny Sunday morning staring at a work of art. The canvas was a large china plate. The tools were a knife and fork. The artist was behind the counter dressed in jeans and a white T-shirt. He was wearing an apron with the words 'Lean mean cuisine machine' on it. I think he was called Murray. His work comprised toast, two eggs, a sausage, two tomatoes, a hash brown, some bacon, mushrooms and a sprig of parsley. After I had enjoyed Murray's tableau of delight, so contented did I feel that I did two things. Left a tip and ate the parsley. It was that sort of morning. You did spontaneous things. Halfway between Uralla and Armidale, some seven minutes after leaving Murray's establishment, another spontaneous action threatened to occur and I let my two mates disappear over a crest before pulling over and enjoying being at one with the Australian bush.

At Armidale the New England Highway continued north to Glen Innes, Tenterfield and the Queensland border. We, however, turned off onto a minor road that would carve through the Cathedral Rock and New England National Parks, heading east-ish back out to the coast. The boys were going to leave me in Grafton and strike south back to

Sydney. But first there were the 200 kilometres between us and our parting.

The signs hinting at alien settlements in the bush continued to amuse me. Wongwibinda, Woolomombi, Dundurabbin and Buccarumbi. Say these correctly first time and you're a better person than I. The road through Ebor to Billy's Creek was so typically Australian that I needed to enhance my cultural experience with music. The bike was equipped with an iPod on which were downloaded 492 songs. It was a motley collection, I grant you, but in planning the trip I knew that, at some point, I'd crave some local flavour and that point was now, cruising through the bush, with laughing kookaburras high in the trees, pesky wombats playing hide and seek in the undergrowth, koalas nursing their young. I was certain that Rolf Harris was in there somewhere, painting it all. And thus it was that I endured 2 kilometres of Rod Stewart's 'Waltzing Matilda' before I ended this well-meant but disastrous attempt at some cultural connection.

We ate fish and chips in the main street of Grafton, wiped our greasy mouths on the backs of our sleeves and shook hands. 'Bloody good ride, Mr Throttle, good luck for the next bit,' by which Steve was referring to the remaining 16,000 kilometres. I rode north and found the Summerland Way. It was exactly 100 kilometres to Casino with only one small settlement called Whiporie that caused me to use the gear lever for the only time in that stretch. I would like to devote two more pages to the Summerland Way. It represented a sixth of the whole day's ride and deserves a comment. The problem is, I can't think of a single thing to say about it. The landscape was neutral, the road had few bends and I saw and spoke to no-one. My iPod jammed so I rode in silence. I simply left Grafton and arrived in Casino, end of story really. Standing at the petrol station in Casino, pump in hand, nozzle in tank, I thought about the past 100 kilometres. I wondered if large chunks of the journey would be like that. Unremarkable. Featureless. Routine. In fact, the Casino run would be the last time I would be stuck for words, but I wasn't to know that at the time.

In Lismore I made a navigational blunder: I trusted my instincts. Equipped with a Garmin GPS, a book of maps and several road signs up ahead, I ignored these resources, went with my gut and branched off in a direction I thought would bring me out on the Pacific Highway at Bangalow. I repeated the name 'Bangalow' so many times in my head that when I saw a sign to Goolmangar, Chinese whispers took over. Bangalow . . . Bangalar . . . Balmangar . . . Galmangar . . . Goolmangar. I sped off down the wrong road. I realized the error when I got to Goolmangar, a collection of three or four houses and not much else. Three things occurred to me as I pulled over and switched off. I couldn't smell the ocean, I was certain the Pacific Highway wasn't this covered in dung, and there was an old chap leaning on a gate grinning at me. 'How's it going?' I said. 'Hair-gama. Yullust?' 'Yip. Lookin' for the Pacific Highway.' 'Nah worries. Gaback ta kays. Righta Dunoon. Strayta Mullumbimby. Or yicken carry onna Nimbin. Get some hooch. Nah arnly jarkin ma. Through Nimbin ta Murwillumbah outta Tweed.' I knew this friendly guy was speaking English but I simply had no idea what he was saying. I recognized the word Nimbin. 'Thanks a lot, mate.' 'Sludder ma,' he called and ambled into his house. 'See ya later, mate,' I finally translated and returned the farewell. Sludder, sludder, sludder. As I rode off towards Nimbin, I mentally filed away this handy phrase in case I needed to converse with locals again.

As I got to Nimbin I realized the old fella on the gate had, in fact, not been jarkin'. The jark was on me. It was like riding through a wormhole in time, back to the 'sixties. The main street was full of craft shops selling essential items like bongs and hookahs. In the window of a café was a sign that said 'Practise Safe Lunch — Use A Condiment'. There were some tourists, but most women I saw wore long flowing kaftans, and had bare feet and close-cropped hair. I could swear I heard Peter, Paul and Mary over the street's musack system. I've since read that Nimbin is the self-labelled 'Alternative Capital of Australia'. Here's what Nimbin says about itself on the town's website: 'Nimbin provides an example to the world of how communities working together can find creative, sustainable solutions to the many environmental and socio-economic dilemmas facing us all as we plunge into the new millennium.' As I rode through town slowly, I thought it just looked like a haven for spaced-out druggies, but I accept this was probably a shallow and prejudiced view. It's just that, to a casual observer — albeit from behind a tinted visor — businesses called Big Bong Burger Bar, Finger Limeing Good, the Nimbin Hemp Bar, Pot Art Tattoo and Church of the Holy Smoke made it seem as though a certain culture dominated this pretty yet quaintly old-fashioned town. And it appeared the New South Wales police thought so too. As I rode over a small humpback bridge going out of Nimbin, I saw a convoy of no fewer than five patrol cars parked in a lay-by scrutinizing every vehicle coming or going. I was tempted to weave my bike over the bridge, call out 'Peace, dude' and see what happened.

At Murwillumbah the road forked right to Coolangatta and left to the Gold Coast via the back roads. I turned left. What an inspirational decision that was. Beyond Chillingham the narrow road looped up into the hills, having run out of valley. Without warning I crested a hill to see a cattle-grid, a small house with a vegetable patch by a fence and a rusting tilted sign that said 'Queensland Border'. But what was the house? A border post? And were vehicles meant to stop? That raised an interesting question. What were the border formalities in Australia anyway? I hadn't really thought about it.

I clanged across the grid and pulled over to take a photo of the sign. A man came to the door of the house and stood there. He wasn't dressed in a uniform and did not point a gun at me or ask for a bribe. In fact he wouldn't have known if I was entering Queensland or leaving. I called over to him, 'Just taking a pic.' 'No worries. Sludder ma.' 'Sludder.' And with that exchange of pleasantries my first border crossing was complete. I was now in Queensland.

The road zigged and zagged through an endless series of gullies and ranges as it passed Natural Bridge. I saw my first sugar cane and it was as if, by virtue of my having passed a rusting border sign, the tropics suddenly started. I suppose it is called rainforest; the foliage became more leafy and palmy. The road tracked out into the Numinbah Valley. I stopped to check the map and saw a long winding drag ahead towards the Hinze Dam and beyond that Nerang. Settling in for the last stretch as dusk fell, I passed a sign to Mudgeeraba and took it to be a shortcut. In fact it was anything but. The twisty, narrow mountain road curved up and over a range of hills. On the descent I glimpsed, through the breaks in the eucalypt canopy, the distant high-rises of Surfers Paradise. It was then that I swallowed a wasp.

I say wasp, but that's probably building it up in my mind. Let's call it an unidentified winged object. I was coasting down the interminable procession of downhill corners and had my visor up. I was enjoying the cooling evening air and being on this switchback road on my own. I have no conscious recollection of having my mouth open but I suddenly gagged as this UWO slammed into the back of my throat. Shock turned to disgust which turned to horror as I involuntarily swallowed and down it went. I'm not saying the UWO's experience was any less traumatic than mine, but spare a thought for the accident potential as I tried to regurgitate this writhing denizen of the night while staying in control of the motorcycle on a dark, twisty road. The more I retched, the further it progressed to its horrific, slow, eventual death in my intestines. It must have been a sight. But I learned two lessons that night. One, never ride at insect feeding time with visor up, and, two, if I ever pass a Big Bong Burger Bar again, I will stop and consume their daily special. I think this poor winged creature would have appreciated something in there to numb it during the ordeal.

BIKE'S FUEL FOR DAY: 64 L, costing $85.
RIDER'S FUEL FOR DAY: The Drover's Big Breakfast, an orange,
    Mars bar, 3 L of water, fish-and-chip meal for lunch
    and a pie. And one unidentified winged object.

Chapter 3

Gold Coast–Mackay

DAY'S RIDE: 1,052 kilometres.
JOURNEY TO DATE: 2,060 kilometres.

TODAY I HARBOURED intentions of having a crack at qualifying for the basic level of entry into The Iron Butt Association in America. 'The Iron what?' you ask. Here's what it's all about. The IBA is an organization for extreme endurance motorcycle riders who do nothing more than put as many miles under their tyres as they can, in the shortest possible time. Their trademark event is the two-yearly Iron Butt Rally in which invited contestants have to ride at least 1,000 miles (that's 1,600 kilometres) in a 24-hour period . . . and then continue to do this for 11 consecutive days. In less than two weeks they virtually circumnavigate America. I read a book about it written by one of the all-time Iron Butt achievers, Ron Ayres. This is a guy who rode a motorcycle through all 48 contiguous states of the US in 6 days and then for the hell of it popped up to Alaska to knock off the 49th state. That was 10 years ago and his record for this '7/48' endurance feat as they call it still stands. One whole chapter is devoted to methods of minimizing delays with tips for taking power naps on the side of the road to fueling up in under five minutes. Here's an extract: '. . . park at the pump so you don't waste time having to walk around the bike, while you're filling the main tank with your left hand remove the auxiliary fuel tank cap with your right hand, only use pay-at-the-pump gas stations as you may end up in a queue at the cashier behind someone buying groceries', etc., etc. You get the picture.

There was no small part of my psyche wanting to know how someone could ride a bike for 1,600 kilometres in 24 hours and what sort of mental and physical state they'd be in, both during and after such a slog. It sounded worthy of further research. The 1000/24 is known as the Saddlesore 1000 and anyone can enter, anywhere in the world, merely by producing evidence of achievement in the form of petrol receipts and a witness at either end. If you achieve it you get a certificate, a pin and, more importantly, your name on the prestigious Iron Butt Association's roll call of endurance riders. I decided to have a crack.

I left Mudgeeraba at 7.15 a.m. At 7.21 a.m. I had gassed up at the local petrol station, and the automated receipt served to crystallize my official Saddlesore 1000 start time. I had calculated that 1,600 kilometres north of where I was happened to be Innisfail, just south of Cairns. I had to be there by 7.21 a.m. the next day. Up to half the ride would take place at night. I could allow myself several stops, but my average speed for the next 24 hours had to be no less than 71 km/h. Until then, the furthest I had ever ridden in a day was 750 kilometres.

Adrenalin pumping and emotions bouncing around, I rode unnecessarily aggressively up the four-lane freeway from Nerang, past Dreamworld, Sanctuary Cove, Beenleigh and Logan, swerving in and out of morning commuter traffic heading for Brisbane. The freeway ate up kilometre after kilometre and it was good stuff. The bike felt good pounding along at 120 km/h in overdrive sixth gear and was revelling in the challenge. My brain constantly reworked the calculations each time my GPS ticked over 50 kilometres. 1,650 kilometres to go. Average speed 120 km/h. Potential rest stop in 4 hours, of 25 minutes only. And on it went.

My palms were sweaty inside thick gloves and I started to prepare mentally for the big hurdle looming in 25 kilometres' time. I refer of course to the toll plaza on the massive Gateway Bridge spanning the Brisbane River as the freeway splices through the outer city. I heard the voices. On one shoulder the little red devil said, 'You know you're going to drop the bike', yet the little blue angel on the other side said, 'Stay cool, pull up, pop it in neutral, off with your right glove, hold bike steady with left hand, stay gloved, undo zip on tank bag gently, remove wallet, hold in teeth while taking out coins . . .' And so the approaching toll plaza preyed on my mind as the overhead signs indicating which lane to get into loomed larger. At the toll plaza the motorway was eight lanes wide. I headed for the purple lane, which was for 'manual' payments. Naturally there was a queue behind me as I decelerated up to the booth. I ungloved the wrong hand, steadied the bike on the throttle which revved it loudly, couldn't unzip the tank bag, by which time the attendant commented, 'You know you need three hands, mate?' I merely handed my bum bag to the lady and shouted, over the noise of the thundering semi-trailer idling behind me, 'Take what you need.' I finally accelerated ridiculously fast out on the other side of the toll plaza as this awful rite of passage mercifully came to an end. I knew my next toll plaza would be when I came back into Sydney in five weeks' time. I had 16,000 kilometres in which to get my act together.

The freeway surged northwards and it renamed itself the Bruce Highway. I saw about as much of Brisbane as anyone sees of London from the window of a fast train from Paddington. However, I had to remind myself that this was not a sightseeing day. The miles blurred into each other as I simply kept going. Turn-offs to iconic resorts flashed by. Caloundra, Bribie Island, Maroochydore, Noosa. The Bruce kept tracking relentlessly northwards and I sat on it like a suckerfish along for the ride. I kept doing the mental gymnastics, calculating stopping allowances. I committed to a ten-minute stop every three hours for the first nine hours. I figured by then the going would be getting a fraction gritty.

My initial goal was to ride 350 kilometres non-stop. I was assuming there would be a novelty element which would mean that the adrenalin would obviate the need for any stops. At 350 kilometres I duly pulled over in a lay-by and hopped off. I didn't know what to do. Should I be doing press-ups, star jumps or just be having a sit down? What do the Iron Butt pros do in their power-rests? I shuffled around checking my tyres, for what I don't know, and took a quick pee in the bushes. I wasn't quite ready to test the technique of taking a comfort stop while still riding. That earned itself a whole page in the Iron Butt book. I mounted up, set my next mental goal and took off like a bat out of hell.

Towns came and went. Nambour, Gympie, Maryborough, Childers, Gin Gin. I became perpetually unsettled at my inconsistent speed. The highway was variably a dual-lane carriageway or single lane. The speed limit signs chopped around as if some disgruntled roadworker had had a bad day at the office. The open-road limit was posted at 110 km/h, and in such areas I naturally idled along at 120 km/h. Then, for no apparent reason other than that there was a school down a side road, you were posted down to 80 km/h for the next 5 kilometres. The continual changes in speed restrictions played havoc with any natural rhythm and I felt the 1,600 target slipping away from me as I had to chug through these towns in third gear, stopping for ladies with prams, school buses and — the scourge of Iron Butt wannabes — those Stop/Go men at roadworks. The spectre of being given a speeding ticket also hung over me. In fact, the only cop I had seen in the 2,000 kilometres since Sydney had been one earlier that day, pulling over a guy with no shirt on in a Holden. That'll teach him to cover up next time.

I sped through a small town between Gympie and Maryborough called Tiaro and racked my brains as to where I had heard of that name before. It had to do with UFOs but I couldn't recall the details. I've now researched what happened there and it's one of those controversial did-they-or-didn't-they media beat-up mysteries which Australia is expert in conjuring up.

Three adults called (and I use initial letters only to hide the identities of Keith and Amy Rylance and Petra Heller) 'Mr K', 'Mrs A' and 'Miss P' were sleeping in a house near Tiaro. It was midnight and a warm breeze was wafting over the town. Miss P heard a sound coming from the kitchen, saw a bright beam of light under the door and assumed Mr K was making himself a cheese sandwich. She went to tell him to quieten down. However, instead of seeing Mr K slicing bread, she found (with concern) that aliens were carrying Mrs A out through the window on a sort of stretcher towards a hovering UFO.

Miss P closed the window, poured herself a glass of milk and watched some TV. No wait, that's not it, I'm trying to recall what happened next. That's right, she screamed her lungs out and woke Mr K (who, by the way, had slept through his wife's abduction from their double bed). 'She's gone where?' asked a disbelieving Mr K. If it weren't for the nearby crop circle, some light scorching around the kitchen window and Richard Dreyfuss digging up his garden, Mr K would have gone back to bed. Instead they rang the police who came out to the property, shone their torches around and interviewed the couple at length, suspecting foul play.

Suddenly the phone rang and it was the Mackay police, saying Mrs A had staggered, looking dishevelled and lightly scorched, into the BP station on the highway outside Mackay. The thing here is that Mackay is 800 kilometres north of Tiaro. 'What the f***?' The Tiaro policeman put into words what everyone was thinking.

Mrs A later recounted her experience. 'I was in a brightly lit room. In walked a guy, of slender build and about six feet tall, wearing a full body suit with black holes for his eyes, nose and mouth.' In a calming voice he told her she would soon be returned to a place not far from her home. The last thing she remembered hearing before drifting off to an anaesthetized sleep was 'Scalpel'. I made that last one up, but that's about the drift of Mrs A's testimony. She had strange triangular marks on her inner thigh and her hair was growing out to its original colour, whereas she had dyed it only a week before. In other words, she was showing signs of having aged a few days, not the few hours she had been missing. And how did she get 800 kilometres north of her home?

Enter an organization called The Australian UFO Research Network. Two investigators were assigned to check out this alleged alien abduction. Unfortunately, according to their website report, they received little cooperation from the abductee and associates who claimed they had a 'Men in Black' experience, were being followed by a sinister dark brown 4WD and therefore had to lie low. The affair received quite a bit of media attention before petering out. Most people thought it was a crock, the police brought in a dingo for questioning, and the Tiaro visitor centre sold out of blow-up alien dolls. Only in Australia.

The miles rolled on. I passed a signpost to a settlement called Goodnight Scrub. Every creek I crossed seemed to be named either Sandy Creek, Alligator Creek or Twelve Mile Creek. I never saw creeks One to Eleven, and was so bored somewhere near Bundaberg that I mapped 12 miles after crossing another Twelve Mile Creek to see why it was called that. Is it 12 miles from somewhere? Is it 12 miles long? Are there 12 creeks in the mile?

I felt I should be thinking more about Australia. I didn't want to blast through without learning something about this huge continent and country. I had heard that the only country name that starts with an 'A' but doesn't end with an 'A', is 'Afghanistan'. Now was the perfect time to disprove that. As I motored along I tried to think of as many countries as I could with names starting with 'A'. I came up with the bleeding obvious . . . Austria, Argentina, Algeria. Then the not so bleeding obvious . . . Albania, Andorra, Angola, Armenia, Antigua. And then, in a moment of ultimate anal retention, I thought of Azerbaijan. Thus I disproved the *Trivial Pursuit* question, which presumably was printed before the ruckus that split up the Soviet Union. This was indeed turning out to be a journey of knowledge, a quest for enlightenment and a search for the forbidden truths; such as, did you know that there are no words in the English language which rhyme with 'month', 'silver', 'orange' and 'purple'?

As I rode along in a state of neutrality mile after mile, the calculations turned to the prospect of riding through the night. It was part of the challenge, there could be no doubt about that, but the whole adventure of this Saddlesore 1000 started to lose its charm as I envisaged a lone ride at 3.00 a.m. along a dark highway with grazing wildlife all around ready to commit suicide.

Dismissing the night-riding concerns, I plugged on, stopping only to top up the tank each time I'd clocked up 150 kilometres. A crucial part of the Saddlesore achievement is securing proper documentation in the form of petrol receipts. These slips of paper must provide evidence of the time, date and location by means of a computer-generated docket from the till. A hand-written slip is useless, for obvious reasons. I say this because I was now filling up at a place called Benaraby, specifically at a small store with a single pump. I could have kicked myself for not considering the odds of the Benaraby store having a computer. The young man in dungarees strumming a banjo on the verandah should have been a warning sign. 'G'day,' said the lady at the counter, 'You got pump one out there?' 'Yes,' I replied, looking back out at the single pump and wondering where pumps two and above were. '$22.50, love.' I handed over the cash and she looked at me for further instructions. 'You wouldn't have a till docket would you?' I asked with a growing realization that my Saddlesore attempt was about to strike its first hurdle. 'No worries, I'll write one out for you,' and she grabbed a brown paper bag used for selling pies and wrote on it, '$22.50 Benaraby'. That was it. I could see the Iron Butt judging panel in America struggling to accept this as a computerized time/date/location stamp from Benaraby. 'You wouldn't have a . . . like sort of stamp for your store would you?'

'Yes dear, over there.' She pointed to a stand of souvenir stickers for nearby Lake Awoonga Caravan Park. I rode away from Benaraby having learned a key Iron Butt lesson.

After passing the turn-off to Gladstone, my next goal was Rockhampton. I had done 630 kilometres and was feeling jaded. My limbs were aching and I couldn't stomach any more Corrs and Cranberries on the iPod. I was on one of those stretches where there were no towns, no cars, nothing to remark on, and to relieve the boredom I stretched out my boots closer to the speeding road surface to see if I could make just the tiniest contact with my heel.

Eventually the dusky lights of Rockhampton hove into view and I promised myself this would be the big halfway rest stop. As I cruised through the city centre, I noticed an enticing sign saying 'Fish Meals. Big Ones' on a shop, so I pulled in. As I was tucking into my Big Fish Meal an older gent, maybe 60-ish, wandered across after having given the bike a good look-over. 'I'm winning the lotto tonight. Twenty-seven big ones. Maybe I can get a bike and we can go together? I only ride BSAs. And what about them Norton Commandos, eh? And maybe Ducatis. Not Harleys. Twenty-seven mill is too much for one person. They should spread it around. You going far, mate? Do you want me to ride with you out of Rocky? Maybe I could take that one [pointing at the lady serving behind the counter]. Ah, don't worry about me, mate, I'm always on the stir.' I looked at the lady behind the counter for unwritten instructions. Do I humour the old chap, who I guessed was called something like Gus or Wilbur? Or do I tell him to sod off, that I had allowed myself only a 20-minute rest stop and that he was ruining it? The lady rolled her eyes and I took it that he was a Big Fish platinum customer and not one to be offended. 'Good on ya, Gus, have a chip,' I said with my mouth full. 'See ya, off to get me lotto ticket,' and he disappeared out into the night. I rode out of Rockhampton a better person.

As the lights of Rocky slipped below the treeline, the blanket of darkness fell with a vengeance. There was no dusk, it just turned black. And wet. There were no lights of any sort as I plugged north. I felt vaguely uneasy about the road surface, but tried not to imagine slippery patches where there probably weren't any. I couldn't decide between having the light on dip or on full. Dip was better for the immediate riding zone, where you are looking 50 to 80 metres ahead, but full beam highlighted, albeit in a dimmer light, the whole road ahead.

At the very point when I was contemplating the whole road-kill issue and why riding at night in Australia is not officially recommended, the bike jolted over something on the road. It would be true to say I suffered an involuntary bowel movement. In Australia they refer to it as 'packing oneself'. To this day I don't know what it was. I had a mental image of a flattened animal. It wasn't fresh, as the bike did not lose its harmony. But the bottom line was that I had run over something and, more significantly, that I had not seen it in my lights.

And to round off the trilogy of night-riding joys, there were the trucks. These are not the famous road trains, just your normal articulated heavies which come out at night and travel in packs. Without exception they assumed I was an oncoming car minus one headlight. And that headlight seemed to be on full beam, so in a safety-conscious act of enforcing road manners, they clicked their whole arsenal of 18 halogen headlamps onto full whack just as I spurted past. Therefore, every time I passed an oncoming truck, I suffered a blast of full beam which blinded me and a vortex of road spray which soaked me, and for a further 500 metres or so I was seeing stars before my vision readjusted.

The distance from Rockhampton to Mackay is 400 kilometres. That was 400 kilometres longer than I wanted to be on the road. And the reality was, I was only halfway along my Saddlesore route. Those 400 kilometres took 5 hours. There is little civilization between these two towns. I saw a distant mine brightly illuminated. I imagined wandering stock and low-flying bats. At 10.30 p.m. I reached Sarina and just made it before the petrol station closed. The Mrs Mac's sausage roll, with its 25% meat content, tasted wonderful. But I knew, mounting up and riding out into the night again, that the Saddlesore had beaten me. I was still 700 kilometres short of Innisfail and tired beyond belief. The night riding was taking its toll and I was covered in flies and moths.

At 11.00 p.m. I mercifully changed down gears as I coasted into Mackay. I had ridden 1,050 kilometres and was spent. I don't know how these Iron Butt guys do it. Maybe they have a technique for sleeping while riding along at full speed on their inter-states, but I take my helmet off to them — 1,000 miles in 24 hours, for 11 days consecutively. That's like circumnavigating Australia in under two weeks. I'd still like to see them fuel up at Benaraby, though.

I found the local campground, pitched my tent in the dark, slurped water out of the gents' hand basin in the ablution block, left the bike keys in the ignition, took off my padded jacket, crawled into the drooping tent and lay down on my uninflated thermarest pad.

And frankly, that's the last thing I remember.

BIKE'S FUEL FOR DAY: 64 L, costing $85.
RIDER'S FUEL FOR DAY: Bacon and eggs for breakfast, bag of chips, Mars bar, 4 L of water, fish-and-chip meal for tea, Sarina's heavenly sausage roll and a Coke.

Chapter 4

Darwin
Katherine
Turkey Creek   Mataranka
Broome   Croydon
                                Cairns
            Threeways   Mt Isa
Karratha   Mackay

Overlander
        Kalgoorlie   Ceduna   Gold Coast
                          Port Wakefield   Walcha
Perth   Madura   Goulburn Sydney
    Jerramungup
            Mt Gambier   Cann River
                Melbourne
                          St Helens
                          Hobart

Mackay–Cairns

DAY'S RIDE: 743 kilometres.
JOURNEY TO DATE: 2,803 kilometres.

I HAVE NEVER slept so deeply. Having said that, I have never also slept in boots, so this first night under canvas had broken more than one paradigm. For my $17 camp fee, I fully intended to use all of the facilities this establishment offered, so I trundled off to the communal ablution block. This was the first time I'd looked in a mirror for 48 hours, and it would be truthful to say there was no small wear-and-tear issue happening. But why should I worry? Beautiful people don't tend to ride motorcycles, swallow wasps and pee at the side of the road.

'Jeez, that's a big mongrel. Inline four GS? Yep, reckon so.' A friendly

33

camper called Grant watched me pack up and lumber around like an idiot doing everything twice. I was still recovering from yesterday's marathon ride, and still half asleep. The campground was full of what I've heard are referred to as 'grey nomads', or persons in their golden years who just go around and around Australia towing a caravan. I would pass plenty of them on the road during the next five weeks, all pootling along at 80 km/h.

Grant, the particular grey nomad who was chatting to me, was a friendly guy and had time to kill. 'Is that a twin carb?' The fact was, I simply didn't have a clue how many carburettors my bike had, overlooking the obvious point that it was fuel-injected anyway. So I replied, 'Yip'. Unfortunately he knew his bikes, specifically the suspension thereof. He was a retired shock-absorber fitter from Dubbo. When I found that out, I knew with a mounting resignation the question that would come. I quickened the pace rolling up the tent, but I wasn't quick enough.

'You got rear spring preload and rebound damping by the look,' Grant said, peering somewhere in by my back wheel. I pretended not to hear, frantically racking my brains for something sensible to say about my bike's suspension. 'And cartridge type, oil damped on the front.' He was now peering at the front forks. 'Find it chatters in the sweepers?' 'Does it what,' I replied. 'This is what you do, mate. Revalve the stock compression stack, get rid of one of the 3-inch shims, shim the bushings out to remove free play. That'll give you real front suspension. You want 30–35% sag for touring. But don't shag around with harder fork springs if you're replacing the rear factory shock with . . . with . . .' he was clearly searching for my technical assistance. 'A different one?' I added, feeling like a git. 'Nah, I was going to say a smoother one, maybe an Ohlins.'

I was desperate either to add something intelligent to the conversation or else simply to ride away. I chose to add to the conversation and immediately wished I hadn't. 'Well, mate, I'm carrying a fair load of luggage so I've got the preload wound right out.' 'Wound out? Mate. You want to switch to a shorter suspension dog-bone.' The term dog with a bone had occurred to me as well. 'Mate of mine', Grant kept going, 'had awesome sync on his V-twin right through the RPM range.' I knew he was changing the subject to fuel injection and I knew as much about fuel injection as I did about asparagus-growing in Mackay. 'Right through the range?' I asked, simply not wanting to be rude enough to tell him to bugger off. 'The differences in airflow patterns through the intake track which includes airbox, throttle bodies, manifolds, heads and valve adjustments are right b******s. The sync on your V-twin here, less than half an inch of mercury is fine. That means three to four inches on a homemade rig.'

Another grey nomad, Bruce, had by this time strolled over. 'Morning men. Grant, mate, how's it goin'?' 'Good, mate.' 'Up for nine holes before some grub?' 'Sounds the bee's knees, mate. I'll go and tell the handbrake', by which I knew he meant his wife. 'Sludder ma', which translates from Australian to 'see you later, mate' in English. Say it fast a few times and you'll see what I mean.

Demoralised by my exposed ignorance of anything remotely mechanical on my bike, I set my GPS to find the shortest way out of Mackay. Five minutes after leaving the camp I approached a set of traffic lights at an intersection. To this day I cannot explain the motor reaction which took place in my brain, but the end result was that I simply accelerated through the red light as if it wasn't there. Perhaps I was preoccupied with trying to determine if my sync was right through my RPM range, I don't know. But there were no fewer than four vehicles crossing my path when I snapped to and instinctively slammed down hard on the rear brake. The bike's rear tyre screamed in pain and a small wobble developed. I narrowly missed the first open-mouthed driver's car which was also braking hard. Some inbuilt survival gene instructed my throttle hand to get with it and I accelerated again, this time leaning first left, then right, as I weaved between two criss-crossing cars. Had I been pursued by hundreds of police cars you would have thought it was the Blues Brothers on two wheels. I spurted out the other side of that intersection needing to change two things. Down a gear and my underwear.

The road north from Mackay was fast, straight and bordered by endless sugar cane. Mile after mile of cane crops waving in the light breeze were punctuated by red gravel side roads and miniature train tracks under a blue sky without any hint of a cloud. This set the scene for a 200-kilometre opening ride — often called a blat — while I was fresh, eager and at peace with the world. After my road-safety lesson back at Mackay I felt a little bullet-proof. I was to learn that it was a good policy, while such a semi-euphoric state exists at the start of each morning's ride, to capture the moment and put on as many kilometres as possible. You just want to stand up on the pegs and sing hymns while riding. In my case I settled for Queen on the iPod, but you get the drift.

I decided to ride along one of the red gravel roads between the sugar cane and turned off. However, once off the main highway, the air was transformed into a cauldron of sweaty, oppressive heat, and immediately I felt sweat trickle down into my nether regions. I stopped in the middle of the cane-bound road and attempted a smooth transfer into hot-weather gear, entailing undressing down to my undies. The padded gear was tossed onto the road shoulder and I fossicked through the panniers trying to remember where I had stowed the Draggin Jeans jacket, Draggin Jeans jeans and Draggin Jeans gloves. Draggin Jeans is a brand of motorcycling apparel made in Australia, by Australia, for Australia, and I can see why. The farce of changing gear brought home to me my packing limitations. A memo was duly logged to self that this packing had to be more military and organized. I got away with standing on a deserted roadside in sugar cane in my undies, rooting through my panniers looking for my hot-weather gear, but I wouldn't want to try it on, say, the freeway.

I fuelled up outside Bowen, scoffed down an egg-and-lettuce sandwich, congratulated myself that I was eating plenty of greens, and quaffed a cold Coke. To round off the culinary fiesta, I threw down the daily multi-vitamin pill, with the Coke of course, and rashly bought a blueberry muffin on the way out. Both bike's and rider's tanks were duly full to bursting leaving Bowen as I idled back onto the Bruce Highway heading for Townsville.

Settlements whipped by. Home Hill, Ayr and finally, after 400 hot and sticky kilometres since Mackay, I decelerated into Townsville, riding past the obligatory outskirts signs for Kentucky Fried Chicken, Barrier Reef cruises and a business called Joe's Car Lockup in Cairns. This last one made me laugh out loud as Cairns was another 400 kilometres away. This would be the first of about five signs for Joe's I'd be seeing. If I ever meet Joe, I might suggest he restrict his advertising to, say, within 10 kilometres of Cairns. On the other hand, his marketing strategy may be spot-on. Had I a car, and had I needed to lock it up in Cairns, there would be nowhere else I would think of going.

I bypassed Townsville as a quick mental calculation told me I was running too far behind to make Cairns by dusk. After my Rockhampton to Mackay night-time ride yesterday, I was squirrelly about after-dark travelling. I'd also lapsed into a slow speed, which I defined as below 100 km/h, and there was no reason for it. The thing is that when you're the only vehicle on the road there is no context for speed. If you have a vehicle in front, you mentally wind it up a bit to catch up and overtake. If there is a vehicle behind, you likewise speed up as we all know it'll be a cold day in hell when a male driver gets overtaken. So trundling along at 95 km/h enjoying the view was fine for grey nomads, but Twisting Throttle was falling behind schedule.

It was a pity I had to ignore Townsville. You'd think I could have paid Queensland's second largest city a little more lip service than a few roundabouts and waving to an old guy mysteriously pushing a supermarket trolley with what looked like a gearbox in it up the bypass.

When I was reading up about places that I would pass through on my ride, one bizarre story made Townsville stick in my memory. Here goes with what I can recall of it. There's a sunken ship called the *Yongala* which went down in a storm off the coast in 1911. One hundred and twenty crew and a racehorse called Moonshine did not live to tell the tale. No-one did, actually. The wreck is now a popular diving attraction, but the problem is that the marine life is getting too up close and personal with humans. In 2001 one of these divers, and I'll mask his real identity by calling him, say, 'Dick', was scuba-ing around the wreck when a massive potato cod swam up out of the gloom. The potato cod is so called because it tastes lovely with chips. Actually no, if you see a picture of one of these monster cod you'll see the resemblance to a potato. These fish grow up to two metres long and can weigh more than I do. So here was Dick, enjoying his dive, when this potato cod swims up to him and swallows his — Dick's — head. One minute he is looking through his goggles at tropical coral, next minute he is looking down the gullet of a fish. Apparently the cod did not bite Dick's head off as such, just sucked it a bit and then swam off, bored. Dick, in turn, surfaced, caught the next boat ashore and found the nearest lotto shop to buy a ticket.

It was this recollection from the guidebook to Queensland which occupied my thoughts as I weaved through the Townsville traffic. I wondered if that's where the expression, 'You're a bit of a dickhead,' originated.

It was 3.00 p.m. and I still had to travel 400 kilometres to get to Cairns.

I passed the surreal sight of a big kangaroo lying on the roadside on its side with its legs in the air — as if it had been standing upright one minute, then just toppled over. So here's the question. What caused it to die in this position? If it had been run over, then it would surely have been pancaked. If someone had hit the kangaroo, and it was a fair size, then did they merely stop and drag it by the tail to the roadside? And why was it so oddly puffed up like a child's soft toy? This one looked as if it had been stuffed. I suspect decomposition had worked its magic on the poor roo but it was such a perfect display of taxidermy it seemed more than accidental. Several photo possibilities crossed my mind, as did stabbing it to see what would happen, but I was 10 kilometres down the road already when that thought struck me.

The sky was azure blue and the sun was illuminating everything. The tarmac was like a ribbon of glass. The surface was smooth and soporific. I clicked out of my reverie clipping along at a more respectable, if slightly illegal, 115 km/h. A white ute flashed its lights as it sped past me and I slowed down to 95 km/h again for the next 25 kilometres before I realized there wasn't a radar trap after all. I thereupon wished a plague of locusts would destroy the sugar-cane plantation belonging to that ute driver.

The route north was split into beautiful arithmetically symmetrical goals; these being Ingham, Tully, Innisfail and then Cairns. The towns were all 100 kilometres apart and perfectly placed to aim for as the next 'get off and rest' stop. Slowing down through Cardwell I got a shock, as the sea was right next to me. This was the first time I'd seen it since Surfers Paradise, and I'd had no idea I was actually on the coast. As I rode closer to Innisfail, I noticed there were no road signs. Then one appeared around a bend, saying 'Cyclone Area: no road signs'. The damage from the recent cyclone was completely obvious — from palm trees with no palms, to blue tarpaulins covering roofs. It was like riding through a petrified forest as the roadside woodland looked decimated. Funnily enough, the sugar cane and banana trees were still upright. I had thought the sugar-cane plantations would have been levelled, but maybe they were just a very dexterous plant and simply sprang back upright after it was all over.

As I took the wrong bypass out of Innisfail and slogged through an industrial area to find the Bruce Highway again, darkness fell like an iron curtain. If there was a dusk, I missed it. My bum was sore beyond belief and no amount of onboard callisthenics could relieve the crushing soreness. I wasn't game to stand up on the pegs after dark. There was no choice but to endure the constant stream of fast-moving traffic, so I just tucked in behind a semi-trailer, enjoyed the slight buffeting which was cool, and counted down the miles to Cairns.

Cairns's lights appeared on the distant horizon, and in no time I was riding past Best Westerns and Red Roosters and desperately looking for Joe's Car Lockup. Cairns represented the northernmost point of my trip up the east coast, and from here it would be a westward turn towards the Gulf of Carpentaria across the Cape York Peninsula. I badly needed to repack the panniers, do some washing and send emails, so I pulled into a cheap-looking motel. The neon sign had the 'o' out, so I knew it was the sort of establishment where I could clean my bike with their towels and no-one would know the difference.

'Got a room for a single?' I asked the proprietor who was wearing a white singlet. 'Yep, got one room left, number 15, but it's only got a single bed,' he said with an expression that seemed to be apologetic. That assumption plus the sign on the car park saying, 'Be Warned. 24 Hour Security' told me I wasn't checking into the Hilton. What the heck — the fan works, there's a Subway next door, a sign in the bathroom saying 'No Smokking', and under Room Service in their compendium is listed a telephone number for someone called Jasmine.

I dropped onto the bed in my riding gear for a quick rest.

And thus I spent two nights in a row sleeping in my boots.

Bike's fuel for day: 39 L, costing $57.
Rider's fuel for day: Egg-and-lettuce sandwich, muffin, Coke, 3 L of water (two bottles and a refill from the tap at Ingham BP), a foot-long sub, one bag of chips and two Mars bars.

Chapter 5

Darwin
Katherine
Turkey Creek
Broome
Mataranka
Croydon
Cairns
Threeways
Mt Isa
Mackay
Karratha
Overlander
Kalgoorlie
Ceduna
Gold Coast
Perth
Madura
Port Wakefield
Walcha
Jerramungup
Goulburn
Sydney
Mt Gambier
Cann River
Melbourne
St Helens
Hobart

Cairns–Croydon

DAY'S RIDE: 569 kilometres.
JOURNEY TO DATE: 3,372 kilometres.

I'M SITTING HERE on a rock, surrounded by bush and gum trees, somewhere in the vast nothingness at the base of what is officially called Cape York Peninsula, that pointy bit of Australia up on the right of the map. Papua New Guinea is only another 140 kilometres north of Cape York Peninsula's tip, but it might as well be on Mars for the likelihood of the tarmac traveller to reach the top. The seal ends a small way up the Peninsula at Lakeland and thereafter it's a gravel road turning into a 4WD track called the Telegraph Road. In the wet season, which I should properly refer to by its technical name 'The Wet', the road is impassable. In the dry season, surprisingly named 'The Dry', which is now, it is not for road bikes like Suzuki V-Strom 1000s.

The area covers 137,000 square kilometres and has a population (so they have apparently counted) of 18,000. It is a big empty hunk of landscape. For some bizarre reason the whole area has a mystical lure for me, and firing like a missile across its base today was a fraction unsatisfying.

On a family holiday in Cairns a few years ago, I had a yearning to 'get out amongst it' as the locals say and hired a conventional two-wheel-drive car off Budget. The map I found in the glovebox had no-go zones all over it in red where insurance would be invalid and there was no possibility of roadside assistance. One such prohibited route was the Bloomfield Track between Cooktown and Cape Tribulation. I loved every minute of it. There were fords, weirs, washouts and unsignposted forks. From that day I marked Cape York Peninsula as unfinished business.

As I sit here on my rock pecking away on the keys on my laptop in the fading light I realize it remains unfinished. My next visit here will have to involve a trail bike with auxiliary fuel tanks, knobbly tyres, a mate or two and some insect repellent. For now I'm just content to be out here with my bike, my tent, cans of cold beans and pineapple and Windows Solitaire.

In Cairns this morning it was another blue sky, balmy morning temperature and filthy helmet visor. I went out to the bike and was aghast to see the windscreen, fairing, headlights, mirrors and indicators covered in dead flies or little moths. I remembered being spattered the previous night coming into Cairns through the darkness and I'd ridiculously assumed it was spots of rain. Back into the motel unit and, using their towels and my Visa card, I scraped and cleaned it all off. The next 15 minutes were then spent cleaning the motel towels.

It was a poignant left turn out of Cairns towards Kuranda, at Smithfield. Poignant because that roundabout represented the end of the trek north, and I, in a moment of dramatic impulse, leaned the bike over Valentino Rossi-style to exit the roundabout: simply to add occasion to this left turn and the start of the westward heading. Equally momentous was seeing the GPS settle on the little 'W' compass heading and not 'N' as I had become used to for the previous five days up the east coast from Sydney. It's the little things, trivial to others, which bring a tear to the biker's eye.

The pull up the hill past Kuranda and to Mareeba was wonderful. Wonderful because I was in second gear, leaning over and in the shade. I passed under the Skyrail gondolas and flashed a quick salute to whoever was up there, probably no-one. It was that sort of morning and zest was running high. The Queensland rainforest soon disappeared and I was riding across the Atherton Tablelands through Atherton, Ravenshoe, Mt Garnet.

I crested a hill to find the hillside dotted with huge wind turbines, turning slowly like massive Ferris wheels. Out in the middle of nowhere I saw a man standing at the side of the road holding a 'Stop/Go' sign. The sign was on 'Stop'. I stopped, as you do in a conformist society, 20 metres or so this side of him. Nothing happened. The road ahead was empty and long. I idled the bike up to him. 'Morning.' 'Morning.' 'Lonely job you've got there.' ''Tis a bit, mate.' 'Roadworks up ahead then?' 'Not really: grass cutter.' The next three minutes passed in silence. I switched off the bike and we existed together out in the heat just waiting for something to happen. Then, bizarrely, having received no communication of any sort, he flicked the sign to 'Go' and I was off with a mutual cheery wave. Five kilometres down the road was a tractor mowing the road verge, completely off the bitumen and a further five kilometres on was a reciprocal 'Stop/Go' man with fluoro vest. A nod and I accelerated back up to 110 km/h.

There were no cars for miles either side of the Stop/Go zone, and, in the absence of anything else to occupy my mind, I became tormented with the question why I had been held up. And it remains a mystery how these blokes communicate. Do they seriously choose to do this job or is it occupational health and safety for road users taken to extremes? The solitude and meaninglessness of Stop/Go guys governing straight stretches of desolate roads would trouble me for the next 2,000 kilometres before I let it go.

Past Mt Garnet I saw several signs warning of road hazards, namely tree kangaroos, cassowaries and 50-metre road trains. Also, the road re-engineered itself. By this I mean it reduced from two lanes with a dotted line in the middle down to one single strip of tarmac with massive red dust verges of shoulders.

You are called on to adjust your driving technique, and the new driving technique is this. Blat along the tarmac strip until you see an oncoming vehicle. Make an assessment of how big it is. If it's a mere car or ute, you can stay on the tarmac; they get their left-hand wheels in the dust, you get a single (index) finger wave as you pass, and that's it. If it's a 'grey nomad' pulling a caravan or a school bus, then you both slow right down and mutually get your wheels in the dust. Then the single-finger wave and that's it.

The interesting protocol comes when it's a road train which, by definition, is a truck pulling up to five trailers. The first sign of one of these coming towards you is what looks like a dust cloud way in the distance. I have now learned to react as follows. Button off completely, get totally onto the shoulder and, if it's hard-packed clay, keep riding with visor down and vents closed. If the shoulder is gravelly, dusty grooves, simply stop. The road train does not get off the tarmac strip for anyone or anything. It has a momentum that means it cannot stop inside a kilometre. I couldn't see whether the drivers waved, as they are sitting several storeys up. They probably didn't, as they were driving the animal at the top of the food chain. On a bike I am a krill equivalent in the ocean of road users.

After I'd passed several oncoming road trains, I started to prepare for when I had to overtake one going the same way as I was. At this early point in my road-train anxiety experience, I planned to simply pull over, have a drink and let him get miles ahead. I had only spent a morning on these narrow roads — known for some historical reason as beef roads — and I wasn't fooling myself into thinking I had the experience, or guts, to take on a 50-metre juggernaut with 20 times the number of wheels I had, at 110 km/h, in gravel.

I passed a lay-by with a huge yellow road train parked in it. I turned back and circled it twice before seeing the driver, in the traditional hi-viz vest, tightening wheel nuts with a spanner the size of a spade. 'OK if I whack off a photo of your rig [note the attempt to communicate in road-train jargon] with my bike?' the krill asked the whale. 'Go for it, mate,' he said without looking up. I felt like an idiot tourist, but it was too good a photo to miss as this thing dwarfed the bike. As it was pointed the way I was riding, I got going quickly to avoid the need to pass it and thus confront my looming demons. According to the 'how to pass road trains' literature you find in roadhouses, you need to allow a visible kilometre in distance, drive on the shoulder and watch out for the vortex of dust generated if the road train's wheels temporarily hit the shoulder. This is probably not the last time I'll be writing about road trains.

It was a long, straight haul across the base of the Cape York Peninsula westward towards the Gulf of Carpentaria. I aimed for Georgetown, another 200 kilometres away. I clicked the bike up to 130 km/h and didn't pass or meet anyone else for 150 kilometres. I saw live kangaroos bounding across the road in the distance and whooped with joy. For some odd reason it now seemed as though I was in the outback proper. I rounded a wide sweeping bend, known to motorcyclists as a sweeper, and had to brake hard to avoid a herd of cows on the roadway. They had humps like camels and I spent the next 40 kilometres congratulating myself both on not hitting one and on renaming them 'cowmels'.

You get an abnormally long time to think on a bike.

I came across a dead kangaroo on the roadside in the same petrified state as the one I'd seen the other day. It was like a child's soft toy that had fallen over on the road. I stopped, took off my helmet and posed with it. The stench made me retch.

Georgetown came and went. I had lapsed into an inertia that caused a sort of soporific laziness. This meant that I couldn't be bothered changing down gear or, in the absolute extreme, pulling over to stop. It was this state of mind which meant Georgetown came and went.

Otherwise I would have called in at the roadhouse, quaffed a Coke and bought a fridge magnet. After all, this was about the only populated place in the 500-kilometre slog across the York. The Savannah Way forged on.

Tens of miles would pass without a single thing moving in the unfolding landscape. Not even a bird. There could have been a nuclear holocaust and I wouldn't have been any the wiser until I reached the next roadhouse. In all probability, they wouldn't have known either. The vegetation was sparse and dry. There were periodic side roads off to Lord knows where and I decided to ride down one simply to relieve the tedium of the tarmac. It was hard-packed red clay. Eventually I turned around but got into some soft bulldust. The bike heaved over and lay there like a pregnant cattle beast. I squirmed out, dusted off and tried to lift it back up, but it weighed 300 kilograms and stayed down. I took off luggage until it was light enough to get upright. There were sounds in the bush which were possibly kookaburras, but, whatever they were, the sound they made was both musical and taunting as if they were chortling at this alien in their landscape trying to jump-start his spaceship.

The sun was now sinking and more miles rolled by with absolutely no change in the terrain. An hour before I had been on the same road in the same landscape. An hour later the road and the landscape would still be the same. It was 190 kilometres to Croydon, the next roadhouse. I set that as my goal and, spurred on by the hastening purply dusk, decided to camp out in the bush that night. Croydon, a blip of a settlement, flashed past and I irrationally thought about stopping at the pub for a cold beer. I got a wave from some boys playing in the dusty street.

About 10 kilometres past Croydon I saw a side road, which looked little used. I headed up it for 5 kilometres and idled into a clearing among the spiniflex and scrubby trees. I set up camp for the night and soon afterwards the most stunning sunset presented a majestic prelude to the inky blackness of being out in the middle of nowhere with no artificial lights to pollute the horizon. The flies started to swarm, so I slumped into the tent.

Looking out of the tent netting, open to get what little air might be eddying around in the humid night, I looked up to the stars. It was like a glow-worm cave ceiling. The Milky Way was bright and massive. The Southern Cross seemed close enough to touch. I was adamant that if I kept looking there would be a shooting star, it was that sort of moment.

There was an orchestra of insects in the bush, each trying to outdo the others. It was too enticing to remain huddled inside a tent, so I clambered out in bare feet and undies. The orchestra stopped and I didn't blame them. I thought about snakes — briefly — but took a punt. Immersed in the blackness with the curtain of twinkling stars above and the resumed cacophony of tree life, it seemed a pity not to be sharing the moment.

BIKE'S FUEL FOR DAY: 22 L, costing $31.
RIDER'S FUEL FOR DAY: Two Mars bars, bag of chips, two bottles of water, full Camelbak, tin of cold baked beans, tin of pineapple.

Chapter 6

Croydon–Mt Isa

Day's ride: 657 kilometres.
Journey to date: 4,029 kilometres.

I'M BACK IN CIVILIZATION tonight after a lonely, hot and fast day at the office. I'm in a motel room in Mt Isa, and I refer to it as civilization because I've eaten my way through an obscene amount of Kentucky Fried Chicken and accessories, such as the Colonel's coleslaw and similar nutritional offshoots. I swear this was a meal from heaven as I was hungry beyond belief. I realize I'm turning into a dietician's nightmare, but the Burke and Wills roadhouse didn't sell any cholesterol pills so what can I do? I've stuck my boots over the bike's mirrors to air them out, and my other deadly weapons — socks, T-shirt and gloves — are draped over the motel room's fan which doesn't work but makes an excellent airing rack. Thus the room smells of fried chicken, sweaty feet and the 'Pacific Breeze' air freshener I found in the toilet which I thought would be useful to spray in my aromatic helmet. Granted, it wouldn't be the ideal venue in which to woo a woman friend, but I challenge anyone to ride all day in 30+ degree temperatures and remain boyishly fresh at the end of it.

This morning out in the bush I had woken at 6.00 a.m. with spinal issues. Basically, my back was sore because I'd been lying on one of my boots all night without realizing it. It was a good reason to start the now interminable process of equipping the bike, tying everything down and hoping the bike would start. It always did.

By 7.00 a.m. the sun was getting a mite warm and I wanted to get moving to cool down. I opened the laptop on the bike's rear rack and downloaded some photos from my digital camera to free up the memory card. I switched on the cellphone, intending to send a few emails and upload the photos to my website, and again got a 'no service' message. I laughed at the futility of it. The nearest settlement of any size was probably back on the east coast some 600 kilometres away. I stripped off my shirt and again the tree insects became mute in shock. I had to top up the Scottoiler reservoir with more hot-weather oil. This is the gismo that drips oil onto the chain and extends its life. It had run dry and I had to prime the tube by blowing air down it. I almost passed out, because it was like blowing up a kid's paddling pool while enjoying a sauna.

From Croydon to Normanton is 140 kilometres, and it went by in a flash. The first hour in the saddle every morning is always comparative bliss, as the seat feels soft, the iPod plays Roy Orbison and the world is never quite awake in the outback. This was the Savannah Way and it ended at Normanton, a dusty speck of a place, which seems to exist to mark the crossroads with the Matilda Highway heading south.

I had harboured a Burke-and-Wills-esque yearning to see the Gulf of Carpentaria and the only option was to ride to Karumba, an impossible 140-kilometre round trip. I contented myself with photographing a sign pointing to Karumba and turned to the vexing question of what to eat in Normanton.

Outside two derelict buildings, which sort of inferred you could buy something to eat therein, squatted several indigenous Australians. I waved, but they simply looked at me. I followed a sign to a bakery and found it up a side street. It looked as though it actually made bread, but when I went inside they only had one steak-and-mushroom pie and a pack of tomato-and-cheese sandwiches. I bought both. Thus the Normanton bakery, at 9.00 a.m., had run out of stock. I asked if I could fill my Camelbak with drinking water. The girl said no, as they have to boil all their water, presumably meaning they don't give it away to tourists free of charge.

In the main street of Normanton there is a big fibreglass crocodile called Krys the Croc that is modelled on the biggest croc reputedly ever caught. It was shot in 1958 by a woman called Krystina Pawlowski, hence the name Krys given to her victim. The story goes that she found the animal basking on a sandbank in the Norman River. This croc was 28 feet long and 13 feet around its girth. Mrs Pawlowski was no random hiker who happened to have a shotgun handy when she stumbled upon the basking croc. She and her husband Ron were crocodile hunters and shot 10,000 saltwater crocodiles in the killing frenzy of the 'fifties and 'sixties, before Australia moved to protect the animals in the 'seventies. The Pawlowskis became staunch conservationists eventually and I'd love to know what turned them around. I suppose a woman can have only so many handbags.

I fuelled up at a BP garage that had four pumps of which three were out of order. In front of me was a rental van branded 'Wicked', which is a chain of backpacker Toyota Hi-ace vans with pithy sayings painted on the back. I know this, as I often overtook these vans. This van's saying was, 'Why are they called haemorrhoids and not ASSteroids?' The driver was a hippie-type American, and his girlfriend wore a long skirt and had bare feet. She looked at my bike and said, 'Cool'.

Normanton also presented me with a moment of truth. Here's the geographical overview. If a crow wanted to get to Darwin it would not fly down to Cloncurry, turn right along the Barkly Highway, track over to the Stuart Highway, turn right again and wing its way north to Darwin. It would fly along the real Savannah Way directly towards Darwin. And this latter route filled me with two things. Excitement and dread. My slight misgiving, as I sat at the junction just outside Normanton, was that this road was both a sinisterly dotted line on the map and was signposted with warnings like 'take extra fuel', 'this is not a highway, drive to the conditions' and '4WD recommended'. I was — albeit perhaps heat-affectedly — entertaining the idea of having a crack at this road in the interests of not backtracking. With a roadhouse called Hell's Gate and remote settlements with names like Doomadgee, who could resist the lure of the outback? On the other hand, every piece of advice I had received or researched on the net about travelling in outback Australia included three critical things to take with you when attempting a route like the Savannah Way. Extra fuel, a satellite phone and someone else. I had none of these. I turned onto the Savannah Way. Three kilometres up the red gravel road, I came upon what proved to be the show-stopping sign. 'Road Closed. Water Over Road 37 km.' This had to be a sign from above saying, 'You mug, stick to the programme'. Fair enough.

Back on the Matilda Highway heading due south it was 200 kilometres to the next slice of civilization, the Burke and Wills roadhouse. This was 200 kilometres of utter and absolute nothingness. For as far as the eye could see, there was sheer flat desolation. This was where I finally understood the meaning of the Australian outback's 'big sky'. It is hard to describe, but here goes. You are sitting on a motorcycle looking ahead. At the bottom of your field of vision you have an inch of windscreen and, above that, a further inch of road ahead. The remaining 90% of your vision is just azure blue sky. In the movie *The Truman Show*, Jim Carrey sails towards a huge blue cloudy sky. It is like that. Perhaps it is the lack of landmarks or elevation which creates this effect.

I rode into this big sky stunned at the bigness of it. Fittingly the iPod clicked into 'My Sharona' and I was fast entering a state of Zen cantering along at close to 140 km/h. The road was narrow with the usual red dust shoulders. It was well surfaced and I could see at least 5 to 10 kilometres ahead to the vanishing point, which evaporated into a shimmering, hazy mirage.

This was when I nearly had my first accident. I am almost too ashamed to include it in this book, but it goes to show the soporific state of mind that I was in as I cruised through this landscape. The road opened out into two lanes to allow for passing. In the middle of this stretch was a gentle curve. Not a corner, just a mild veering. I could see it coming up 5 kilometres away. On the curve I over-corrected and found myself on the wrong side of the road heading for the shoulder. I leant further over and stupidly touched the brake. In short, my line was totally wrong and if something had been coming the other way events would have been interesting. In fact, there was not a vehicle in the next 70 kilometres. I was shocked that I had forgotten how to corner properly. I had ridden into the bend upright and with my mind in neutral. I would have been safer on a horse. To make matters worse, the iPod started playing Abba and I took my punishment from the motorcycling gods accordingly.

I passed over a river that had pelicans swimming in it. Then I saw, up ahead, a cluster of birds on the road. These morphed into eagles tugging away at the entrails of a dead kangaroo. At the last moment they reluctantly lifted into the air and I felt their animosity at being terrorized away from their lunch. The big sky was still massive. I felt as though I was a gnat on something huge. The sheer remoteness should have troubled me for fear of things like punctures or breakdowns. In fact, the opposite emotion engulfed me. I was stripped down to T-shirt and cool, aerated gloves. The tube from my Camelbak delivered warm but refreshing water into my mouth as warm air gushed through my open helmet visor. The bike pounded along to a rhythmic swish of the tyres on the smooth road. As far as the eye could see there were scrubby spiniflex and lifeless gum trees dotting the horizon. I passed over dry creek beds with names like Snake Creek, Dingo Creek, and the innovatively named Dry Creek.

I coasted into the Burke and Wills Roadhouse. These roadhouses are oases — dusty, untidy collections of facilities usually comprising pumps, a café building and a barren camping area. There were a lot of vehicles at the roadhouse, parked in shade under gum trees. There were at least 10 grey nomads in 4WDs towing their cut-down caravans. Then there were three massive road trains that I eyed up as, sinisterly, they were pointing in my direction, inferring that I might have to overtake them if they left before I did.

I tanked up with the most expensive fuel yet, and bought a fridge magnet to prove I'd been there. There was a stench of fried food in the café that seemed out of place. I lay down under a gum tree, took off my boots and socks and slugged down a lime fizzy drink. I heard the thunder of an engine starting up and in a scene reminiscent of the movie *Duel*, two of the three road trains moved off. The cabs were dark and I couldn't see the drivers. By the time they had driven 100 metres, they had changed gear four times. The remaining road train was a sheep truck with three trailers. I rode over to get a photo. There was no driver but the trailers were full of sheep that didn't make a sound. I knew how they felt.

It was 181 kilometres to Cloncurry where the Matilda collided with the Barkly. I rode away from the roadhouse contemplating how I'd pass these monoliths up ahead. The tarmac strip was impossibly narrow; however, there were periodic stretches where the road opened out into two lanes which would allow a strategic, but very quick and pre-planned, passing attempt.

I'd always known that this moment was going to come and I looked on it as a rite of passage. It briefly crossed my mind to drop my speed to, say, 100 km/h and let them outpace me. As I rode along, I summarized these options like a small boy summoning up the courage to punch the schoolyard bully. It came down to a man or mouse call. 'And Twisting Throttle eats cheese for no-one,' the little red devil on my right shoulder whispered. I accelerated towards my demons.

Within 20 minutes I found myself in the slipstream of the rear road train. It was travelling at 85 km/h. After 15 kilometres of what can be described as mounting apprehension, a two-lane stretch appeared, the truck went left, I went right and it was ridiculously easy. The driver raised a finger off the wheel, as is the custom, and I waved back nonchalantly in empathy with a fellow outback road jockey. The rite of passage was over, I had been blooded, and the next road train was overtaken in similar fashion with a Bruce Springsteen number blasting out from the iPod. I yelled out 'You're the Man!' in a pathetic display of self-actualization. In fact, my throttle hand was coated in sweat.

Over the next unwavering 150 kilometres, as I sped through the flat, unrelenting landscape, I encountered several vehicles. This was where I tried to get a feeling for the protocols of waving, an issue which had been troubling me for a few days and one which I need to explain simply to get it off my chest. Here goes.

Lonely Planet Outback refers to the 'one-fingered salute', which is not the same as the city road-rage version. It's a different finger and a different message. You casually lift your index finger off the top of your steering wheel in an acknowledgement of the other vehicle that is sharing your road space if not actually pulling over for you. On the bike I started waving exuberantly with my left hand but felt as though I was farewelling a loved one at a train station, so I tried to tone it down. In the end, after several variations, I actually put my left hand on the bike's windscreen and lifted my index finger.

Then I went through a series of vehicles whose drivers didn't wave back. Each time this happened, I suffered an irrational anger at being snubbed and changed my policy to being the respondee. Let them wave first. Needless to say, drivers would wave and by the time I waved back, we would have passed each other and I was similarly wrenched by the thought that they might think I was unfriendly. For some perplexing reason this whole system became an all-consuming issue for me to the extent that when a white speck appeared on the horizon I would swear to get the wave right. Not too soon, not too late. To this day it ranks up there as an art form with ballet and origami.

It was hard to perfect this art form, but I desperately wanted to get it right because it affected my state of mind as I rode through the nothingness. If a driver didn't return my wave, I got angry. I would then take it out on the next vehicle by spurning them like a sulky teenager. Then, at the last minute, they would lift their finger and I would be angry with myself for being so petulant. The only solution was to wave every time and take the snubs on the chin. Tinted and dirty windscreens didn't help my nano-second analysis as we sped past each other at a combined speed of up to 250 km/h. Nevertheless the waving policy would stay with me until Tasmania — where no-one bothered.

After an eternity, the intersection of the Matilda and Barkly Highways hove into view near Cloncurry. I turned right onto the Barkly, the ribbon of tarmac that would carry me the next 750 kilometres to its end at the Stuart Highway, the turnoff for Darwin. As I accelerated up to speed on the Barkly, there was an immediate change in dynamics. A dotted line appeared down the middle of the road, there were unnecessarily oppressive 100 km/h signs and, the hardest thing to stomach, cars on my side of the road. It was a fast 120 kilometres to Mt Isa and I tucked in behind a speeding Corvette as it sat on 125 km/h. After an hour the Corvette and I crested a ridge, and in the distance in front of us, splattered on the plateau, was Mt Isa, dominated by the two huge chimneystacks of the mines.

It was time for an accommodation treat and I coasted into a motel to ask about their rooms. 'Sorry, mate, we've only got a self-contained flat left for $120, which you can have for $100.' 'Thanks, but that's a bit rich for me,' I huffed and rode away. At the next motel they had one room left, for $99. I grabbed it, rapt with my bargain. That'll be the day I pay $100 for a motel room. I may have suffered road-train anxiety, been snubbed by non-waving drivers and had my dreams of riding the Savannah Way crushed, but my pride was intact.

Bike's fuel for day: 53 L, costing $78.

Rider's fuel for day: Pineapple ice-block, steak-and-mushroom pie in Normanton (town motto: 'We never waste road kill'), three tomato-and-cheese sandwiches, lime drink, melted Kit-Kat bar, Kentucky Fried Chicken in Mt Isa, unknown quantity of warm water from my Camelbak.

Chapter 7

Mt Isa–Threeways

DAY'S RIDE: 636 kilometres.
JOURNEY TO DATE: 4,665 kilometres.

I'M SITTING AT Threeways Roadhouse, so called because at the road
junction of the Barkly and Stuart Highways you can go three ways.
To Alice Springs in the south, to Darwin in the north, or back to
Queensland in the east. To the west there is nothing. I am sitting under
a tree laden with squawking crows in the campground behind the
Threeways Roadhouse. There are a few other caravans and pup tents
here, plus two or three road trains resting up out front. The campsite
cost me $4 and another $5 refundable if I handed back the key to the
toilets. Tempting though it is to keep it, I'll give it back tomorrow
morning. I can use the $5 back.

The sun has dropped below the tree line and the now familiar
golden glow of the half hour or so before the black curtain descends is

filtering through the gum trees and bathing the site in a dappled orange hue. Some peacocks, a lone violinist playing Vivaldi, and some cold Chardonnay would round off the scene perfectly.

It has been a lonely day but a memorable one. Lonely because there was no meaningful town or human habitation for over 600 kilometres. Memorable because I didn't want there to be any. I waxed lyrical yesterday about riding into the 'big sky'. Today the sky was bigger. I can only assume it was bigger because the landscape as far as each horizon contained nothing more than about a foot high. Imagine a prairie without end and a thin line bisecting it. This was the Barkly Highway bisecting the Barkly Tablelands in Northern Territory, but I jump ahead.

From Mt Isa it was a fast and no-fuss 188 kilometres to Camooweal. Here's an interesting fact. In that 188-kilometre ride I never left Mt Isa. 'What the . . . ?' you ask. Sure enough, the Mt Isa City Council administers an area of 43,000 square kilometres, and Camooweal, 188 kilometres to the west, is an outer suburb. This makes Mt Isa technically the third largest city by area in the world, ranked behind Chongqing in China and Wood Buffalo in Canada. The Mt Isa people rushed to get this into the *Guinness Book of Records* claiming, with some daring poetic licence, that it was in fact the largest city in the world. This from an outback town which doesn't even have a Burger King. On the home page of the MICC website, they announce some repairs to the shade structure in the park, a new roundabout being built and the AGM of the chamber of commerce. I'm not belittling this awesome town. It's just that, for a city council which boasts of being the largest city in the world by area, the reality is a fraction lower-key. It's like Timbuktu claiming that the whole Sahara is within its city limits simply because there is nothing out there to offer any sort of counter-claim.

I had focused on Camooweal, outer suburb of Mt Isa, a lot in that 188-kilometre stretch and had built it up in my mind to be more than it was. I fuelled up at the only store and rashly treated myself to a breakfast of bacon, eggs, sausages and toast. I ordered a tea, and the lady brought it over in a brown mug with the tea bag still in it. 'I'll let you do the rest,' she said and, apart from taking out the tea bag, I'm not sure what she had in mind.

While I was wolfing down this heavenly meal, a red Commodore with mags pulled up outside and an aboriginal lady jumped out and came into the store. She was wearing an Adecco top and bright blue track pants, and had bare feet. She went to the instore ATM machine at which she stood for what seemed like five minutes punching buttons. No money came out, she went out of the store and drove off. I'm not sure why that even registered with me, but it's almost as if I'm looking for stereotypically downtrodden Aborigines, such is my dismal level of education about the indigenous situation in Australia. It wouldn't be the last time on this trip that I would labour with an inadequate understanding of Aboriginal lifestyles, but at least I'm prepared to admit it. Sitting there, scooping up my last grilled tomato with a piece of toast, I naturally assumed she was out of cash after spending it all on booze. In reality the woman at the ATM was probably only getting a balance and doing a savings account transfer. No wonder they have a PR problem.

The distance from Camooweal to the Northern Territory border is 13 kilometres. I stopped there for the essential photo op. There was also a rental van parked at the border. I said hello to the couple and guessed they were Dutch. That put out the woman, who sniped that they were Danish, not Dutch. Thus ended my only chance of extended communication for the next 500 kilometres. They showed me their van's layout inside but did not ask anything about my trip.

On the other side of the border, the landscape changed with a jolt. The scrubby bushes and clumps of trees disappeared completely and I rode into a prairie-like vista with the road in the distance not even visible to the naked eye. It was breathtaking. I kept braking in the middle of the road to take a photo, trying to capture the sheer scale of the theatre I was a mere speck in.

There are no open-road speed limits in Northern Territory and I felt obliged to increase my illegal average of 120 km/h to at least 140 km/h. Passing the open-road signs, I accelerated up to 190 km/h for no other reason than that I was allowed to. Out there no-one would care. In fact, out there no-one was there. I thought about another small twist of the throttle to say I had gone 200 km/h. On the edge of my comfort zone already I buttoned off, rationalizing that I could wait to do that over Sydney Harbour Bridge on the way back.

I kept inventing slogans to justify my recklessness as I hurtled along through the flatness. 'In this space no-one can hear you speed.' 'Speed thrills.' 'Faster than a speeding bullock.' And speaking of bullocks, or is that bollocks, a cattle-truck road train pounded towards me, a dot in the distance that after five minutes whacked me with a compression wave. The driver waved and I felt exhilarated by the recognition. At last I was in the brotherhood of highway users. The iPod was playing Sonny and Cher and I sang along to 'Don't Go Breaking My Heart'. Firstly I did Sonny, then I replayed it doing Cher. Then I replayed it again and did both parts resorting to a falsetto for Cher. Solitude was taking its toll. There was a black strip of something in the road which I couldn't avoid running over. It may have been a dead snake or a bit of tyre. I'd like it to have been a snake so I could say to people I had run over a snake, so for the record it was probably a python.

The road stretched out ahead as far as the eye could see and it shimmered in a watery haze. The miles blended into a vista of unrolling sameness. Nothing varied, it simply was exactly the same as it had been 10 kilometres before. Each time I glanced down at the GPS, another 10 kilometres had passed — and I glance down a lot as I ride. Out here I was an insignificant traveller in the landscape and I couldn't stop thinking about people who get stranded in the outback, thinking they can walk for help. The futility of trying to beat this bigness is laughable.

I reached Barkly Roadhouse with my fuel light flashing. This came as a shock as I had racked up just over 280 kilometres from Camooweal whereas I can usually get 350 to 400 kilometres off a tank. I took it that the higher speed and slight headwind had made the difference, so this was a lesson. At Barkly Roadhouse I bought petrol and an ice-block, and had a wander around. The toilets were labelled 'Blokes' and 'Sheilas'.

At the pumps I chatted to the owner of a 4WD truck towing a 4WD caravan. He introduced himself. 'Hair-gama,' he said. (To understand, you need to translate that greeting from Australian into English. I'll do that for you in the next chapter.) Standing at the pumps chatting with Murray I decided to exorcise the mystery about these perpetual travellers. Over the past week I had tucked in behind so many of these travelling couples, fondly referred to as 'grey nomads', that I needed to research things for my own knowledge.

Murray and his wife were on the road for nine months and just flitted wherever the fancy took them. They had been countless times around Queensland and were now striking out for pastures new in Western Australia. The wife was not so full of it. She complained of a sore bottom from day after day of sitting, and wanted to go home to Gympie. The husband ignored her and kept his hand on the bowser. The wife told me I had to see what sounded like Coomagee. I asked where it was and she said it was in Arnhem Land and I should head for Alice Springs — which was in the opposite direction to Arnhem Land. I nodded with thanks and wasn't rude enough to argue with her about her directions. I wished bon voyage to the geographically challenged nomadesse and thought about how long the road ahead was going to be for these two, so tetchy with each other.

After buying the now traditional fridge magnet at Barkly, I mounted up in the unrelenting heat and idled back out from the blissful shade to the bitumen ribbon that was the Barkly Highway. I looked wistfully down the Tablelands Highway, a 380-kilometre stretch of narrow tarmac that goes from Barkly through to Cape Crawford. This cape is, of course, several hundred kilometres from the coast — as it would be.

This route represented another of my subconscious wants in my trip planning. The Tablelands Highway was as desolate and remote as they come, with nothing in the way of shelter, driveways to farms or even corners. It sounded great. But I didn't contemplate it due to my fuel concerns. A distance of 380 kilometres was already on the outside of my known range, but the morning's drag across the Barkly Tablelands had dealt me a sobering lesson about fuel economy. I rode one kilometre up the Tablelands Highway to say I had done it, took a photo, and rejoined the Barkly pointing the Suzuki's nose towards the end of the road at Threeways, 186 kilometres away.

In this 186-kilometre stretch there were four bends. I define a bend as a section of road where you have to actually steer with the handlebars. The angles of most bends were so obtuse that you merely steered straight ahead and did a hint of a lean to change the bike's angle by several degrees. On each real bend I shrieked with joy as this gave me two things to do at the same time: lean over and shriek. This was the longest, straightest road I had encountered so far. It simply went from A to B direct. It was as if a scalpel had sliced a line through the nothingness and called it a road. And why should there be any corners anyway? There was nothing to corner around.

I was riding due west and the sun was low in the sky. It was frying my head inside the helmet so I opened my visor for some air. Immediately a bright green fly flew in and perched on the lining in my helmet close to my ear but just at a spot where I could see it out of the corner of my eye. I found myself chatting to it. The outback is the ultimate leveller for all forms of life. The fly depended on me for a lift, and in turn I may have needed to eat it. We coexisted, Colin and I, as he hitched a ride for 95 kilometres in my helmet. He then suddenly — without warning or any word of thanks — flew out and away. Britney Spears had started playing on the iPod. It may have been a coincidence.

I reached the T-junction at Threeways Roadhouse at about 5.30 p.m. and cut the ignition. That was it for the day. The bike was spent and I was knackered. I set up my little tent and a dog defecated a metre away. I saw a bigger tent with a BMW bike and sidecar parked beside it. Sitting at a wooden table surrounded by pots and pans were a couple who lent me their tomahawk to bash my pegs into the stony ground. I bashed away and the pegs bent. I pretended to get them in and returned the tomahawk. The bike couple were sidecarring around Australia the other way round, and were taking several months to do the trip. I was dying to ask how they transported their wooden table and waited for an opening. They asked nothing about my trip, and after a long, hard day crossing the Barkly I felt a little jilted at the lack of reciprocal interest.

And thus I found myself sitting at a formica table inside the roadhouse, it having got too dark outside to see what I was doing, tapping on my laptop after downing a hamburger. I was feeling too tired to make conversation with anyone in the roadhouse café, although as I glanced around there were some suitable targets. A family came in. The young kids hopped over and sat down at the long table where I was perched at one end. Their mother gathered them up and moved them to a table on the other side of the café. I suspected I'd learn the reason why when I looked in the bike's mirror the following morning.

Desperate for some intellectual stimulation, I got out my fridge magnets and arranged them on the table in alphabetical order. I was so tired that I struggled with the order of Barkly and Burke and Wills. I'd ordered a vanilla milkshake and had a banana one delivered. My hamburger was actually steak and gristly as hell. It tasted wonderful. I just didn't care any more. Tiredness is the valium of motorcyclists and I was groggy on it.

As I lay like a cadaver in my tent, my last conscious thought was about Colin the fly. I hoped he had got another lift back to his family.

BIKE'S FUEL FOR DAY: 43 L, costing $74.
RIDER'S FUEL FOR DAY: Bacon, eggs, sausages, toast 'n'
     tea at Camooweal Roadhouse, bag of Cheezels,
     Fruju ice-block at Barkly, unknown quantity
     of warm water from my Camelbak, a steak
     burger and chips, banana milkshake.

Chapter 8

Threeways–Mataranka

DAY'S RIDE: 564 kilometres.
JOURNEY TO DATE: 5,229 kilometres.

I̱T'S 9:00 P.M. and I'm in a place called Mataranka for the night. I'm sitting slouched on my bike seat, bare feet up on the handlebars, parked among a grove of palm trees in this campsite down by the Roper River. The encroaching dusk is rendering the sky a canvas of purple and pink hues, while the night-time bush orchestra is warming up. Competing with the insects and far-off unknown animals that yowl are a group of grey nomads corralled half a kilometre away in the motorized caravan park. I can hear their Chardonnay glasses clinking from here, and, although I accept this may be my overactive imagination, I thought I heard a flush toilet too. How the other half live. Somewhere near here is a thermal pool out in the bush called Bitter Springs.

I've tied my tent between two trees rather than using the traditional poles, as the whole experience out here smacks of Robinson Crusoe. I've just downed a jumbo can of tinned pears in syrup without using any cutlery, as I don't carry any. I tried using a tent pole to skewer a pear, but it fell off and is now wedged between my exhaust pipe and seat. I'm lying back now, head resting on my top box. My helmet is perched on my bike mirror and through the speakers I can hear the faint crooning of the Eagles. There is some rustling in the trees by the river and I can barely make out some bats flitting about up there. Stretched out on my bike in the sultry night-time air, pear juice staining my T-shirt, the intoxicating 'Hotel California' in harmony with the chorus of insects, and the bright Southern Cross standing out in a mass of twinkling stars carpeting the now jet-black sky, I close my eyes and relive the day's ride from Threeways.

This morning I woke up at 5.30 a.m. to look out of my tent flap, bleary-eyed and sweaty, at a greying dawn sky. The same dog that had soiled my site the previous night was hanging around again and, as at my bush camp several nights ago on Cape York Peninsula, my back was killing me. I can't help lying on things and last night it was my armoured riding jacket shoulder pad. The jacket was my pillow but had migrated during the night to become my mattress. I was so unconscious that I hadn't noticed the discomfort during the night.

I cast sidelong glances at the sidecar couple packing up as I was determined to see what would happen to the wooden table. Sure enough, the legs were unscrewed and the wooden top slid in underneath the sidecar.

Having remembered to claim back the $5 that I had paid as the toilet key deposit, I got on the road and immediately passed a sign to Darwin, 969 kilometres away. I briefly considered another 1,000 kilometres-in-a-day slog like the Gold Coast to Mackay epic, but I didn't want to move too quickly along this stretch of the journey. I wanted to head up some side roads to explore a bit more. The sky was blue, with an amazing white cloud formation spreading over the horizon like one of those rolling clouds in alien invasion movies like *Independence Day* or *War Of The Worlds*. There was a stiffish side wind that caused me to ride at an angle. A road train which was a Shell tanker towing four trailers blasted past me and the compression wave belted me over another few degrees.

The road undulated through the landscape and formed a series of massive long straights. Each straight was about 10 kilometres long, ending in a slight curve after which, and I was always slightly surprised at this, I faced another 10-kilometre straight. I passed a sign in a bush which said 'hot showers' and then another which said 'green grass'. Intrigued, I rode another 50 kilometres and was none the wiser about what these signs referred to. Out here, grass that is green is certainly something to advertise, but who was doing it? Between the grass sign and the next roadhouse there was not one hint of a lawn that you might have thought worthy of a road sign.

I stopped to photograph a dead cow. It was as if someone had dropped a crumpled cow costume on the side of the road. The stench was overpowering and I wondered why it had dropped dead right there. It seemed as though someone had sucked the cow's insides right out of it with a vacuum cleaner, leaving the rest lying there like a discarded pantomime suit. Did the cow just fall off a stock truck, had it been struck at night by a passing road train, or had it simply dropped dead from . . . what? Dehydration? Age? Boredom? I rode off, glancing at the heap again in my mirror, and asked myself why I had stopped in the first place. Dead road kill, which most road kill probably are, was starting to become an obsession.

The iPod blasted a song into my helmet speakers that I banged my head around to like a crazed punk rocker. All I remember is 'Whip it, whip it good'. As the road continued, the bike thumped along with the rhythm. Whip it, whip it good. Before long I was simply shouting out to the empty landscape, 'Whip it, whip it good'. I don't know who sang the song or what the other words were, but it became a pulsating anthem as I replayed it repeatedly like a demented druggie. Looking back, I was simply being a moron and should have been watching the road.

I fuelled up at the Renner Springs roadhouse and encountered my first language difficulty in this foreign country. I bought the petrol and wanted a pen. The girl simply did not understand what I was asking for. 'Pump number 1 gas and a pen, please.' She brought out some souvenir pins of the roadhouse. 'Pen, not pin,' I had to physically pick up her own pen to show her what I wanted. I felt as if I was in Timbuktu.

And speaking of linguistic challenges, here's one for you. Back at Barkly the grey nomad I had talked to at the pumps had greeted me with 'hair-gama'. Since then, I have been greeted at least half a dozen times with the same 'hair-gama' at these roadhouses. Your challenge is to work out, before this chapter ends, what they are saying. Here's a clue which worked for me. Say 'hair-gama' to yourself fast, imagine you're addressing a true Aussie truckie or roadhouse counter girl and pretend you're a local by adopting their Australian twang. It will come, but you have only a few pages left to win the bet.

Between Renner and the next speck of a settlement called Elliott, there were four bends. Approaching the last bend I found myself behind a grey nomad. He was going 95 km/h. I was going 140. I pulled out to pass with the bend 200 metres away. In the past 60 kilometres there had been three vehicles coming the other way. With these odds it seemed ridiculous to err on the side of caution. I erred. Around the bend came a road train. Tucked in behind the grey nomad, all I could rue was what would have happened if I had yielded to the lull of the odds of the open road. If there had been a lotto shop nearby, I would have stopped and bought the lot.

Newcastle Waters and Dunmarra were marked on the map but I don't know why. The first I knew of each of these specks was a sign, 'Thanks for calling'. The Stuart Highway was unrelenting in its perpetuity. The road had no end and simply kept ploughing on. I would have loved to have an aerial perspective of the land. I imagined looking down on the tiny motorcycle as it moved like an ant in slow motion. I was now riding in *The World's Fastest Indian* style. That's sitting back on the seat as far as possible and hunched down behind the screen. It did nothing for aerodynamics but was a relief for my aching posterior.

And then I collided with and killed a resident of the outback. Here's what happened.

I believed it was a bat that whacked into my helmet. Either that or an eagle. It felt big. Very big. In reality it was a dragonfly of some sort. I had my visor down, and looking back I can visualize the last nano-second before the dragonfly disintegrated into a thousand body parts on the thin plastic shield in front of my face. Its expression was both frightened and quizzically resigned to its death by visor. It was such a jolt that I pulled over and took off my helmet. It was as if someone had spattered me with yellow porridge. I then addressed the question of how to clean it off. Where were motel towels when you needed them? I rinsed off the visor with water from my Camelbak and scooped off the debris with my Visa card.

Here's what I now know about Australian dragonflies, or should I say *Austrophlebia costalis*. Firstly, they have between 10,000 and 50,000 individual eyes within their compound eye, so called because it can see in multiple directions at once. Two compound eyes equal up to 100,000 individual eyes all looking in different directions. And it still didn't see me coming? In some cultures, such as those of the Pacific Islands, dragonflies are cooked with onion and are said to taste like crayfish. And I, culinary cretin, simply wiped its remains off my Visa card onto a bush. The dragonfly lives up to four months as an adult, which you would have to say is not a lot of time to form lasting relationships. If I were to be alive for only four months, one thing I would not do is take risks like hovering over the Stuart Highway at windscreen height. You'd want to maximize your time on earth and preferably see out the whole four months, wouldn't you? But here's the best fact. One Australian dragonfly has been recorded as being the fastest flying insect ever, clocked at 58 km/h. A few questions spring to mind. Who timed it and how did they manage it? When they caught up with the speeding dragonfly did they say something like, 'Going a bit quick, aren't you sir?'

So to recap. Here is an insect which has up to 100,000 eyes and a 360-degree field of vision, is the fastest known flying insect and has a vested interest in not taking risks due to its very short lifespan.

I rode away reflecting on this carnage and how, in the cosmic universe of existence, you can always be in the wrong place at the wrong time. With the whole of the outback to choose to hover in, this dragonfly had made a fairly poor choice.

A turn-off to the day's 'must-do attraction' came into view. I refer to Daly Waters. I don't know why, but this place seems to attract tourists for no other reason than it is a place tourists are attracted to. There is nothing there except a pub that is an icon. I hate overly touristy places which label their toilets 'Dunnies' and have sandwich boards outside saying 'G'day mate, ya gotta come in'. I went in.

'Hair-gama,' said the barman. 'Hair-gama,' I replied. I had a pint of XXXX at the bar and saw a Contiki bus pull up. Out poured a throng of young tourists. They immediately formed a rugby-style grouping outside the pub, placing no fewer than 30 or 40 digital cameras in the roadway for the tour leader to click off group photos on each. Cars had to veer around the tour leader in the road. Someone shouted 'All aboard team!' and they flocked back onto the bus. Daly Waters was no richer for their visit and no-one even bought a fridge magnet.

On my way back out to the main road I passed a sign that pointed down a dirt road saying 'To the Stuart Tree'. You're only alive once, so I turned left and rode up the road. Eventually I came to a clearing where there was a low iron fence around a tree trunk that had a lean on it. This was the Stuart Tree. There was a plaque explaining who Stuart was and why this tree trunk was important. To repeat it here would make my head slump forwards onto my laptop keyboard with drowsiness. I realize that is an ignorant thing to say and I do not mean to belittle Australian history.

Stuart in fact was a major explorer of his time, 1862 to be exact, and one of the ones that staggered around in the outback before finally making it out the other side. In Stuart's case he made it in two years from Adelaide to Darwin. Passing Daly Waters he spurned the pub — and faced with paying $4 for a pint of XXXX I don't blame him — instead stopping at this leaning tree. The plaque at the base of the tree stated he carved his initials on the trunk. I was stumped if I could find them among all the Kylies, BJs and 'Gunter was here' scratchings. I memo'ed self to avoid these side-trips in the future.

Larrimah, my next self-imposed goal, was 80 kilometres away. It turned out to be a store and that was it. The sun was getting low and the endless highway plugged northwards. Tony Christie and I belted out 'Amarillo'. I headed for Mataranka knowing I'd be falling off the bike by then. I passed a sign warning of brolgas on the road. The sign indicated it was a sort of stork. Maybe I had wiped a brolga off my helmet 100 kilometres back?

Mataranka is famous for its hot springs where you can soak luxuriantly in 35-degree pools out in the bush. I was covered in a slimy film of perspiration after slogging on in my padded jacket, too lazy to change into my Draggin hot-weather jacket. I could feel my possum-merino-blend socks slide around in my boots. Even at 140 km/h I could smell myself decaying in the heat. I rode past the hot springs sign, feeling hotter for even looking at it. I followed a sign to Bitter Springs campground that was down by a river.

'Hair-gama,' I got in first to the proprietor. 'Hair-gama,' he thankfully responded. I truly felt in sync with this country. I bought a site for $4 and rode, standing up on the pegs, through a bushy track down to the river. A flood had recently come through, and the ground, while looking lawn-like, was boggy. When I put the side stand down, it sank and the bike listed over, saved only by my leg and the knowledge that

I'd be too tired to right it if it dropped.

I found a hard patch of ground, did the obligatory snake, spider and croc check, pitched camp, topped up the Scottoiler, did the tyres, checked the oil, finished a bottle of warm Fanta, opened my can of pears, climbed up on the bike to stretch out, and reflected on a big day's riding, during which my biggest achievement, a few minutes before, there in Mataranka, was being understood by a local with, 'How're you going, mate'. Hair-gama. I take it you just lost my bet.

BIKE'S FUEL FOR DAY: 40 L, costing $66.
RIDER'S FUEL FOR DAY: Packet of chips, meat pie, fish and chips, Fanta, Magnum ice-cream, lemonade ice-block, can of pears, unknown quantity of warm water.

Chapter 9

Mataranka–Darwin

DAY'S RIDE: 483 kilometres.
JOURNEY TO DATE: 5,712 kilometres.

AH, DARWIN. CIVILIZATION. Stopping at red lights. Using my indicators. Looking in my mirrors. Not daring to ride 10 kilometres on the wrong side of the road just to relieve the boredom. I'm not saying it's exactly a culture shock to be here, but I rode into town with such a sense of occasion that I'm embarrassed to look back on it. A lady in a 4WD cut me off at a roundabout while talking on a cellphone and the bizarre thing is I warmed to her. It just underlined the feeling of achievement of making it across the badlands into Dodge City.

This morning I left Mataranka with a cheery yet deep-throated 'sludder ma' to the petrol station guy who equally cheerily fleeced me with the dearest petrol yet. I suppose the same principle lies behind why there is simply nothing fresh to buy at these outposts. After 1,500 kilometres since Mt Isa and my last fresh food — in the form of Kentucky Fried Chicken coleslaw — I would have sold my sister for an orange, anything with lettuce or, and I accept I may be hallucinating here, watermelon. Simply put, everything has to be trucked in and Darwin's fruit and vege store would probably baulk at daily deliveries to places like Mataranka. Therefore the food on sale is frozen, fried and freshless, but then again what else could you expect? Also, in complaining about the limited range on offer, I have to bear in mind who the main customers of these roadside eating establishments are. It is unlikely that a road-train driver would arrive and order an avocado-and-cream-cheese bagel.

My nostrils were flared for Darwin. It was going to be an easy 450-kilometre ride and I was determined to take it easy. I had had enough of blasting through the landscape and I guessed there would be a little more to see than the usual nothing. A tall tree would be nice.

As I rode towards semi-civilization, I also noticed civilization's other features imposing themselves, a process which I call 'de-outbacking'. For example, virtually no-one waved any more. The one-fingered salute stopped just before Katherine as the traffic intensified to one oncoming vehicle every five minutes. There were also mystifying speed restrictions; for example, the imposition of a 110-km/h limit in this state with no speed limits for no apparent reason other than there was an intersection. I spent a lot of time mulling over the mathematical probability of a vehicle speeding along road A that intersects with road B, like the one I'm on. If both were travelling at 150 km/h and they collided exactly on the junction, the odds of avoiding that by limiting the speed on road B to 110 km/h seems a little like bettering your heads/tails odds by flipping a coin two feet higher.

The long-distance motorcyclist gets a lot of time to mull things over. Not all of them make sense.

I pulled into Mobil Katherine and topped up. I decided to celebrate arriving at an actual small town — defined as having a mayor and a post office — the first one since Mt Isa several days previously — by having a coffee in a proper café. I rode up and down the main street, but there was no café. I saw groups of indigenous persons sitting under trees in a park and on the low wall outside the post office. I waved at one guy who appeared to notice me on the bike, but he simply looked away. Katherine was the place I'd be returning to in a few days as it's the turn-off to the Victoria Highway into Western Australia.

The other memory I'd have of Katherine was repeating half an hour. I noticed that the time on my petrol receipt was out of whack with my watch. I have no idea when I rode into a different time zone but at some time since I'd left Queensland, time had gone back half an hour. I think it was when I crossed the border into Northern Territory, although I can't remember any handy sign.

It was a few kilometres after Katherine that I invented Bikesthenics. To explain. Whenever I got off the bike, after a long stretch in the saddle, such as at a fuelling stop, to pose for a photo by road kill or to irrigate the roadside verge, I would suffer an agonizing minute or so of back spasms as my creaky frame adjusted to an upright gait again. Simply put, sitting for hours on the bike was seizing me up and I had to introduce some form of fitness regime into the journey to stay loose and supple. My left toe, which changed gear, and my left index finger, which twitched at oncoming traffic, were in fine condition, but the rest of my body was essentially sedentary for most of the day.

I went through some get-fit options bearing in mind the situation. Some press-ups in the middle of the deserted highway, a power-walk 1 kilometre into the outback, turn 180 degrees and 1 kilometre back, some sit-ups with my feet wedged under a particularly heavy piece of road kill. I badly needed callisthenics yet I didn't want to leave the bike alone. And thus my keep-fit programme called Bikesthenics was born. I have popped a couple of Bikesthenics exercises in the picture pages so you can try them at home. If you haven't got a motorcycle, your barbecue trolley or ride-on lawnmower will do just as well.

The 100-kilometre stretch to Pine Creek was wonderful riding. The sun was not too hot since it was mid-morning, the road was built of light-coloured chip that made me think of a yellow brick road, and the iPod blessed me with sing-along greats. I even karaoke'ed along to the lyric-less *Deliverance* theme. Snigger you may, but this is possible. Dang-dang dang dang dang dang dang dang dang. Dink-dink dink dink dink dink . . . and so on. My heart was soaring with wellness, the bike leaned over in corners like a swan on the wing, and the sipping water from Mataranka in my Camelbak was still cool.

But things were about to get even better.

Yes, I refer of course to an egg-and-lettuce sandwich waiting for me at Pine Creek.

Pine Creek is off the highway and you have to be committed to a hard left turn to go there. Normally that's too much effort and unnecessary hardship on the brakes. However, a sign that advertised Mayse's Café was enticing for its by-line, 'Free coffee for drivers'.

This little gem of a café, 100 metres up a side road, had a food choice which made me realize that the long hours in the saddle had sapped my decision-making skills. I stood there like a complete idiot mulling over whether to order the egg-and-lettuce sandwich or the ham-and-cheese sandwich. Then there came the agony of choosing tea or coffee. 'Hair-gama,' said the lady as she gave me a mug of hot water and popped in a teabag. I was used to this method of tea-making. My role was to crush the teabag there and then on the counter. Had they served cappuccino I'd have been standing there frothing up the milk as well. Then I saw another cabinet with — and I am not making this up — banana cake in it. Pine Creek was a culinary Shangri-la, this small café was a temple, and I felt like Livingstone stumbling across a McCafé in a clearing in Kenya.

I sat outside at a picnic table in the shade, scoffing this smorgasbord of freshness while coloured birds pecked at my banana cake.

I then walked along to the public toilets, where on a low fence sat about a dozen Aboriginal men with stubble and red eyes, wearing old jeans. They all waved and murmured to me in friendly greeting, and I was so variously thrilled and surprised that I was fleetingly tempted to sit down and start a conversation. Why I didn't can probably be put down to guilt about having fed my face with nice food and the inbuilt radar telling me to just take a pee and get back on the bike. It troubled me as I rode out of Pine Creek that they were probably just normal blokes having a smoko, yet I had categorized the situation according to what I remembered about indigenous Australians from schoolbooks read 40 years previously.

Plunging northwards up the Stuart Highway I saw a sign pointing down a side track to McDonald Airfield. I was sick of highway riding and fancied a detour through the bush. The road was narrow and overgrown but nevertheless paved. I had no idea how far away the airfield was, but assumed it was one of many derelict World War Two airfields that dotted Northern Territory. I had a full tank and a full belly courtesy of Pine Creek, a warm balmy breeze in my face, and a jaunty swagger to my riding position. In short, the day — no, life itself, dammit — was full of zest.

Motoring carefully along the pot-holed road out in the bush I stood up on the pegs, opened my visor and enjoyed the ride further off the Stuart Highway into nowhere. The road passed by a billabong and I pulled over. I can't explain the sudden fixation, but I desperately wanted to see a snake, preferably from a distance. Kicking the side stand down, I took off my helmet and listened to the sounds of the bush. A blowfly landed on my face and I had to physically pat it away before it would move.

I set off through the bush on foot, carrying my helmet, and struck out for the far side of the billabong. There was an outcrop of rocks halfway around, and it occurred to me that this would be Snake Hilton if anywhere was. I put on my helmet, reasoning that if a snake lunged I would be protected. I was also confident that days of poor hygiene would work in my favour. I listened in silence but heard no slithering. I lifted up several large loose rocks to see if anything was underneath.

I saw a few ants and a bright blue beetle. I picked up a branch and levered over more boulders, assuming that's what David Attenborough would do. Apart from a twisty vine I saw nothing resembling a snake and was racked with disappointment.

I went down to a small sandy beach at the billabong and dabbled my hand in the water. As a precaution against lunging crocs I put on my helmet for the second time. At once a small dragonfly flew inside the helmet and lost its way. It started tunnelling into my ear and I jerked off the helmet, digging it out with my finger. The dragonfly was squashed in half with its head and wings lodged in my ear cavity. I found a small twig and levered the remains out easily.

I made my way back to the bike through the bush, pushing through a swampy area which covered my boots in a silty mud. It was crushingly disappointing not to have had a more personal encounter with Australian wildlife other than a blowfly, a blue beetle and two halves of a dragonfly.

By the bike was a metre-high conical termite mound. I perched my helmet on the top of this wizard's hat while I scraped mud off my boots with a branch. When I started to ride off, I felt a tickling in my ear and assumed the dragonfly's abdomen was still in there. It turned out to be tens of ants which had got into the helmet off the termite mound. I stripped off my Camelbak water backpack, took out the plug and emptied the lot over my head. It was wonderfully refreshing and washed away the ants. The sense of being dangerously close to nature was overwhelmingly exhilarating and I can't explain it. Perhaps it was a reaction to days in a 'safe' environment with little risk-taking.

As I rode around a bend I found myself literally on the disused airstrip. It was built in 1942 by the Americans' 43rd Engineer Regiment. B25s flew from this airstrip on missions to Japanese-occupied Timor and Penfoei. The pilots were Dutch and the crews Australian. I rode up and down the sloping airfield, dodging pot holes and loose gravel. I could still feel some activity in my left ear, but I rode away towards the Stuart Highway, too lazy to stop again. I named my aural passenger Colin, after the green fly that hitched a ride back on the Barkly. Later, in Adelaide River, I scooped out Colin — who was by that time dead.

There are probably more pleasant ways of ending your life as an ant.

The little roadside communities flicked past as the traffic built up towards Darwin. Emerald Springs, Hayes Creek, Adelaide River. Before Adelaide River I had seen a side road leading over a railway line. I took a photo of the bike straddling the line as I wanted a daring 'what if?' picture of this famous track that runs from Darwin to Adelaide.

As I rode slowly into Adelaide River, what should thunder past but the Ghan train and I couldn't believe my luck in seeing this rail icon in the flesh — or steel. I braked hard and floundered with my gloves trying to snap off a photo. The digital camera wouldn't turn on in time and the train had gone. I did a U-turn and chased the train. The track veered away from the road just as I was catching up. I wasn't sure how I would take a photo with both of us travelling at about 140 km/h. I accelerated to 170 km/h, frantic in my intention to get a picture of the Ghan. After 15 kilometres of this lunacy, and heading back towards Pine Creek fast, I crossed an overhead bridge under which the railway line passed. I had no idea if the Ghan had been through or not. I U-turned once more and struggled again with the gloves, and all of this was happening in slow motion. The Ghan came out of nowhere and thundered under the bridge. I just got the camera out in time and snapped like mad as it disappeared up the line.

I rode back sedately into Adelaide River on a complete high. Adrenalin was surging so fast that I choked after over-sipping out of my now-refilled Camelbak.

The ride into the greater Darwin region required a slight re-familiarization with urban traffic after so long out in the hinterland. The road itself was a dual carriageway and I was being overtaken in the slow lane by cars the likes of which I hadn't seen for a week, defined as anything not white in colour, not towing anything or of which the driver was under 30.

As I entered Darwin proper, I felt like an astronaut returning to

Earth after spending a year in space. I passed Repco, Beaurepaires, Toyota and a mall. At the first set of traffic lights since Cairns 3,000 kilometres back, I prepared to slow down for the red. It turned green as if welcoming me to the end of the trek north. I rode past a park with kids playing soccer, a boy-racer car with blow-off valves dragged me off at a roundabout, and there was a formed kerb at the side of the road instead of a dusty red gravel shoulder.

I pootled into Darwin city centre and ended up riding along the Esplanade looking up at the Novotel and Holiday Inn. Had I been on Mars the landscape couldn't have been more alien. The road ended in a park. I idled into the park and nudged up against a fence overlooking a vista of the Beagle Gulf and the distant Timor Sea. I dismounted, put the bike on the side stand, and gazed out at the sparkling turquoise ocean with some islands faintly etched on the horizon. I had just reached the northernmost point of my trip. The fence stopped me falling into the sea.

I was reminded of Forrest Gump. I'm not big on pioneering history, but the stories of Burke and Wills and their ilk reaching the ocean became very relevant to me now as I leaned on this wire fence in Darwin. Imagine what they felt after slogging for years through the outback, bush, desert and finally mangroves before staggering onto a remote beach, and looking out to sea knowing they couldn't travel any further.

Any similarities between these explorers and Twisting Throttle instantly ended as I toddled off in search of a Burger King.

Darwin represented two things: the point where I had to turn around and go back south, and cashing in on a self-promised treat. That treat saw me in a swanky motel for two nights as I had a rest day off the bike.

My meagre articles of clothing — being two pairs of boxers, a T-shirt, a pair of shorts, my riding jeans, my merino riding top and hot-weather gloves — swished around in a washing machine for $2. It was 34 degrees and there was a deep blue pool just outside my door.

I couldn't go for a swim as my shorts were in the wash. I was standing at the washing machine and peeled off the T-shirt I was wearing, adding it to the machine and feeling like that sultry stud-like guy in the laundrette in the Levis ad. If there had been any insect life in the trees outside it would have gone quiet at the sight.

Back in the room I dialled for a pizza. After complaining about road-house fried food for days, I chose pizza to eat. The irony hit home as soon as I'd hung up and I was ashamed. I looked at myself in the mirror, shirtless and unshaven, and resolved to stop the rot. Nutrition was the first thing on the list. The next day I would look around Darwin, find a supermarket, buy and eat a whole lettuce, a box of bran flakes and a pallet of oranges. I would shave, trim toenails, do 20 press-ups and learn T'ai Chi. I would clean the bike with the motel's towels and swim in the pool to wash my boots. I would send a letter to Mum, meditate, convert to vegetarianism and watch a *Sound of Music* DVD.

The cleansing process had started and I had one day in Darwin to become normal again.

But that would be tomorrow. Tonight I dine on Mexican pizza, drink Tooheys beer from the mini-bar, watch a Bruce Willis movie on Sky, and burp loudly. And I have to tell you honestly, my friends, it doesn't get better than this.

BIKE'S FUEL FOR DAY: 33 L, costing $51.

RIDER'S FUEL FOR DAY: Banana cake (shared with birds), egg-and-lettuce sandwich, ham-cheese-and-tomato sandwich, pineapple ice-cream, mug of tea, Mexican pizza (discarded olives), 1 L of Coke, garlic bread, bottle of Aqua's Gold water with hint of lemon, three beers, unknown quantity of warm water.

Chapter 10

Darwin–Katherine

Day's ride: 696 kilometres.
Journey to date: 6,408 kilometres.

As I sit here in my $19 cabin at Katherine Caravan Park, I look around the room. There is — in clockwise order — a bunk, a chair and a cricket. I had been too late arriving in Katherine to mess around with a tent site, as the sun had already dropped below the tree line and darkness was only a cricket's breath away. I'd also needed the extra tent-pitching time to reflect on the day's events. Today I have suffered the heart-wrenching loss of a riding companion, come unnecessarily close to being part of a bushfire experience, and seen my first Australian wildlife that wasn't curled up lifelessly at the side of the road.

It had been a quick 35 kilometres from Darwin to the Arnhem Highway turn-off to Kakadu National Park. I had factored in this 420-kilometre extra loop because I wanted to be able to say I had gone to Arnhem Land. It was an inexplicable yearning and I can only peg it back to a Social Studies project on Arnhem Land that I once did as a kid at school, and the seed has always been there. In fact, the tarmac tourist can only get as far as Jabiru, which is like saying you've done Singapore after having a cup of tea in Changi Airport's transit lounge. Nevertheless, I accelerated away up the Arnhem Highway with a cheerful heart, my visor open and pumping out a tuneless 'Black Betty' by Ram Jam on the iPod.

Shortly before I reached the wide Adelaide River, I came across signs advertising tours to see the Jumping Crocs. I suspect that crocs that jump are no more than hungry ones lurching out of the water as the tour-boat crew dangles hunks of meat off the side. But that's not the interesting point.

The first sign said to turn off five kilometres on the left. I passed a second sign that said to turn off six kilometres on the right. Then came a sign that said, 'You're getting near the famous jumping crocs cruise, only 3 kilometres on the left'. A fourth sign said, 'Get ready to turn off on the right for the spectacular jumping crocs tour'. Then there was a signpost pointing up a road to the left saying, 'This is the turn you've been waiting for, come on up to see the jumping crocs'. Around the corner was another sign, 'You idiot, you missed the jumping crocs turn-off'. And then lastly, as the river itself approached, there was a sign pointing to the right saying, 'Here you are, start slowing, jumping crocs turn here'. I could imagine that 500-metre stretch of highway being campervan chaos as people stop, reverse, do U-turns and mill around wondering where to go for the jumping crocs. It must work as there was a boatload of people on the Adelaide River presumably enticed into seeing these jumping crocs. With two competing jumping croc businesses on either side of the road, you'd have to say things were ripe for a merger.

I rode through the Kakadu wetlands which, to be honest, looked like a swamp with cabbage trees. I saw a sign for Wonderful Wetland Walks and didn't stop. This will sound uncharitable, but anyone who's just experienced jumping crocs 50 kilometres back is unlikely to gain the same adrenalin rush walking through wetlands. I'm sure it's a truly wonderful wetland walk, but often wonder is in the eye of the owner.

At Corroboree I fuelled up, and as I was pulling out back onto the highway I saw three kangaroos bound across the road ahead and start grazing by a fence. Excited beyond belief to at last see live wildlife in Australia, I sped up to them, threw the bike into neutral and coasted to a silent stop some 50 metres away. Quietly I fumbled for the camera — and then the roos looked up at me. I basically had them cornered. They were up against a metre-high fence on two sides and the highway on the other, with me blocking their escape. This would be a David Attenborough moment. I started up the bike again and idled towards them, slightly smug that at last I'd get my first wildlife photo that wasn't a carcass lying near a white dotted line. I don't know what I expected would happen, but the roos appeared to regard me with something I interpreted as disdain, looked at one other, then leaped the fence. Within seconds they were gone from sight into the bush. I laughed with embarrassment at my naïveté, thinking I could ambush native Australian wildlife in their own habitat. I hoped no-one had seen the encounter.

As a further reminder that I was not really a resident in the landscape through which I was passing, around the corner a white ute, covered in dust, braked hard coming off a side track as he gave way to me on the highway. I waved at the driver. As far as it is possible to tell at 130 km/h, I saw an Aboriginal boy, who could have been no more than 12 or 13, at the wheel. Consistent with my usual cultural success rate of bonding with Aborigines on this trip, he just stared at me.

I was conscious of just blasting through Kakadu without doing more exploring. I passed a sign to Bird Billabong and screechingly did a U-turn. The one problem I had with many road signs there is that everything is wonderfully signposted but no distances are indicated. I headed up the red gravel road not knowing if Bird Billabong were 6 or 60 kilometres away. But the name was too enticing to ignore. I'd see birds, and of course they would probably be in or on a billabong. I never reached Bird Billabong. I gave up after 10 kilometres, realizing the stupidity of assumption. The billabong was obviously there long before the Arnhem Highway. The designers of the highway would not route it close to Bird Billabong, taking it miles out of the way, simply because people might want to see it. Therefore, to assume it would be just off the road was silly.

I rode back feeling out of sorts after a morning of bad decision-making. I just wasn't connecting with Australia. First live kangaroos and then a billabong had evaded me. I resolved to think about things more before charging off on a whim. However, it was a whim that saw me enter a half-hour period just before lunch that caused me more than a small amount of stress. Here's what happened.

Up ahead I noticed some smoke wafting across the road. All up this highway I had been struck by the miles of burned roadside bush, blackened tree trunks gnarled in a still-life death frenzy in a macabre tableau, a carpet of soot underneath black, skeletal bushes and lone green shrubs which had, miraculously, escaped the fire.

In what proved to be a spectacular error of judgement, I rode up a track to get closer to the smoke and, sure enough, 50 metres ahead I saw a burning tree trunk. The flames were half a metre high at the most, and the surrounding bracken-like undergrowth was merely smouldering. Leaping off the bike and grabbing the digital camera I strode up to the conflagrating scene. It reminded me of a farmer's burn-off, but there was no farmer. Suddenly the flames danced across a patch of dry grass within a metre of where I was standing and a wall of fire rose three metres high, crackling and spitting. I needed to urgently change two things. One, my position, and two (yet again!), my underwear.

This was where events turned a little pear-shaped. I dashed back to the bike and in manoeuvring it to do a U-turn on the narrow and rutted track, I dropped it. The expression 'dropping a bike' is motorcycle jargon for it falling over and you springing off it to avoid going down too. The reason it dropped was probably that my mind convinced me I would drop it. It lay there like a beached whale. The dry, burning grass was popping like firecrackers, although the flames were not really moving my way — but I wasn't looking anyway. I had to offload two of the three panniers to lighten the bike in order to lift it up. This entailed fumbling for keys and unscrewing a communications cable. Sweat stung my eyes inside my helmet and I fleetingly wondered how I would explain to followers that the trip had regretfully and spectacularly come to an end in Kakadu with exploding fuel.

Of course, the danger was probably not that real; however, I have experienced less tense moments. When you flee the bogeyman in a nightmare, it feels as if you are running in treacle. I felt the same sensation as I haplessly went through the motions of getting the bike upright, turning it around on the narrow track, reloading it and listening to the little blue angel on my left shoulder telling me it wouldn't drop again. All the while that little red devil on my right shoulder was shouting to me that the fire was almost upon us. I could barely see out of my visor for the perspiration drops. Riding away from the scene, I surfed the iPod for something to calm me down. 'A Whiter Shade of Pale' did just nicely.

I rode into Jabiru after 219 kilometres of Arnhem Highway. A full tank of premium unleaded, a mince pie and a Pepsi later, I was back on song, putting the Kakadu Konniptions of the morning behind me. It was 200 kilometres back to the Stuart Highway, and I stripped down to T-shirt and no gloves, ready for the ride west. This is where my second issue of the day revealed itself. A close encounter with a bushfire was one thing — had it gone badly for me, I would have been the only victim. Not so my next bout of trauma. It happened like this.

In sorting out my tank bag, I discovered that I had lost my right-hand padded glove. The left one was there, but not the right. I unpacked everything on the roadside and slowly the implications of the loss dawned on me like a wave of utter dread. This glove had left Darwin on my hand, and somewhere in the Kakadu, where I had switched gloves to the hot-weather pair, it had dropped off the bike. I have a checklist that I follow religiously whenever starting out after a pullover, to ensure that nothing is left perched on the rear luggage. This checklist had somehow failed and now I had lost a friend through my lack of attention.

It is a difficult thing for the armchair traveller to understand, but tour riding gloves are more than just $50 pieces of kevlar and nylon. This glove had been with me for 6,000 kilometres since I'd left Sydney, and now it was out there in the Kakadu, alone and frightened, padded fingers probably reaching for the sky, and the last sound it had heard was my bike accelerating out of sight. I racked my brain to think of where I might have dropped it. It could have been at any number of pullovers on the highway in the last 100 kilometres. Maybe it was at the bushfire site? But wasn't I riding gloveless before that? I momentarily considered riding back down the way I had come, but it would be like finding a needle in a haystack — and it was possible that that particular haystack was on fire.

I rode in fourth gear for about 10 kilometres, getting my mind around losing this glove. I could get a new pair in Perth and in the meantime the hot-weather ones would be fine. It wasn't that. It was something on a deeper emotional plane. This glove had twisted the throttle for me day in, day out, had braked when I wanted it to, had symbolically started us out on each leg of the journey by pressing the electric start button. And because of my carelessness, the glove was now lost, abandoned to the bush and finished.

I could visualize the glove lying in some dead grass, looking up at the twinkling stars, resigned to its fate. I hoped it could forgive me. Over the next 20 kilometres on that highway out of Jabiru I composed a tribute to my right-hand glove that I would like to share:

To Glovey

Today I lost a friend.
A sad and lonely way to end
the journey for you, my glove.
You were my right arm
or the end of it anyway
and we didn't deserve to part today,
when the trip is only a third done.
All you'll see now is the setting sun.
You twisted the throttle with your padded grip.
You braked for corners, you steered the ship.
You were my one true glove.
And now we say our last adieu.
Farewell Glovey, rest in Kakadu.

I stood up on the pegs, fast-forwarded to a suitably mournful and dirge-like Enya number on the iPod, and for exactly a kilometre I saluted my lost companion.

But I knew I had to move forward. For example, the next pressing question was where could I stop to take a pee?

I came up to a river and saw a car parked on the bridge. An elderly couple were peering over the railing with a camera and then they started to clamber down the bank below the bridge. Why am I writing about this? Let me put this in context. The river's name was South Alligator River. It looked as if Mick Dundee should be paddling about in it. There was a warning sign before the bridge with a silhouette of a crocodile and the words 'next 5 kilometres'. As you left Jabiru, there was large red sign the size of a house saying, 'Don't risk your life. Stay out of creeks and rivers.' I found it incredible that this couple would trek down to the riverbank. Anything for a photo. Imagine what they would do if they came upon a bush fire . . .

Talking about risking your life with crocodiles, there was a pamphlet I had read at Jabiru while I was eating my pie. If you are attacked by a crocodile and are being pulled down in the famous death roll (that's your death, not the croc's) all you need to do is stick your thumbs into its eyes and its jaws will open. At that point you of course remove two things: your thumbs from the croc's eye sockets and yourself from the river.

The road undulated its way through the Kakadu National Park. I felt I should stop to explore something before leaving. I saw a sign urging people to visit Leaning Tree Lagoon. After my experience with the anti-climatic Stuart Tree in Daly Waters, I wondered why Aussies have a fixation with trees on an angle and rode on. Next was a sign to Nourangie Rock, again with no distance indicator. It was tempting. Was it another hanging rock where I could have a picnic and hear haunting pan-flute music? Or was it a rock covered in ancient Aboriginal drawings? Or was it simply a big rock 40 kilometres down a 4WD track which some innovative local had cloaked in superstition and was charging tourists $5 to have a look at? Cynicism won the day and I didn't even change down gear.

Disgusted with my ignorance, I vowed to actually stop and explore at the next opportunity which presented itself. It soon came with a sign pointing to Alligator Billabong and Red Lily Billabong. Billabongs and red lilies are right up there with me. But you don't name a billabong Alligator Billabong without just cause. And then it occurred to me that I'd been told there weren't any alligators in Australia. Why is everything suggesting otherwise? I pootled a kilometre or so down the road towards the billabongs, but a gut feeling and low fuel saw me turn around and head back to the highway for Pine Creek. You can only have so much excitement in Kakadu.

The last chapter of that day's ride was the 90 kilometres back on the Stuart Highway from Pine Creek to Katherine. I passed three massive trucks transporting army tanks, but otherwise the road was all mine. I crouched down behind the screen and my speed crept up to 150 km/h as the wheels hummed on the white tarmac and I sang out loud to 10cc's 'Rubber Bullets'. The highway curved up and over escarpments covered in scraggly gum trees. I say gum trees, but I don't really know what they were. Insects whipped my bare arms and hands, but the freedom was too overpowering to worry about these minor things. Freddy Mercury, Elton John and a techno-Grease megamix fuelled the testosterone as I became the road and the road became me. I was clearly hallucinating and Katherine mercifully hove into view as the sun was making shadows of my bike on the red shoulder. John Denver started up with 'Country Roads' and I knew then it was time to end the madness.

So I invested $19 in a cabin in the Katherine caravan park and unpacked. I had two neighbours. In Cabin No. 1 was Hardy, a transient fruit picker who follows the work. He rakes the leaves in this caravan park and for that gets a cabin and food. He's originally from Christchurch, New Zealand. 'Hereford St, mate', to be exact. He was one of the occupants of a hotel in Frankton in New Zealand's North Island which burnt down in 1995, in which six people died. He was the last one out and sat on the tin roof until it became too hot, then jumped. In Cabin No. 3 was Graeme, who is a miner from Mt Isa. I'm not sure what he does here. He said he had excess skin growth. I wanted to know more. He explained it as a condition where the body produces too much skin, particularly around the eyes and chest. Graeme was grilling his meal of barramundi and onions on the communal barbecue. It smelt tantalizingly beautiful. I bought some barramundi and chips at the garage next door. They tasted untantalizingly awful. Hardy and Graeme went to bed at about 7.30 p.m.

Here in Cabin No. 2, apart from the cricket on my wall, there is nobody else here to talk to. Except my now obsolete and recently widowed left-hand glove. I have some explaining to do and the time is now.

Bike's fuel for day: 43 L, costing $66.

Rider's fuel for day: Leftover watermelon for breakfast, mince pie from Jabiru bakery for lunch, orange juice, two bottles of water, two muesli bars, barramundi and chips for tea, Pepsi, a Camelbak full of warm water during riding.

Chapter 11

Darwin
Katherine
Turkey Creek
Broome
Mataranka
Croydon
Cairns
Threeways
Mt Isa
Mackay
Karratha
Overlander
Kalgoorlie
Ceduna
Gold Coast
Port Wakefield
Walcha
Perth
Madura
Goulburn
Sydney
Jerramungup
Mt Gambier
Cann River
Melbourne
St Helens
Hobart

Katherine–Turkey Creek

DAY'S RIDE: 722 kilometres.
JOURNEY TO DATE: 7,130 kilometres.

TODAY I CROSSED three things. A border, a time zone and the centre line — the latter many times. The border was between Northern Territory and Western Australia; crossing the time zone meant going back two hours; and the repeated crossing of the centre line was due to boredom. The ride of 722 kilometres started with a warm-up 200 kilometres across the flatlands between Katherine and Victoria River, then a 300-kilometre scenery dress rehearsal to Kununurra, culminating in the 200-kilometre main act as I rode, open-mouthed and genuinely goggle-eyed, through the eastern side of the Kimberley.

I'm tapping out today's riding log hunched over the laptop in a small cabin at a roadhouse in the middle of nowhere called Turkey Creek. Its real name is Warmun, but I, and seemingly the owners, like the turkey name better and, besides, that's what it's got painted on the roof.

My cabin cost $30 which I thought a little rich for a fibrolite box kitted out with a slat bed, a bed light with no bulb, a large tin for an ashtray, and a window that won't shut. I've duct-taped my mosquito net over the window and so the cabin stands out from its neighbours as now having air conditioning. In the communal ablution block there is a piece of paper taped up over the basin saying not to swallow any of the water due to calcium. Tonight I go to bed without doing my teeth.

My cabin is one of six in a row. I arrived totally knackered at 6.30 p.m. as the sun was getting low. As I was unpacking, my fellow cabin residents arrived. It was, in fact, only 4.30 p.m. — I had forgotten to put my watch back two hours at the border. My neighbours are off a roadworks gang doing the shoulders 30 kilometres further along, on the road towards Broome. They're up here for six months doing their shoulders and staying in this luxury cabin complex. They swarmed around the bike and I became a ringmaster for half an hour, demonstrating the bike's electronic toys.

Rip, my next-door neighbour, drives a roller and asked to put the helmet on to listen to the Bee Gees on the iPod. As I type, he is still out there in the dark with the headlight burning. I suspect my battery will be flat in the morning, but he's enjoying it. Clay is a young guy from Donnybrook whose job is manning the 'Stop/Go' sign. In Australia they call it 'Stop/Slow' because that's what it says on each side of the lollipop sign. He told me how the Stop/Slow system works and there is more to it than I have given these guys credit for. In previous daily logs I have been less than complimentary about Stop/Slow men. I could now wash my mouth out.

When these guys turned up this evening, one of them looked like an Aborigine. I wondered if this would be my chance to talk to one. In fact, it was Harry, who does some job on the road gang that entails him getting completely and utterly covered in dust and grime. He is literally black at the end of the day. He had a shower — taking care not to swallow any water — and emerged a white man after all.

The fourth worker in this gang is Tony, who's from Adelaide. His house had burnt down and he had almost lost his dog in the fire as well, as it 'catching *ammonia* from the dousing, mate'. He then bought a caravan and towed it all the way up the middle to Darwin, where his daughter Jemma got a job at McDonald's. Now he is working as a grader driver in the Kimberley. You could drive a truck through the missing bits in his story, but to question him would be like asking Lord Lucan what he'd been up to lately.

The new friend I'd made last night in Katherine, Hardy, had urged me to stay at Turkey Creek. Now I could see why. There's a sort of cabin network around for non-tourists and it is fantastic. I feel like one of the boys, while the tourists shack up over at the poncy caravan park. While they sip their Chardonnay from chilly bins we, the roughnecks, slurp water from the outside tap and spit it out, due to the non-swallowing rule. All I have to do is end each sentence with 'mate' and say 'yeah?' a lot. I do a lot of listening. Rip is the only one who asked about my trip. He said he could drive around Australia in his ute in a week, but a bike might take longer because of the bugs at night.

The day had gotten off to a strange start. Twenty kilometres out from Katherine I was struck with a bizarre patch of indecision: I simply couldn't choose between two options presented to me.

The first bout of dithering came when I saw up ahead a small kangaroo or wallaby in the middle of the road looking as though it was cleaning its paws. It did not see me. I could either go left around it, staying on my side of the road, or veer over to the right. It got closer and I fluffed around thinking about what to do. This was all taking place in a few seconds. The animal might either jump to the left side of the road, the direction in which it was facing, or, if you listened to the stories, it could about-face and leap back to where it had come from. I simply couldn't decide in time and rode straight into it on the centre line. Except it wasn't there any more. It was off to the left in a flash and had a second to spare.

Then 'The Lion Sleeps Tonight' came on the iPod. Do I weem-a-way or do the falsetto? I tried to do both. It was a mess.

I saw a boab tree. Should I stop to take a photo or keep going? I was still undecided 2 kilometres past the tree. The only thing I could think of for the next 10 kilometres was how 'boab' is an anagram of 'abbo', and was this just coincidence?

I put this state of pathetic inertia down to the surroundings. From Katherine through to just before Victoria River the landscape was, in a word, neutral. There was nothing remarkable to look at or hope to look at. I knew that 20 kilometres down the road it would be just that: 20 kilometres down the road. And time would have stood still. It seemed I was becoming immune to the sameness of the terrain and merely riding for the sake of riding. Usually I gaze around like a meerkat on wheels. That day I tucked in behind the screen and simply counted down the kilometres.

I passed the turn-off to the Buntine Highway at Willeroo. That wouldn't have registered other than I recalled the name from a news report the previous month about a man who had survived over two months in the outback. Here's how it went.

The 35-year-old man — let's call him 'Wally' to protect his real identity, but whose actual name might have been Rick Megee from Brisbane — was driving along the desolate and remote gravel road called the Buntine Highway. The word 'highway' is not to be taken literally. In the distance he spotted a sole figure waving him down. He stopped and picked up the hitchhiker. At some time in the journey as they bounced over ruts and tree roots the hitchhiker offered Wally a drink from his canteen. That was the last thing Wally recalled.

Some time later he regained consciousness and noted with concern where he was: namely face-down in a hole, covered with a plastic sheet with rocks and dirt piled on top. 'What woke me up were four dingoes gnawing at the plastic sheet trying to get to me,' Wally reported later.

Over the next 10 days he walked cross-country in search of water and help, regularly passing out from heat exhaustion. He found a small stagnant dam and decided to make camp — consisting of some sticks with which he fashioned a crude shelter against the sun. Each day before darkness fell, he went out and caught lizards, grasshoppers, frogs and little brown snakes. He ate those with gusto for his one meal a day. 'I ate leeches raw, straight out of the dam. The only thing I sort of had to cook was them frogs. I slipped them onto a bit of wire and put the wire on top of my shelter, let the sun dry them out till they got crispy and then just ate them.' Wally stayed put, enjoyed his carnivorous diet and waited.

Two months later, workers from the remote cattle station Birrindudu happened upon the dam and out of the bush stumbled Wally. The workers, hurriedly throwing a tarpaulin over the cannabis plants in the back of their ute, greeted this walking skeleton with the classic Aussie salute, 'What the f***?' Wally was given three things. Two cans of Fosters and a flight to Royal Darwin Hospital.

The outback had taken its toll. He weighed 45 kg, had lost half his body weight, and introduced the nurses to his imaginary friend Dave. The doctors were a little sceptical of his story until Wally complained that there was only one fly in his soup. Northern Territory police were looking into Wally's claims but had found no evidence of criminal offences. The commissioner, in a press conference, was reported as having said, 'Not another b****y dingo case'.

It was Gregory National Park and the Victoria River roadhouse that snapped me out of the funk. The National Park because it had speed signs on corners, which meant I had some leaning to do; the roadhouse because it had a blackboard on which was scrawled those heavenly words 'All-day breakfast'. 'Hair-gama,' I greeted the roadhouse man. 'Hair-gama,' he replied. 'All-day breakfast please.' 'You want tomato with that?' 'Is the pope a Ca . . .' As I wiped the last trace of egg off the plate with the final bite of toast, I wondered if life, defined as a full belly and a full tank of premium, could get any better on the road. It soon did.

The Gregory National Park was a series of brick-red escarpments that towered above the small, thin line of tarmac undulating through this prehistoric wilderness. The sun was high in the sky, creating no shadows, and the landscape was like a creased piece of canvas, dabbed with hues of red, brown and green, across which an ant — that's me on the bike in this metaphor — was slowly wending its way. As the red cliffs surged close to the road, I found myself making out faces in the formations. Around a bend, three or four eagles were on the road feasting on a carcass. As the last eagle flew off, surly and resentful at the intrusion, it left its lumbering lift-off so late that I could have kicked it as I sped past.

I stopped at the turn-off to the Buchanan Highway, a 420-kilometre no-fuss gravel road that traverses the never-never through Top Springs, emerging at Dunmarra on the Stuart Highway. As I pulled out my camera, a ute towing a caravan arrived in a massive red dust cloud and out clambered a husband and wife. Without a word being spoken, he trotted over and shook my hand. 'Good on ya, mate, that's the way to do it, just watch the crossing at Coolibah and you'll like Jaspers, that's only 54 clicks from here.' He assumed I was about to tackle the Buchanan on the bike and the one-sided conversation had gone so far that I couldn't find any part of my ego ready to admit I was only taking a picture of the sign. I rode off up the Buchanan, standing on the pegs like an adventure rider, looking in my mirrors begging them to drive off towards Victoria River to avoid me having to overtake them if they went my way to the west. They departed northwards, praise be. I turned around and deftly exited the Buchanan Highway feeling like a namby-pamby. Road tyres, an inadequate fuel range and the fact that I'd be heading back towards Queensland were fairly good reasons to miss the Buchanan, I argued.

At Timber Creek I fuelled up. At that moment a coach pulled in and out climbed at least 40 senior citizens. The women headed for the roadhouse store, the men pulled out cigarette packets. About half a dozen of them came over to me. In the next 10 minutes I learned more about Nortons and BSAs than I care to know. I pulled up next to a road train that was a bulk fuel tanker which had just refuelled the petrol station. The driver was checking his toolbox. I asked him if he was allowed to self-fuel and he talked to me about inputs and outputs — and I still have no idea if he could fuel up his truck from his own three fuel-tank trailers. He asked me what the bike's fuel usage was. I said 17 kilometres to the litre and asked what his was. He said 800 metres to the litre. The mouse duly bid goodbye to the lion.

The Victoria Highway forged through open grassland, across small escarpments and over countless creeks, mostly dry. Snake Creek, Dingo Creek, Emu Creek flashed by and I counted six Sandy Creeks. I saw a large lizard in the middle of the other side of the road, frozen in terror or merely sunning itself safe in the assumption I would observe the road rules. I did and we passed as friends. Approaching the Western Australian border I knew the open speed limit was coming to an end and pushed it up to 200 km/h as a last token gesture. I had never ridden at that speed and it felt unsafe. I imagined patches of melted tar. Riding into the Western Australian border station was like taking the bike in to get a fitness certificate. I was asked if I had worked on a banana plantation in the last six months, and whether I was carrying on board any honey. That was a no and a no, and I passed into Western Australia, a state the size of India, with a clear conscience.

I rode through Kununurra and past the turn-off to Wyndham. The road became the Great Northern Highway and this would be my yellow brick road all the way to Perth. Perth was so far away it didn't feature on any road signs. The furthest town signposted was Port Hedland, 1,500 kilometres down the road. I saw a snake on the shoulder, did a U-turn to investigate, discovered it had a bite out of it and wasn't moving so decided to add it to the photo library of wildlife carcasses I had seen.

The last chapter of the day was a 200-kilometre slice of motor-cycling heaven as the Great Northern carved its way through the eastern flanks of the Kimberley. What I called escarpments in the Gregory were mere stopbanks compared with the Kimberley's ranges. The sun was going down fast and the broken red rock faces of the tree-strewn cliffs were dappled in shadows, creating the most wondrous plasma of colour you'd ever see in Mother Nature. It was like something out of *Planet of the Apes*. A pterodactyl cruising high above the tree line on a thermal would not have made me turn my head. Pillars of upthrust rock dotted the horizon and ever present were the endless escarpments of red and brown cliffs.

The road lost its dotted line and I became reacquainted with my friends, the wide red dusty shoulders, last seen in Northern Queensland. But there was nothing on the road to overtake, so I rode through the primeval landscape unchallenged. The V-twin motor on my bike thumped away somewhere down under my seat, my brain thumped around in my head with tiredness and Meat Loaf thumped out of my helmet speakers with 'Bat Out of Hell'. How about that for the perfect anthem as the bike streaked through the dusky haze of the Kimberley, eagles soaring high above the cliffs on lazy warm thermals and grazing wildlife looking up through the scrub like startled meerkats as the alien machine carved through their territory?

And so it was that Turkey Creek roadhouse suddenly materialized around a bend, nestled in trees in the middle of this desolate yet alluring landscape. It was time to stop, slurp their water without swallowing and invest in a $30 cabin.

Turkey Creek is the gateway to the Bungle Bungles, the term 'gateway' being defined as having brochures and a helicopter which does scenic flights over them. The cost is $800. That's another 26 cabins. I'll think I'll just get the fridge magnet.

Bike's fuel for day: 49 L, costing $82.
Rider's fuel for day: Brunch — bacon, eggs, sausages, tomato, toast and coffee at Victoria River, two muesli bars, bottle of water; tea — hotdog, chips, lemon cheesecake, Fanta at Turkey Creek; supper — 10 biscuits and bottle of water; full Camelbak of water drunk during ride.

Chapter 12

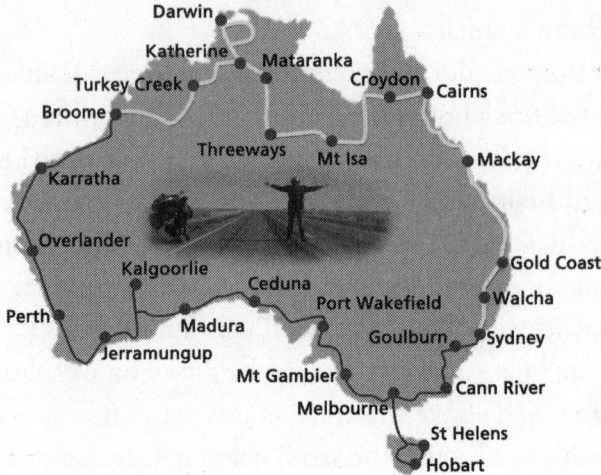

Turkey Creek–Broome

DAY'S RIDE: 865 kilometres.
JOURNEY TO DATE: 7,995 kilometres.

I CAN'T REALLY describe the feeling that came over me when I clicked the bike into neutral, put my foot down to stop it easing forward and raised the visor on my helmet. Where was I? At the end of a boat ramp in Broome. Had I ridden a further 10 metres, I would have been in the Indian Ocean. I looked out on a sparkling blue vista. The sky was deep blue, the ocean was shimmering blue. There is something special about seeing the sea after so long.

So long? It was pathetic. It had only been three days since I was in Darwin, but it seemed three times as long. I suppose the journey into Western Australia and here to Broome had been so hot, long and dry that it seemed as if I'd walked all the way. To gaze out to the horizon and look for Africa was a defining moment. That's three out of four coastlines cracked, only the south edge to go.

'You can't park there, mate,' a lifeguard complained. I was jolted out of my reverie, kicked the bike into first, and rode back into Broome to look for a cold shower and for water you were allowed to swallow.

That morning at 5.00 a.m. my cabin neighbours at Turkey Creek, the road gang, got up. The cabins were separated by walls made of tissue paper. Therefore at 5.00 a.m. I got up too. They were on the road with their graders, rollers and 'Stop/Slow' signs by 6.00 a.m. I passed them 30 kilometres down the road at 6.15 a.m. and they all gave me the road-gang salute — one finger raised. I in turn stood up on the pegs and rode through the 30 km/h roadworks zone between them feeling like a visiting dignitary. Not a huge show of emotion between us, but I felt the bond.

This was the first time I had ridden so early. I worried about wildlife but saw none. I also saw no other vehicle for 160 kilometres all the way to Halls Creek. The sun was so low it cast shadows across the highway like an unending avenue of black and white stripes. Before being lit up by the sun, the escarpments were a dark ochre and the landscape was muted. It had not woken up yet and I was sorry for disturbing it so early. A flock of brightly coloured birds swarmed across my path and swooped high into the sky. I told myself they were rosellas because that's the only brightly coloured bird over here I could name.

I rounded a corner to find a creek flooding across the highway. It looked shallow and crossable. I braked and thought about options. Options? Turn around and do what? I rode through and it was ridiculously easy. It's strange how being on your own magnifies risks. I reached Halls Creek at the time I'd normally be rolling over in my sleeping bag, crimping another five minutes' snooze. I fuelled up at the store and went in to pay. Aboriginal citizens buying all the fried food the store could dish out besieged the counter. Hotdogs, pies, chips and sausage rolls. And this at seven o'clock in the morning. For the store to have trays of this food ready suggested that they knew their customer base. Across the road was a park where a huge number of Aboriginal locals were squatting, sitting and being generally motionless. The thing that struck me was that they were dressed in such bright clothing, from purple track pants to Fijian-like flowery shirts. I'm not sure what Halls Creek, a hamlet in the middle of nowhere, offered these residents. Perhaps they were well-off . . . I don't know. Whatever, they could certainly spend up for breakfast.

I set off into the Kimberley for the 290-kilometre run to Fitzroy Crossing. I now thought of my goals in 200-kilometre increments. A 100-kilometre stretch is like riding down to the shops for a pint of milk. The sun rose in the sky and instantly the landscape was whitewashed. The road was a light-coloured chip, and the tall grass, waving languidly in the soft breeze, was bleached. I struck a rhythm, which was mesmerizing.

The Proclaimers screeched through my helmet speakers and the music was too harsh for the ride. I surfed forward on the iPod. Cat Stevens, Boston, the Moody Blues and I rode through the morning. I even let 'Mull of Kintyre' run through unforwarded. It was that sort of ride. Gentle, undulating, leaning left, leaning right, entrancing. After listening to the Drifters I almost fell off, I was so laid back.

I flowed into a valley between brick-red escarpments. The road dropped away onto a flat plain of nothingness. In the distance were mesas, flat-topped plateaux, shimmering like a mirage. I could have been in Africa. Had a gazelle darted across the road, I wouldn't have blinked.

What was blinking, however, was my fuel light. A zephyrish head-wind combined with my load reduced my fuel range. I had 65 kilometres to go to reach Fitzroy Crossing roadhouse, where I would be able to suck lifeblood up from the well of petroleum waiting for me there. Should I slow right down and ride in fourth gear to conserve fuel, or would that use more? Should I blast along at 140 km/h and shorten the misery of not knowing?

I couldn't keep my eyes off the blinking fuel light. It was the bike communicating with me like a warning of some impending seizure.

The GPS counted down the kilometres and I started assessing what would be an acceptable walking distance if I coughed to a halt short of Fitzroy. A sign to Ngalingkadji, an Aboriginal community way out in the bush, appeared. They wouldn't have a BP station there, but maybe a jerry can. Irrationality was a by-product of tension in the cockpit. I switched off the iPod pretending this would conserve fuel.

I surged into Fitzroy with the bike on the verge of having a coughing fit. As the bowser nozzle gushed unleaded relief into the parched tank, I reviewed distances here in Western Australia and mentally adjusted the refuelling policy. Simply put, where there happened to be a petrol pump I would stop and top up.

At Fitzroy I bought a Mrs Mac's jumbo sausage roll and an ice-block. I pulled over under a tree in a park to enjoy this feast. 'What you doing, fella?' A small shirtless Aboriginal boy stood there, also with a jumbo sausage roll in his hand. 'Riding around Australia on this motorbike, son.' 'Is that far?' he asked. I got out my road atlas, found a map of Aussie and traced a line around the outside. 'Where you from?' 'From New Zealand.' 'Sydney?' 'No, New Zealand.' He called to his two mates under the tree. 'This fella's from Sydney.' 'What's your name, young fella?' I lapsed into native jargon. 'Curtin,' he said. I've spelt it 'Curtin' because I didn't want to think of him as a 'Curtain'.

His two mates wandered over and I went through my demo of the toys mounted on the bike. They each tried the helmet on, and Curtin stood there, a metre tall, little brown body with a big titanium-coloured helmet on, listening to 'Crocodile Rock'. 'Where do you live, boys? Fitzroy?' 'Nah, down there in bush.' I took that to mean an indigenous community out in the sticks. The boys clambered up on the Suzuki. I showed the oldest one how to start it and then press the kill switch. Curtin kept listening to Elton John. 'How far to Broome?' I asked, knowing the answer. 'Which way's that, then?' they asked me. They ran after the bike as I pulled away from our shady tree.

The last I saw of Curtin and pals, they were tucking into their jumbo sausage rolls under the tree in Fitzroy Crossing.

I forged on towards Broome under a hot and angry sun. Everyone else seemed to be having a siesta, as the road was almost deserted. I heard later that the state's highest temperature was 35 degrees at Fitzroy. And those degrees were concentrating themselves in my helmet cooker and down my back.

I was riding in a merino-fleece top that was meant to be cool in hot weather. It was slimy with sweat and became untucked from my jeans. I was so uncomfortable I didn't know it had ridden up to just under my neck. For I don't know how long I was riding along with my stomach and chest exposed. I wondered why women covered their small children's eyes as cars passed. I cringe now at the thought of it.

The straights were so straight I couldn't even see the end of them. The road just evaporated into a watery nothing as mirages hovered on the distant tarmac surface. I rode through a smoky haze, which turned out to be a sizeable fire crackling through the tinder-dry undergrowth a metre from the road edge. For kilometres it was as if a scorched-earth policy had been followed, with wisps of smoke curling up from blackened stumps. There were thousands of termite mounds for as far as the eye could see. They were man-sized lumps of brown dirt and it felt as though I were riding through Cerberus's litter box. The road was still white, which made me feel hotter.

The iPod blasted out the Blues Brothers and Bryan Adams. Finally, a techno version of Venga Boys forced me to end the agony and I pulled over in the shade of a massive boab tree to glug down the last half-bottle of water.

Mercifully, Willare Bridge roadhouse soon appeared on the horizon and the slog was over. Watermelon and fresh ham sandwiches now elevated this august establishment to five-star status. It was nectar. The watermelon was soft, brimming with sweet juice and tasted beautiful. I ate two big pieces and let the juice stain my top. I felt as unhinged as Jack Nicholson in *One Flew Over The Cuckoo's Nest*. In reality this was caused by riding too many long miles in the hot cauldron that was the southern Kimberley.

By contrast, the 200-kilometre stretch into Broome was forgettable. I say that because I can't remember a thing about it. I remember the turn-off to Derby on King Sound and recollected that you fly over this part when you're doing a long haul to Singapore from New Zealand. I looked up wondering if anyone was up there in a 747 looking down on a parched and arid landscape wondering if anyone was down here. That's the flight where you start your nap over Sydney and six hours later wake up to discover you're still over Australia. Derby to be exact.

Reaching Broome and the west coast of Australia, I had this thing in mind: to do what Forrest Gump did and ride literally to the end of the country. I GPS-ed my way out to Cable Beach, which is like the Surfers Paradise of Broome. I rode to the end of a boat ramp with only a 10-metre beach between me and the lapping surf of the Indian Ocean. I asked a guy to take a picture, which he did, but it turned out to be of a hotel behind us. I asked him if he would take another one, this time with me and the bike and the Indian Ocean in it.

It was time to crash. I crazily asked about a motel room at Cable Beachside Resort and the coiffured receptionist quoted me $295. It was probably her way of refusing me as a guest in such a swanky place. I hadn't shaved for a few days and my helmet hair was sweatily plastered to my head, but I believe what clinched it was that my merino top was still around my neck.

BIKE'S FUEL FOR DAY: 57 L, costing $94.
RIDER'S FUEL FOR DAY: Two muesli bars, jumbo sausage
    roll, mango ice-block, two slices of watermelon,
    ham-cheese-and-tomato sandwich, two bottles
    of water, Trumpet, full Camelbak of water.

Chapter 13

Darwin
Katherine
Mataranka
Turkey Creek
Croydon
Cairns
Broome
Threeways
Mt Isa
Mackay
Karratha
Overlander
Kalgoorlie
Ceduna
Gold Coast
Port Wakefield
Walcha
Perth
Madura
Goulburn
Sydney
Jerramungup
Mt Gambier
Cann River
Melbourne
St Helens
Hobart

Broome–Karratha

DAY'S RIDE: 839 kilometres.
JOURNEY TO DATE: 8,834 kilometres.

T HE CONVERSATION WENT something like this. Him: 'I'm going to get a bike like this, with all the toys, and tour Europe, hopefully with her.' Her: 'I've got a lot of sailing to do first. Maybe I'll crew a bit through the islands, then come with him on the bike.' Him was a young English guy from Birmingham who looked a bit like a surfie. I'd peg him as a Rick or a Danny. Her was Katherine, a 19-year-old backpacker who had sailed in the Greek Islands and was besotted with it. It was the same wishful thinking you hear in backpacker common rooms everywhere. These two had wandered over as I was pitching my tent at the Karratha Caravan Park after another 800-kilometre day in the saddle.

He drooled over the bike . . . dusty, covered in squashed flies and ready for a rest. That was me of course, but the bike had some flies on it, too. I chatted away to the two backpackers as I stooged around, making an effort to put the pegs in the right places. Him and a pal were driving around Australia in a car. They'd picked up Her and a pal hitch-hiking at Monkey Mia. That was a week ago. The girls looked on the boys as a handy transport option. I'm no student of behaviour, but I suspect the boys had a few options as well. Ah, the impetuosity of youth. I asked how old they were. They said 19 and 22. They asked me too. I said 39, deducting 10 years. It seemed to work. She listened to music in the helmet and he kept peppering me with questions about the electronics. He said he would be back at 7.00 a.m. to listen to the bike when I left. He never showed.

Today I toughed it out from Broome to Karratha. If you look at a map of Australia, it's like an inch of progress down the coast. Yet 800 kilometres is almost the length of Britain, or the same as riding from Rome to Prague. The point is that in most other countries travelling that distance in a day would get you somewhere — for example, from one side to the other. In Australia it represented just another page turned in my tank-bag map book.

During my pre-departure check at Broome, I had noticed some flaking rubber on the rear tyre. It was down on tread but I felt it would be manageable to Perth, some 2,000 kilometres to the south. There was no other option anyway. Broome didn't have a Kentucky Fried Chicken store, let alone a bike shop. Still, I had a small cloud of concern hovering over me for the first 100 kilometres before the 'she'll be right' wave of resignation finally got me back into my rhythm of nonchalance. I bought a 5-litre jerry can at Roebuck roadhouse, filled it with spare petrol and put it in my top box. There was a 326-kilometre fuel-less stretch to Sandfire Flat roadhouse and I didn't want the extra stress of praying the fuel would last.

I passed the regular sight of a dead kangaroo at the side of the road. Now think about this. It is a little-known fact that kangaroos and emus cannot walk backwards. That's why they feature on the Australian coat of arms . . . the country that doesn't look backwards, blah blah

blah. So you're a kangaroo and you're feeding at dusk by the roadside. Something prompts you to want to cross the road, so you set off. You hear an increasingly loud sound and you look up to see a road train's halogen lights bearing down on you. Your best option is to get back to the original side of the road to get out of its way. But biologically your curse is that you can't go backwards, so you are rooted to the spot in a sort of neutral gear between forward to certain doom or reverse which won't work. The last thing that goes through your mind, apart from the injustice of this quirk of nature, is of course your ass. I'm sorry, that was crass, but the numbers of dead roos started to obsess me, just in terms of the question 'Why did the kangaroo cross the road?' And to be honest, all I can come up with after kilometres of mulling it over is truly 'To get to the other side.'

The Great Northern Highway is only tens of kilometres from the coast in places, but it might as well have been a thousand. The terrain was unrelenting nothingness. Parched, barren, absolutely constant. A group — or is that a flock? — of black eagles lifted off their road banquet as I bore down on them. This had always been a game of avian roulette between me and the highway birdlife in Australia. As if planned, the last eagle to lift off suddenly swooped back over me at a height of inches above my helmet. I involuntarily ducked and noted that the eagles were now one up.

I passed a sign saying that there would be stray cattle around for the next 120 kilometres as the road was unfenced. Sure enough, I saw a lone cattle beast grazing in the brush. But here's the question: How does the farmer round up these cattle when the need arises? In an area the size of Sri Lanka, his cattle could be strung out for over a hundred kilometres. How does he find them? And how does he herd them? And to where? It's not like they graze in handy groups.

With the cattle-herding mystery still preying on my mind, I reached Sandfire Flat roadhouse after 300 kilometres of mental endurance and wondering why A-Ha called their song 'Take On Me'. Is it just me, or does that title not make sense?

Sandfire Flat is a true oasis as there is nothing on either side of it for at least 200 kilometres. You have to stop there. The place has a captive audience. They can charge what they like, and they do. I fuelled up a dry tank. I had not needed to call upon my jerry can, but I was grateful for the backstop nevertheless.

And that was when I saw the blackboard. All-day breakfast. I was hungry beyond belief and I don't mean for salad. I reached for my wallet. I got talking to the lady behind the counter, who was in the process of fleecing me for my fuel. She'd been up from Perth working at Sandfire Flat for seven months. Given that there is no human habitation for at least 200 kilometres in any direction, I asked what she did on her days off. 'There's a lot here,' she replied. 'In seven months I still haven't seen it all.' I asked why she worked roadhouses for a living. 'If I go back to Perth my kids give me hell.'

I ordered an ADB and she winked as if to say 'You look hungry, I'll give you the works, mate.' Now I don't believe you should expect any high standard of food presentation in a place like Sandfire Flat roadhouse, given that parsley isn't grown out here, but my stomach simply refused to acknowledge grilled tinned tomatoes on, and in, a pile of baked beans, which were, in turn, spooned on top of fried onions. Also under there somewhere were two eggs and some toast. It was unfortunately a case of quantity over quality, but I think I was given the deluxe helping so I didn't want to be seen not eating it. Inwardly I was retching.

I carried my plate outside to a picnic table under a tree where I gave thanks that a few birds fluttered down and took off with my hash brown and bacon. I ate the sausage, one egg, some toast and slurped the tea. The rest I shovelled into the 40-gallon drum that was the bin. I waited 10 minutes, took the plate back inside with a light burp for effect and complimented the lady on the breakfast. 'No worries,' she said, and looked pleased.

From Sandfire Flat it was back out onto the highway, for the 300-kilometre stretch to Port Hedland. At Pardoo roadhouse I tanked up, and a brace of backpackery sorts poured out of a minibus branded 'Planet Outback Xtreme'. The driver rounded them up and said, 'This is a petrol stop, just hold off buying anything until we stop at Sandfire for lunch.' It's obvious which roadhouse slips him some commission.

A strange thing tended to happen each time I rested up at a roadhouse. For the first 20 or so kilometres after hitting the road again I would feel incredibly sleepy and lethargic to the point of wanting to pull off the road and have a snooze, preferably under a shady tree. Bizarrely after the 20-kilometre mark I was humming again and full of zest. It was just that first 10 minutes of head-nodding stupor I had to survive without falling off. I would come up against the state-sponsored powernap signs in Victoria, but here in Western Australia the fatigue warning signs didn't really pose a solution, they just warned you that you were about to fall asleep at the wheel . . . zzzzzzz.

You get the point.

The problem was that I simply couldn't afford the time to stop, find a shady bush, park up, de-glove, etc., stretch out on the ground, have a few winks and then reverse the process to get going again. And the danger would be that I'd be too comfortable, fall into a deep slumber and wake up when a dingo was licking my face.

And that, my friends, is why the Snoozuki Programme was born. How to snooze on a Suzuki without all the rigmarole, including getting off the actual bike itself. It was brilliant. I could pull off the road, when smitten with one of these bouts of fatigue, throw the bike on its centre stand and adopt any one of about eight positions I invented to have a nap in full gear on the bike. The Snoozuki Programme helped me from that point on, and I wished I had thought of it as far back as Queensland. The bonus was that you couldn't over-nap, as after 10 minutes the clutch lever digging into your calves would wake you in agony. There are a couple of Snoozuki positions shown in the pictures in this book. Feel free to try them in the comfort of your own home. If you don't have a motorcycle, a lawnmower or wheelbarrow will give you the idea.

Back on the tarmac after a quick Snoozuki moment, I wrestled again with the ever-vexatious question of waving protocol. It's time to explain my fixation with this subject in depth, so here goes.

Since leaving Northern Territory a few days previously, I had noticed that I was always the one who initiated the wave. Usually I got a response, but the point here is that it was always me first. So that raised the question, if I didn't wave, would they? And if not, why not? Do they simply not wave in Western Australia or don't they wave to bikes? Is there some unwritten protocol that you acknowledge only a fellow vehicle on your level of the food chain, defined by how many wheels you've both got? I hadn't passed any bikes for over 2,000 kilometres so couldn't test the theory.

So I launched my own survey to exorcise this mounting chagrin. I had 250 kilometres of nothing to do other than balance, stay upright and steer, so it was a golden opportunity. I started by continuing my policy of waving first. Here are the results of my survey.

Truck drivers never wave at anybody. They are too high up in their cabs, probably high on other things as well, and own the road, so why acknowledge the fluff between their toes? With some exceptions, I didn't get return waves from women and men with grey beards. Women with grey beards? Enough said. I never got waves from what could be deemed locals; that is, utes with machinery on the back — such as hoses and agricultural plant — officialdom (being utes with yellow beacons on their roofs), or buses. Perhaps these drivers are on the road so much it is a fag to wave. Or perhaps I was dismissed as a mere tourist and ranked as a krill-equivalent accordingly.

I started looking intently at the fingers of the drivers on their steering wheels as I passed to ensure I wasn't falsely maligning them, whereas they might just be twitching their index fingers — that is, after all, the basic wave here. Some campervans have tinted glass, so they could have been greeting me with semaphore and I wouldn't have known.

Then I stopped waving first. There were only a few drivers who waved at me, but after each of these encounters I felt like a sod for not greeting them back. That's because they waved too late and I couldn't respond in time.

The margin of error of my survey is about 80% and I'm not sure what the conclusion is. I decided to keep waving first. Just like my waving experiences in Northern Queensland, when I got snubbed I had a momentary bout of road rage, but it passed. It was better that way than enduring the 1-kilometre guilt burden of not returning a stranger's friendliness.

Port Hedland was off the road. I could have detoured in for a look, but the whole area was a bleak mining landscape with shunting yards, huge piles of ore and rusting machinery. I rode on through. At Roeburne I had to stop at a police checkpoint. I took off my helmet and was breath-tested. The last time I had had a drink was 2,000 kilometres back, in Darwin. And in the meantime that partial all-day breakfast at Sandfire Flat would have soaked up a lot. I passed the test. I rode away thinking how much I would like a beer, and damn them for putting the notion into my head.

The last 100 kilometres of the day taught me what I already knew: that the last 100 kilometres of a riding day sucks. As a rule of thumb, the 700-kilometre mark in a day's ride is when my bum signs off for the day and makes me know it is on overtime rates thereafter. My back starts to groan and I have to perch way back on my seat, hunched down behind the screen, meaning that my legs ache.

As a ball of aches and pains I tottered into Karratha knowing I had about 10 minutes to find the night's shelter and get off the bike. Thus I was happy when my GPS found the local caravan park for me and I got a tent site for $10. It was right outside the house of the caretaker and I felt like a schoolboy sitting outside the headmaster's office.

There was a small superette attached to the camp. I went in expecting to be able to buy a bag of chips and a Fanta. I saw a pre-packed plastic tray with partitions containing quiche, spring onion, sliced ham, potato salad, coleslaw, tomato, gherkins, boiled egg, lettuce, mayo and cucumber. This was the antidote to Sandfire's all-day breakfast. I couldn't believe what I was seeing. I sat in my camp chair by my slouching tent and ate with gusto. I used my Visa card to scoop out the potato salad and my bike keys to skewer the tomato and gherkins. A few sandflies got in the way — and with a mouthful of gherkin, who could have really tasted that moth? — but never has a meal at the end of a long day on the road tasted so special.

I was on a bulletproof high, my stomach was bulging, and I headed off to the ablution block in such a devil-may-care mood that I bolshily didn't wear footwear in the showers. And to contradict the findings of my waving survey, the campground residents, miners from Karratha, greeted me with a heart-warming 'hair-gama' first. The last thing I remember before slipping into that black hole of fatigue-driven unconsciousness, lying in my tent, was how nice it was to be acknowledged almost as a local. That and had I remembered to take off my helmet?

BIKE'S FUEL FOR DAY: 59 L, costing $98.
RIDER'S FUEL FOR DAY: All-day breakfast (half left) and mug
    of tea at Sandfire, mineral water, Fanta, two
    muesli bars, pre-packed salad tray at Karratha
    and full Camelbak of water drunk during ride.

Chapter 14

Karratha–Overlander

DAY'S RIDE: 828 kilometres.
JOURNEY TO DATE: 9,662 kilometres.

ODAY I THOUGHT about a lot of things. Most of those things were trivial, but I had the time, so nagged them to death in my head. Sometimes I nagged out loud, just to give my mouth and ears some exercise. You see, there was nothing to do other than ride and nag. Nag and ride. The distance from Karratha to where I am now — the Overlander roadhouse in the middle of nowhere, also referred to as Western Australia — was just over 800 kilometres. In that stretch of 800 kilometres there was no human habitation except for a few roadhouses. It was like riding from San Francisco down to Mexico or two-thirds the length of Italy without passing a single house or person doing anything. The one town on the way, Carnarvon, you had to turn off to get to. I didn't, because I was too lazy and too used to pointing straight ahead and going forward.

So, and this is my point, in that desolate, barren and empty 830 kilometres I got a little bored. In fact, I got more than a little bored. I was paralytic with boredom, verging on going mad. That's why I exercised my mind by dwelling on anything and everything. That's why today's log is a little off the wall. You had to be there. You had to be pointing ahead, going fast, dissecting any minor distraction, whether a strangely shaped cloud, a combination of numbers on a number plate as you passed it, or why somebody would name their farm Boologooro.

A lot of the time I fretted over the deteriorating back tyre. I could almost hear the rubber burning off onto the road as I sped along. But what could I do about it? It was like being in a 747 on the way to London and worrying about whether you had left the oven on back home. You just had to put it out of your mind and adopt a fatalistic attitude. What will be, will be. And to complete the madness, at that point I started crooning Doris Day's 'Que Sera Sera'. I pulled over, switched off the bike, stood on the empty deserted highway and wondered if there had been a nuclear holocaust. There had been? Oh well, que sera sera.

I was out of the Karratha campground at 7.00 a.m. No point in hanging around. A quick 'hair-gama' to the only other inmate in the shower block and that was it for human communication until my first roadhouse fuel stop. By 100 kilometres into the day I had seen four dead kangaroos at the side of the road. It was quite a slaughter. The one common denominator, apart from their being dead, was that their heads were missing. I dwelt on this and wondered why. Would eagles peck off and carry away just the head? Could it be possible that when being run into by a truck, the kangaroo gets neatly decapitated? When I saw dead kangaroo number five I had the answer. A dingo was right there on the side of the road gnawing the head off this kangaroo. When it heard me coming it paused briefly, glancing up with slit eyes and a whipped look, then trotted off sullenly into the bushes. It was smaller than I had thought it would be, with quite a silky coat. I thought dingoes were more or less like wolves, but this one was like a small hound.

I tucked in behind a car towing a caravan for a few kilometres before passing it. On the tyre cover of the caravan was written 'Grumpy and Max Gotch, Port Lincoln, SA'. This reminded me of another conundrum of the road. Frequently these grey-nomad caravans have names on them which give them a personal branding. Mostly these names are not real words and I have concluded they are a composition of the names of the occupants. For example, I have seen Shirken, Margiepat and Marygal. The last one had me guessing but I'm thinking Mary and Dougal.

This one that I was following, however, was in a class of its own. I didn't want to overtake it until I had worked out what was going on. Was Max the husband and, if so, had he decided to nickname his wife 'Grumpy'? Surely she wouldn't have consented to that being put onto a tyre cover? Maybe one day Max turned to her and said, 'For God's sake, you are such a grump, Gotch,' and it stuck. But why advertise that your wife is a grumpy woman on a tyre cover? Then again maybe Max is the wife, full name Maxine. Therefore Grumpy is the husband. This starts to make sense. And what's he grumpy about? Is he so grumpy all the time that everyone now calls him that instead of 'darling', 'Dad' or 'Jim'? If so, he must be happy with that nickname to put it on a tyre cover.

What if it's two males? I imagined Jack Lemmon and Walter Matthau up in the cab bickering away.

I overtook the car but the windows were tinted so couldn't see in. I accelerated away from it still mulling over what the Gotches were thinking when they ordered that tyre cover.

An inconclusive encounter but one that somewhat enlivened 20 kilometres of boredom.

I took a photo as I crossed over the Tropic of Capricorn because it seemed worth marking the event. You almost wanted someone to hand out a certificate from a roadside booth as they do in planes when you cross the Date Line. But what exactly is the Tropic of Capricorn anyway, other than a notional line on a map? Why is it a tropic? It means you are exactly halfway between the Equator and the South Pole and I suppose how significant that is, is up to the individual. I always remember crossing the 45th parallel in the South Island of New Zealand, or should I say, driving past the road sign that marks it, and it does give me a slight buzz from a sheer order-of-things perspective.

While I was off the bike taking the picture, I stood first on the northern side of the Tropic of Capricorn sign, then walked 2 metres over the invisible Tropic and stood on the southern side. There was a *Doctor Who*-ish 'passing-into-another-dimension' feeling for an instant, but at the end of the day you could have put that sign anywhere and I would have stopped to take a photo. I mounted up and headed off again.

The landscape was flat, barren and, I hate to admit this, tedious. I was finally sick of the endless spinifexy shrubs and ugly stunted trees. Make up your mind, you foliage. If you're a tree, have things like leaves and, here's a suggestion, be green — not this washed-out grey/khaki. Grow tall and be proud, not bent over and twisted. I was angry and tired of the surroundings for the simple reason that I had been looking at it constantly for days on end and hankered for some colour, richness and life. Suddenly a stroll in a leafy central-city park surrounded by peacocks and scampering children appealed more than it normally would. But, then again, this was Western Australia and it was the dry season.

Every few kilometres I crossed a floodway that was a 200-metre-long depression in the road with height markers along the edge. There were no creek beds as such, but just slight hollows, and it was obvious that in the wet you'd see a fair bit of water surging around. Perhaps the flora springs into life in the wet. I was sorry to have maligned it. In fact, it was I who was in their territory, not the other way around, so a bit of respect was called for. And I pledged to be more upbeat about the terrain.

I stopped at Fortesque, Nanutarra, Minilya and Carnarvon roadhouses to top up. I was still carrying the 5-litre jerry can full of petrol in my top box from yesterday and thought I might get rid of it as the roadhouses were now no more than 250 kilometres apart and thus within my fuel range. How providence worked in favour of Carol and Maggie.

These were the names of the two ladies who were now flapping their arms around on the side of the road up ahead, by a parked white rental van. I briefly thought about the rule in the Australian outback which states that you don't pull over for anyone due to the risk of carjacking, mugging and murder. I pulled over. These ladies were English and upset. They had run out of petrol half an hour ago. I was the first person they had seen. They had ignored the rule about filling up at every roadhouse and had flashed past Overlander. Their van had coughed once and cut out.

In what could only pass for a chivalrous *Gone With The Wind* moment of valour, I whipped out my 5-litre jerry can, glugged life back into the van's fuel tank, handed the can to the ladies, dropped my voice a few octaves to add a bit more machismo than was necessary to the words, and said, 'There you go, ma'ams. See that you fill up that jerry can at the next roadhouse so you'll always have some spare,' and made to mount up. Had I been wearing a hat I would have doffed it. They attacked me. Maggie offered me cash, Carol offered me a place to stay next time I was in Goa, India. I settled for a photo, but got a bonus hug and kiss from a shaken Maggie. After almost flooding the van in their eagerness to hear it splutter into life, they roared off so quickly I didn't have time to get their address in Goa.

I rode on mile after same mile after same mile after same mile. Nothing changed, it was totally and utterly constant. The sky, the landscape, the sound of the bike, the unfolding road ahead. After a 10-kilometre straight I would round a shallow bend and be facing another 10-kilometre straight. It was as if I was some little friction toy that a kid keeps playing with on the kitchen lino. No sooner do you crest a ridge or round a curve, than the same tableau is cast before you again. It was the same in the Barkly, yet different — perhaps because I was fresher back then. I couldn't put my finger on why this southern slog was so tedious. I wondered if the Nullarbor would be as daunting. Since leaving Karratha I had set myself the policy of, on the hour, stopping in the middle of the road and taking a photo of what lay ahead over my windscreen. When viewed one after the other these 10 images look exactly the same with only the cloud formations varying.

I got so bored I started to analyse the iPod songs. I set it to shuffle so I had a little more thrill of the unexpected than usual. I vowed not to fast-forward songs but just to hear them out, warts and all. The trouble is, I knew there was a Glen Campbell in there somewhere. It annoyed me that the Proclaimers had to shout all the time; I wondered what Dire Straits are doing now, and why all Coldplay's line-up sounded the same. And what is '99 Luftballons' all about? If video killed the radio star, what sort of havoc would digital have wreaked on it? And can there be a better sing-along than 'Duke of Earl'?

Between Carnarvon and Overlander I crested a small ridge and saw the same desolate landscape unfolding before me. There were two unique features, however, which stood out from the sameness, and they were the red-and-blue flashing lights on top of a police car. Surprisingly I noticed this at the same time that a policeman was flagging me down. I suspected he didn't want to ask if I had any spare petrol. 'Going a bit quick, mate?' That entrée to the process of being relieved of $100 has to be a universal chat-up line common to law enforcement in all countries.

I listed the reasons why I thought I could be excused for a little excessive speed. Highest on the list was an observation on exactly where we were, namely miles from civilization, on an empty highway with up to five kilometres forward visibility on a dry surface. But this was no time for sarcasm. I knew I was for the high jump. Having read books about motorcyclists going through borders in Eastern Europe I knew instinctively how to handle this delicate situation.

'Here's my licence, Officer,' I said, pulling it out of my tank bag. 'Thank you, Mr . . . let's see . . . Mr Throttle. But you can have this $20 note back.' His partner, meantime, was inspecting the back of the bike. 'Your tyre's a bit dodgy. How far do you expect to get before it blows? That's a blow-out waiting to happen.' I dismounted and made a fuss about inspecting the rear tyre which I hoped would garner me some sympathy. 'Actually that's why I was speeding. To minimize tread wear and avoid a blow out.' That statement was two things. Worth a try and nonsense, but it seemed to have worked. 'OK, your call sir. Good luck, Mr Throttle and take it easy.'

As I did up my helmet, I congratulated myself silently that the tyre diversion had taken their minds off my speeding. Not even a warning. Brilliant. 'Oh, and don't forget this.' He handed me the piece of blue paper headed up 'Traffic Infringement Notice'.

I rode away from that interlude both $100 lighter and even more rattled about my tyre. I had been conscious of the rapidly balding tread ever since Broome. Why, oh why hadn't I changed it in Darwin? The pace of wear seemed exponential. It was as if the last 20% of wear had taken place in the last 200 kilometres. Having a third party, and one in uniform at that, mention the word 'blow-out' spooked me into a realistic roadside assessment of my situation. It was 750 kilometres to Perth. I wouldn't make it on that tyre. Fifty kilometres down the highway was Overlander roadhouse. That would be my goal for today and I'd review the likelihood of making Perth tomorrow.

I rode off and slowed my speed to a crawl. It took an hour to reach Overlander but not before I'd ridden across a cattle-stop, called a grid — and I didn't like the sudden, slight back-wheel skewing that happened. There was also a sort of ripping sound, and I was running through the options of simply dismounting where I was, hiding the bike in the scrub, removing the back wheel and thumbing a lift to Perth and back when finally and mercifully I tapped down through the gears as Overlander roadhouse appeared over my windscreen.

That was it for the day. A day of gritty patience and perseverance. I was so tired after all that mental endurance that I couldn't be bothered getting a tent site. I pushed the barrow out and treated myself to a $45 cabin, a Mrs Mac's beef pie and a Pepsi. I was in that sort of 'couldn't be stuffed' frame of mind and just wanted to crash out. I unpacked the bike and had a decent inspection of the tyre.

I was shocked. Tyres are typically black and they have grooves in them referred to as tread. Mine didn't. The sound I heard crossing the grid had been the last bit of rubber leaving a part of the tyre that was now showing the white canvas lining. That tyre had died and had revolved its last revolution pulling in to the roadhouse. To ride further on it would be courting a life-insurance claim. The journey had thus faltered at Overlander.

Geraldton, 300 kilometres south, was the nearest town where there might be a bike shop. I would have to park up at Overlander, take off the back wheel, catch a Greyhound bus to Geraldton the next day — a public holiday— stay in Geraldton until Tuesday morning, find a bike shop if one existed, get a new tyre fitted to my wheel, find a way back 300 kilometres north to Overlander, fit the back wheel on the bike and resume the journey. This would cost me at least two days. I had three up my sleeve for this very type of curve ball.

I put the bike on its centre stand and removed the back wheel. I would be travelling the 300 kilometres from here to Geraldton three times and taking as my luggage a wheel — whereas most other bus passengers would have backpacks or suitcases. But here's the bright side. I won't have to think about things so much, I can just snooze.

BIKE'S FUEL FOR DAY: 57 L, costing $96.
RIDER'S FUEL FOR DAY: Two muesli bars, egg-and-lettuce sandwich, mug of coffee, jumbo sausage roll x 2, Mrs Mac's beef pie, Fruju ice-block, bag of chips, Pepsi, two bottles and full Camelbak of water drunk during ride.

Chapter 15

Overlander–Perth

DAY'S RIDE: 693 kilometres.
JOURNEY TO DATE: 10,355 kilometres.

HAVE YOU EVER seen a live mermaid? I didn't think so. That's because you haven't taken a Mermaid Watching cruise with the company whose advertising poster I am now inspecting on the wall in the bus shelter at Overlander roadhouse. Munching an early-morning sausage roll and balancing my wheel on the shelter's picnic table I've not got that much else to do but read the advertising posters. The mermaid one sticks out as being a little on the inflated side claim-wise. Overlander is at the turn-off to a massive wildlife area called the Shark Bay World Heritage Park, which is also the most westerly point on mainland Australia. This area has some must-see tourist attractions which, thanks to my knackered tyre, will be never-see attractions for Twisting Throttle on this trip. Hamelin Pool, Denham, Monkey Mia and Shark Bay are the enticing names listed on the road sign tempting travellers to turn along the peninsula highway, but they seem to undo their mystique with the name of the route: Useless Loop.

But back to mermaids. Please bear with me if you know all this already. The dugong is a sea cow. There are 10,000 of them swimming about in Shark Bay. Shark Bay has the world's largest seagrass concentration which is the main diet of the dugong. The dugong's main predator is the shark, and you'd assume it was not called Shark Bay for nothing. Poor old dugongs. Mother Nature giveth with one hand and taketh away with the other. In ancient times, according to the advertising poster, seamen thought dugongs looked a lot like bare-breasted women with fish tails, hence the birth of the mermaid legend. There's a picture of a dugong on this poster I'm looking at right now. I know I've been on the road for a few weeks but I'm fairly sure that if I was strolling along the beach in Shark Bay and spotted a dugong and a mermaid washed up, it wouldn't be the dugong who I'd choose to resuscitate. So this wildlife cruise company will take you out on their boat to spot dugongs feeding on the seagrass and give you a T-shirt which says *I Saw A Live Mermaid*. Frankly it was so crass I'd have ridden the 300-kilometre Useless-Loop round trip to do that cruise. Maybe next time. I'm not waiting here for a bus for the love of it. I have a mission and that mission is costing me two days off the bike.

I climbed aboard the Greyhound bus, which was two hours late, clutching my bike's back wheel. There were an elderly couple, three Scandinavian backpackers, a young girl with a CD player and headphones, a dark-skinned lady with some fruit in a supermarket bag, a nun with a guitar, a small child needing a life-saving operation, and Kurt Russell. OK, I made up those last three, but it did feel as if I were in one of those movies where the hotchpotch gaggle of passengers get on the bus and alight at the end of the journey different people, having gone to hell and back, and in which Kurt manages to save the out-of-control bus after the driver has a heart attack. What was that bus movie with Sandra Bullock and Keanu Reeves? *Speed*? Or is that what I'm on right now, rambling like this? Anyway I can't remember the last time I went on a bus, but it wouldn't have been sharing a seat with a wheel. No-one seemed to bat an eyelid.

The driver was called Dave. He was Irish and forgot to wear a shirt. To explain, the Greyhound bus route is 4,000 kilometres long, from Darwin to Perth. Drivers are stationed at roadhouses along the way and just get on and off as their shifts start and end. Tony had driven the bus to Overlander from Karratha. Dave was relieving him here and taking it on to Perth. Tony gets five hours' sleep here at the roadhouse before relieving the northbound bus driver, and so on. Dave, the Irishman, wearing walking shorts and a white singlet, clambered into the driver's seat and made to drive away. The departing driver, Tony, yelled at him through the windscreen. Dave dashed inside and returned wearing his regulation blue-epauletted shirt.

The 300-kilometre bus ride south to Geraldton was tense. It was tense because I had to make a quick decision, literally while the bus was dropping passengers off and before it pulled away for Perth, as to whether Geraldton would have a bike shop of sufficient size likely to have a tyre that would fit my wheel. I knew nothing about Geraldton and the slight, but rapidly fading, optimism that there would be tyre salvation there really only stemmed from one source. That source was John. John was the caretaker at Overlander. He rode a quad bike around the property collecting the rubbish bins. That elevated him in my eyes to the best expert on motorcycle issues Western Australia could offer. He gave me two things. A stump of wood to chock up my bike while I removed the wheel, and assertive advice that I wouldn't need to go all the way to Perth for a new tyre. 'Nah, mate,' he said with such an air of authority that I wanted to sit down cross-legged and soak up his words. 'Geraldton's all you need. She'll be right. No worries for a tyre, pal.' The proclamation may have lacked any real conviction, but I was marooned 700 kilometres away from anyone else who could help. With John's sage words ringing in my ears, I sat on the bus as it pounded down the highway towards tyre redemption.

And thus, four hours later, I got off at Geraldton.

It was Foundation Day in Western Australia, a public holiday. Therefore nothing was open. I had to cool my heels overnight before finding a bike shop to get a new tyre. I hid my wheel in a clump of bushes near the harbour as I was sick of carrying it around. Geraldton looked a nice place, but my mind was elsewhere. I found a phone booth, looked in the *Yellow Pages*, saw that there was a bike shop in town and noted the address for use the next day.

I found a room at the Batavia Backpackers Hostel. Watching TV in the evening in the common room, I got talking to Ari. He was a Jewish South African electrical contractor working at a gold-mine somewhere near Kalgoorlie. He worked eight days down the mine and then had six days off. This was his first day off of the six. He looked shot.

He also happened to be in the room next to mine. The walls were paper-thin. I heard him come into his room and, without a word of a lie, within five minutes he was snoring as though through a loud-hailer. I lay there in the darkness doing the math. It was 10.00 p.m. Ari snored, according to my timing, once every six seconds. He was just as cacophonous on his inhale as he was on his exhale. Therefore, you could say it was a snore every three seconds. That's 1,200 snores an hour. If I lay awake all night listening to this adenoidal orchestra I would suffer 10,000 snores, thus going out of my mind. I thought about the iPod as a solution and put the earpieces in my ears. I listened to half a Hayley Westenra song before opting for the snoring.

After five minutes of this acoustic hell, I stripped my bed and walked the darkened halls of the hostel, like a ghostly apparition, looking for another empty room. I found one next to a dormitory, saw it wasn't occupied and lay down. Through the wall I heard at least three snorers in the dormitory, the very reason I'd got a single room in the first place. I paced the halls again, clutching sheet and pillow. On the floor below I found a double room that had to be the executive suite as it had a bin and a chest of drawers in it. The door was ajar so I peeped in, but couldn't see if it was occupied. I threw my bedding on the double bed and no-one commented, so I concluded it was mine for the night. I snored myself into a deep sleep.

The next morning I got my new tyre. I sat in the reception area of the bike shop in Geraldton and entrusted my wheel to the good people there. As they carried it through to the workshop, I glimpsed the old tyre for the last time. It was like leaving your aged pet to be put down at the vet's. That tyre had been with me since Sydney. It had done 10,000 faithful kilometres without complaint. It stopped when I braked. It went when I accelerated. It carried a heavy load without fuss and I treated it badly at times. I didn't slow down for those cattle-grids across the road and I didn't check its air pressure every day. And here it was about to be condemned to a heap of old tyres out the back of a bike shop in a small town in Western Australia without so much as a farewell. It wouldn't be the last time I would be racked with a knot in my stomach as I replaced a bike part. I was shocked by my cavalier attitude towards my support team, but then I wasn't quite up to asking the guy behind the counter for a few moments alone with my old worn tyre.

I lay on the lawn in a park under the shade of a spreading elm tree. I think it was an elm, but such is my knowledge of trees it may well have been an oak, sycamore, ash or maple. It wasn't a gum, that I know. As I snoozed in the park with my head resting on the wheel rim, I heard the sound of an engine getting louder over to my right. I glanced over and saw a silver 4WD mount the kerb, steer between two trees — elm, oak, whatever — and drive towards me at speed. Crazily I just lay there on my wheel looking at the approaching missile, thinking, 'This can't be happening.' At the last minute, the 4WD did a braking skid and its two right-hand-side wheels came to a stop half a metre from my head.

'Had you worried, bru!' Out jumped Ari. I would have hit him if he hadn't been both a hardened miner and a good foot taller than me. 'Get a good sleep last night, mate?' I challenged him with this statement laced with sarcasm. 'Oh yeah, not bad, bru,' and with that we shook hands and went our separate ways. Ari to do some 4WD-ing, probably in the Geraldton Botanic Gardens, and me back to my wheel.

Six hours later as I boarded the Greyhound bus with my re-tyred back wheel, to head north back to Overlander, any lingering sentimentality about Ari and his adenoids disappeared. It disappeared because that return trip represented the best entertainment I have had in a long time and it was all in with the price of the bus ticket. Here's what happened.

The bus had arrived in Geraldton at 3.30 p.m. and I got allocated the seat right behind the driver. The blue-shirted goatee-bearded driver was called Kel. The co-driver, who didn't drive but sort of just rode up front to keep the driver company, was called Barry. The bus left on time and within 10 minutes was on the North West Coastal Highway with a four-hour slog ahead of it to Overlander. There is nothing I can say about this bus trip except try to recreate the hilarious repartee that went on between Kel and Barry. Most other passengers were further back, out of earshot and probably dozing as they were going to be on the bus for a much longer stint than my mere four hours. As I was only one seat back, I heard it all and this is how it went.

Kel, who was driving, appeared to be a wordsmith and loved doing crosswords. Barry, apparently, had never done a crossword in his life and Kel was training him on how it worked. Barry had a jumbo crossword book and called out the clues to Kel. I got the impression Barry was not on Kel's intellectual plane, but that might be unfair. It was just that Barry struggled a fraction with the concept of crosswords as you will see. In the fading light at dusk, and thereafter in a small glow from my cellphone, I managed to record their conversation.

> Barry: Story, five letters.
> Kel: 'Fable'?
> Barry: Can't be mate.
> Kel: Why not?
> Barry: There's an 'o' in it.
> Kel: Mate you've got to tell me this when you read out the
>   clue. Where is it?

Barry: What?

Kel: The letter. The 'o'. Where is it in the word? First letter? Third letter?

Barry: Hang on a minute. Fourth.

Kel: So read it out like this. Something, something, something, o, something. That way I can visualize the word.

Barry: Get on with it, mate.

Kel: OK, let me think. Story. Story. Maybe yarns or tales. Is it story singular or plural?

Barry: I'll spell it mate. S-t-o-r-e-y.

Kel: Now you tell me, dopey. Storey with an 'e'. That'll be 'floor'.

Barry: Sprite, three letters. I'll get that one. 'Can', or 'tin'.

Kel: What? A sprite is a fictitious waif-like type of figure often found in fairy stories.

Barry: Yeah, but it also comes in cans, mate.

Kel: Try 'elf'.

Barry: Mate, can a clue be itself as the answer?

Kel: What do you mean?

Barry: Bed, three letters. Might be 'bed'.

Kel: No, mate, it can't be itself. Try 'cot'.

Barry: Cordial, six letters, last letter 'e'.

Kel: 'Polite'.

Barry: What about 'orange'? Orange cordial.

Kel: It's 'polite', mate, not 'orange'.

Barry: Leer, four letters. That'll be 'look'.

Kel: Bazza, 'look' is not 'leer'. 'Leer' is to peer at something in a lascivious fashion.

Barry: Like to perv?

Kel: 'Perve' is five letters mate. Try 'ogle'.

Barry: Giver, five letters.

Kel: OK, hang on.

Barry: What about 'taker'? Giver and taker.

Kel: No, mate, if you're a giver you can't be a taker. One gives and the other takes.

Barry: 'Donor'?

Kel: Good one, mate. Donor it is.

Barry: Won't fit.

Kel: Yes it will mate, 'donor' is five letters.

Barry: Nah, the fourth letter is an 'o'.

Kel: Yeah.

Barry: D-o-n-e-r. Won't fit.

Kel: You're a dickhead, mate.

Barry: You want to start pulling your weight, Kello. I'm giving you the clues — you've got the easy bit.

Kel: I've done more crosswords than you've had hot dinners, mate.

Barry: What's this cryptic crossword here? How does that work?

Kel: It's a lot harder, mate, as the clues are what they call cryptic. Read one out.

Barry: 'We hear it transcends the Shakespearean spirit.' What the hell is all that about mate?

Kel: That's a tough one, let me think a minute.

Barry: And this. 'Choice piece the bird pecked.'

Kel: 'Titbit'.

Barry: How do you get that?

Kel: The bird . . . 'tit', pecked . . . 'bit'. A choice piece . . . 'titbit'.

Barry: 'Train speed modified to a walking pace.' Bloody hell, what's that all about?

Kel: Hold on, mate, give me a second on that one. 'Pedestrian'.

Barry: Where do you get pedestrian out of that, mate?

Kel: Pedestrian is an anagram of train speed. 'Modified' means it's an anagram.

All the time this interchange was taking place, the bus was hurtling through the fading light as darkness descended at 6.00 p.m. Kangaroos and other wildlife were probably lining up to play chicken. The windscreen was spattered with insects of the dusk. Kel switched on the wipers and they simply smeared a film of insect remains across the glass. I wondered how many passengers were listening to the crossword contest and hoped Kel was equally focused on the road. He was a true multi-tasker.

I found myself trying to beat him to the answers but could only work out one that he couldn't. 'Impulsive', 11 letters. I stayed silent, not wanting these blokes to know I was enjoying the eavesdropping. Kel and Barry got us to Overlander and took the time to recommend the chicken-and-vege soup on special at the roadhouse. They unloaded my wheel and I thanked them for the crossword entertainment. I said to Kel it was great because it was so s-p-o-n-t-a-n-e-o-u-s. They headed off for their soup none the wiser for my hint.

The next morning, dawn over the desert arrived in a blaze of colour. I saw this at 6.30 a.m. through half-open eyes as I tottered the 3 metres from my cabin door to the ablution block wondering why the sky was on fire. I was busting — but less of the detail and back to the theatrics in the heavens.

It was a ceiling of orange, red and yellow. It was as if there were a raging bushfire just over the horizon and I half expected deer, rabbits and raccoons to come tearing from the black scrub, escaping the inferno. The sun's golden orb peeped above the darkened bush line and inexorably rose like a morphing, shimmering phoenix. Its rays bathed the dawn's moody greyness first into a half-light of shadowy illuminations, but then, as the orb rose, and the rush of colour in the sky abated, the landscape yielded to the god of light and softened with hues of pale yellow and ochre.

That's not a bad effort at describing a sunrise, bearing in mind I was standing there in bare feet and undies clutching a roll of toilet paper and a toothbrush. It was a truly stunning sight, as indeed was the sunrise. I would have started to recite Latin verse if I knew any. I have seen sunrises before, but somehow out here on the fringes of the desert it was more powerful. I resolved to get up at 6.30 a.m. every morning since I would have been curled up in my sleeping bag if it hadn't been for a protesting bladder. I knew that the promise to rise early daily was an empty one, but this had nonetheless been an inspirational start to the day.

I had a quick shower. It was quick because of the ablution shed's pan-gender system. It had two toilet cubicles, a shower and a basin. Both men and women used it. I was there three nights but never figured out how you avoided being walked in on, as there was no lock on the door. I ended up stamping up the steps, loudly clearing my throat and peeping in through the door. I never found anyone in there, nor did anyone ever walk in while I was inside, which would have been interesting. I'd like to think it would have been a Sean Connery moment, but in reality the screams of the walkee would have silenced the desert fauna for miles around.

After ablutions, I fitted the back wheel on the disabled bike, returned the cabin key to the roadhouse, got back my $10 key bond and spent it on a flavoured milk and a Mrs Mac's jumbo sausage roll. And as I rode out southwards on the highway, I wasn't unhappy about finally getting underway again. To celebrate, I surfed on the iPod to a Billy Joel collection and set myself the goal of being able to sing with him 'We Didn't Start The Fire' by the time I got to Perth, 400 kilometres down the track. Ultimately I did the 'we didn't start the fire' bit and let him do the rest.

The thrice-repeated 300 kilometres from Overlander to Geraldton was a *Groundhog Day*-type experience. I was so sick of that stretch that I didn't look around, just tucked in behind the screen and did the miles as if it were another day at the office. Billabong, Binnu and Northampton flashed by without so much as a glance from me, and I rode into the 440 Roadhouse just outside Geraldton to refuel. I also had a free cup of tea. Why is that noteworthy? Here's why.

All around Australia I had seen signs saying 'Free Driver Reviver 500 m'. They're not talking about a burst of the party drug NOS or oxygen but a free mug of coffee or tea. Fatigue is considered an issue on the roads, probably quite rightly. But I never figured out how this free cuppa system worked and was, frankly, too embarrassed to ask.

How do they know you are the legitimate driver? Do you have to jangle your keys as you stride in? Do you need a sort of sipper mug that you just get refilled at each stop? Is a rider classed as a driver? Why not simply pay $1.50 for a cup of coffee or tea and not be a bludger? All pretty pathetic questions, but I never really sussed this free cuppa thing out until 440.

At that roadhouse there was a trolley brilliantly labelled 'Free Driver Reviver Here'. On it was a hot-water urn, coffee, teabags, sugar, spoons and an empty ice-cream container. I threw caution to the wind and just helped myself trying to look like a Reviver-eligible non-passenger and fatigued. But I couldn't see any milk and must have been blethering around like a lost tourist in a railway station as a large woman in a smock passed and said, 'What's your problem, mate?' 'No problem,' I parried, 'just looking for some milk.' 'In the fridge,' she lobbed, all but adding the words, 'you dork', and carried on delivering a bacon-and-egg toastie to a truckie.

And that added the final — albeit overly frosty, I thought — piece of the jigsaw puzzle to this vexatious process. Instead of pottles of UHT milk on the trolley, there is always a jug of fresh milk in a nearby drinks fridge. The point about all this is that you have to know the system and, once you do, you are a pro. Because all around Australia the system is the same. From Queensland to Tasmania you locate the trolley, you find the fridge, you put your used teabag and spoon in the empty ice-cream container and, after slurping down the reviver, you exit the roadhouse with a 'sludder' to the counter lady — and if you get a 'sludder ma' in return, you're in.

You've received the badge of honour and have entered the roadies' brotherhood. It's an experience on a similar level to getting a twitching index-finger wave from a road-train driver. You couldn't be more bonded if you were a Mason. It's a crazy notion, I admit, but having the free cuppa from the trolley makes a statement that you are a roadie and not a plebiscite tourist who, snigger, actually pays for their drink. It had taken me 10,000 kilometres to suss out the reviver system, but now I would stop every time I saw those blue signs and head for the trolley. As a consequence, I would also have to stop in a rest area half an hour down the road, but let's not go there.

Greenough, Dongara, Eneabba, Badgingarra, Cataby, Muchea. The towns were evenly spaced, but the road mostly bypassed them. Ten kilometres south of Eneabba the highway police flagged me over.

As I de-helmeted, de-gloved and de-iPodded, the cop wandered around the bike. I was waiting for the fateful greeting, 'Going a bit quick there, mate,' but he said, 'Just an RBT, mate,' instead. I thought he meant a rego check, so I pointed him to the back of the bike under the number plate. He knew immediately he was dealing with an intellectual giant and said, 'Random Breath Test'. I blew into the tube and he said something like 'Yokay'. I passed. I would have been a little needled to have failed since my last beer had been drunk in Darwin 4,000 kilometres back.

I was keen to ask if he got anyone over the limit out here at 10.30 a.m. on a Wednesday morning but he was gone, dealing with the vehicles backing up behind me as I re-helmeted, re-gloved and re-iPodded. Why is it that you can never get your gloves on fully when your palms are sweaty?

After Muchea, the Great Northern and North West Coastal highways joined and it was a dual-lane job into impending civilization as the greater Perth suburbs hove into view. This was another exercise in refamiliarization with riding in a built-up area.

The signs you are approaching a city were there, but I had forgotten them. You get overtaken by housewives in 4WDs with cellphones to their ears; there are Holden Commodores with lowered suspensions and blow-off valves; there are roundabouts where you have to seriously entertain the notion of stopping to give way to the right; Beaurepaires, Red Roosters, Toyota car yards, traffic lights; signs pointing to the airport, signs with words like 'bypass', 'alt route' and 'clearway'. The numbness with which you hurtle along a deserted road in the boon-docks is replaced with an antenna on full alert. It takes a while to adjust.

I set the GPS to find a motorcycle dealer in Midland, north of Perth. It found one. This was where I was finally going to bury the memory of Glovey and move on. I picked out a pair of XXL padded gloves and stood at the counter. The sales guy was dealing with a man and woman and the woman was sitting on a Harley Fatboy in the showroom. 'I want to hear it,' she said. The sales guy said, 'We can't really start it up, and anyway the battery is out of it, you know'. 'And how do you get a licence? I'll need a licence.' The guy left them to it and came over to serve someone who was actually going to buy something.

I idled past the dealership's skip and tossed in the partnerless left-hand glove that really hadn't been pulling its weight since Kakadu. I rode away not even looking in my mirror. It was an exorcism. I had pensioned off my has-been tyre in Geraldton and now I had equally cal-lously discarded my obsolete left-hand glove. In the Twisting Throttle support crew you either contribute or you're yesterday's bike part. You move forward. If you're a redundant piece of riding apparel, well I'm sorry . . . skip happens.

BIKE'S FUEL FOR DAY: 52 L, costing $76.

RIDER'S FUEL FOR DAY: Two muesli bars, sausage roll, flavoured milk, Fanta, two coffees, ham-and-tomato sandwich, lasagne and fresh — repeat fresh — salad, ice-cream and pastry.

Chapter 16

Darwin

Katherine

Mataranka

Turkey Creek

Croydon

Cairns

Broome

Threeways

Mt Isa

Mackay

Karratha

Overlander

Kalgoorlie

Ceduna

Gold Coast

Port Wakefield

Walcha

Perth

Madura

Goulburn

Sydney

Jerramungup

Mt Gambier

Cann River

Melbourne

St Helens

Hobart

Perth–Jerramungup

DAY'S RIDE: 796 kilometres.
JOURNEY TO DATE: 11,151 kilometres.

I HAVE NEVER been so cold on a bike. It's ridiculous. A week before I had been riding in a T-shirt, swatting away the mozzies and quaffing two Camelbaks a day to keep hydrated. Today — the last 180-kilometre stretch from Albany to where I am now, a cabin in Jerramungup — was as frigid a ride as I've ever known. It wasn't actually wet as such, just polar.

It makes sense. Where I have gone is as far south as you can get in WA, right on the bottom coastline. The trees are those windblown sort that look as though they are just hanging on to the ground by their roots like grim death. It's the part of the country that gets whacked by the southerly from Antarctica and, let's face it, it is winter.

I have two power points in the cabin. One has a fan heater going full-bore. The other switches between the laptop I'm pecking away at, a small TV with a programme about the soccer World Cup, in which Australia is playing, the kettle and a Playstation. Actually, I made up that last one: I'm looking through rose-coloured glasses at this cabin. Anyway, why not? I knew I'd be finishing at Jerramungup simply because I couldn't continue. It is a lonely and desolate 300 kilometres from here to Esperance across a moor-like landscape. Jerramungup it had to be. And, praise be, there was a sign to a caravan park, and, mercy be, the sign said they had cabins. I was fleeced for $66, but would have paid three times that and married the owner's sister if he had asked. I just wanted heat. I've just had a shower that lasted 40 minutes and still the hot water flows. Jerramungup is one of the good 'uns in my journey log. I don't know what the name means, but I'm positive it would be something like 'Place where cold people get warm again'.

The ride south from Perth this morning had also been chilly. I simply couldn't get warm and I shivered on the bike. My fingers were cold in my cold gloves and my feet were cold in my cold boots. This meant everything in between suffered. It would have been a nice ride in summer, but I wasn't concentrating on the scenery. I just aimed for a roadhouse that had hot drinks. The highway tracked along the coast but I didn't see any sea. Mandurah, Myalup, Binningup and Bunbury came and went. I was still cold and realized I was wearing the wrong gear. My padded trousers were lying rolled up in my tent bag. The more I fantasized about those trousers, the more they became dual electric blankets waiting to be wrapped around my legs. But the cold does something to your brain. It represses something, possibly motivation. Inertia just smothers you. I plugged on, setting new mileage goals in the interests of making sure it would be another 700- to 800-kilometre day.

I broke the spell and pulled over when I saw a sign saying 'Emu Pies'.

Positive that emu would be another disappointing variation on chicken, I dismounted and looked for the shop. It was closed, but a lone emu patrolled the nearby paddock, craning its long neck over the fence like an inmate on death row seeking a last meal. Except I was looking at the next 100 pies plus some feathers. And that summed up the mood of the morning somehow. One minute I would have killed for a hot emu pie. Then, as I looked at the pies-in-waiting looking back at me with quizzical, sad eyes, I felt like opening its gate to let it free. I rode away glumly.

Back on the road again I found myself considering the status of the pie. It is true to say that I had been eating a fair swag of pies and pie offshoots, namely the tasty Mrs Mac's jumbo sausage roll. Not only were they a potential impulse purchase when displayed at points of sale when I was paying for fuel, but there is nothing like a hot pie or sausage roll to sit around warming your intestines for many hundreds of kilometres.

Their nutritional value is another issue. About the time I was pounding along near Binningup on this cold, overcast day wondering whether the pie industry had gone too far in making pies out of emus, a debate raged in Australia as to what defined the word 'meat' as in 'meat pie'. Here's the — if you'll excuse the pun — guts of it. A meat pie must contain, by law, at least 25% meat. 'Meat' officially means any part of the animal's, such as an emu's, carcass. Also, and this is for any chicken-pie enthusiasts reading this, it also may include a bird foetus. Mrs Mac's, my favourite sausage-roll manufacturer, is leading the charge to have 'meat content' changed to 'meat flesh content'. 'Meat flesh', by formal definition, includes, of course, muscle tissue and any rind, fat, blood, nerves, connective tissue and skin. But if you don't include offal in the definition, then you kiss goodbye to steak-and-kidney pies, so it's not straightforward. The fuss started when the New Zealand Commerce Commission did a scientific test on Mrs Mac's pies and found 27% meat content, not 31% as stated on the pie wrapper. Mrs Mac's said, 'Yeah, but what do you mean by "meat"?', and the libel lawyers reached for their books. The other little-known fact about meat pies is that meat can be from any animal so long as it's not killed in the wild, which presumably is why you don't see Mrs Mac's kangaroo pasties in the warmer at petrol stations.

So to recap. When I buy a meat pie in Australia, I sort of assume that it is full of tender chunky beef — albeit minced — cut from the choicest part of a cattle beast recently and hygienically slaughtered in a humane, government-controlled facility. On the other hand, an average pie costs $2.20, if it doesn't have cheese, so what can you truly expect? It's just that hearing the words 'foetus', 'offal', 'gristle', 'skin' and 'blood' in the same sentence as 'meat' cools my pie ardour somewhat. And then the question has to be asked: if a pie has to have 25% meat content, and if we sidestep the issue that it could be camel, hare, dugong and so on, then what's the remaining 75% I'm eating? Allow 20% for pastry, 10% for gravy and that leaves just under half the pie consisting of . . . what? Frankly, it makes you think or, at minimum, makes you squeeze more tomato sauce over your pie.

I rode on considering a move to vegetarian pies. But what defines a vegetable . . . ?

Boyanup, Donnybrook, Kirup, Balingup. The towns were spaced at about 40-kilometre intervals, but I still plodded through. Cold, neutral to the surroundings, stamping my boots on the foot pegs to see if that would help. The sky was overcast, gloomy and pouting. I pulled into Bridgetown to refuel. A sour-faced woman who wouldn't look at me was behind the counter. I had to ask her for the key to the men's toilet. Toilets are usually locked at these places, and for some reason you actually have to ask for the key in order to use them.

In one sentence I requested a vegetarian sausage roll, a cup of tea and the toilet key. She charged me $5.80 and I wondered if I had to pay a bond for the key. I asked her if she would mind taking some coins off me. Without looking at me, she nodded. I spilled out my coins onto the counter. She took that as a cue to count them. She divided all the coins into dollar piles and I could see there was $5.75.

Strangely, she then mixed them all up again, and sorted them into piles of each denomination. Not unexpectedly, it still came to $5.75. I was, therefore, five cents short. I hoped for a discount, perhaps if I offered to forego the toilet-key hassle. 'Got another five cents, mate?' I handed over a $50 note and got all my coins back.

I enjoyed this lady's riveting company for about 10 minutes and not once did she meet my intense, scrutinizing gaze. It was like one of those movies where the young couple from the city move out into some backwoods rural village and come up against taciturn murmuring locals.

And then the gods of sunshine beamed and the earth became a lovelier place. I rode through Manjimup into the Shannon National Park. Instantly there was warm sunshine on my back and a blue sky overhead. The National Park was stunning — that is, what I saw of it from the twisty undulating highway wending its way through the stands of karri trees. It was like riding through an avenue of leafy sentinels. The tall trees with their bare trunks and thick canopies towered on each side of the road. I knew there was a treetops walk around there somewhere; that is, a place where you can walk through at canopy level on suspended walkways. At Walpole there were the Treetops Motel, the Treetops Play Centre and the Treetops Walkway Cafe. I had to be close. Sure enough, there was a sign to the Valley of the Giants and the treetops walk. I saw a sign pointing to a Youth Hostel which said 'Tingle All The Way Hostel'. I laughed out loud, thinking the owners had a bit of an over-inflated view of the impact of their hostel on customers. I realized later that the trees around here were actually tingle trees. Yet again my extensive knowledge of Australian flora came to the fore.

The Mt Frankland National Park sort of followed on from the Shannon. It was a motorcyclist's dream. The well-cambered road twisted and turned in gentle arcs and gradients, not slowing you down, weaving through the miles of regal timber standing at attention like soldiers lining the trooping-the-colour route. But majestic and wonderful as the ride through these National Parks was, it was something else that preoccupied me throughout most of the day.

And that was placenames. Specifically my question is this. Why is it that virtually all placenames in this part of Western Australia end in 'up'? Listen to these. Noggerup, Narrikup, Mumballup, Kirup, Nannup, Dinninup, Wokalup, Mayenup. Who thinks up these names and why do they have an -up fetish? I switched off the surroundings and my mind went into overdrive. I imagined in the olden days a committee of squires at the local shire inn. One was an old fart who yawned a lot. Another had the hiccups. Squire 1 says, 'Right gents, what'll we call that village down there?' Squire 2 calls out, 'How about Nogger?' Squire 3 hiccups, 'Hup'. Squire 1, 'Aye, that'll do, Noggerup'. And so on.

But it's not just the -ups that had me obsessed. What about these? Yarloop, Bowelling, Dumbleyung, Wickepin, Popanyinning and the incredible Dwellingup. You start expecting that hobbits leaning on pitchforks will appear at the roadside as you approach somewhere like Badgebup. Then you think you've ridden into a Famous Five yarn when you pass signs for Grimwade, Windy Harbour, Cliffy Head, Witchcliffe and Conspicuous Cliffs.

I took a photo of Yornup, a speck of a hamlet not even indicated on the map. You wonder what the residents of Yornup think about their name. Are they in fact ecstatic with it? Possibly these '-up' names are rooted in some historic local connection not involving anyone with the hiccups. I then spent the next 25 kilometres making up other placenames that you could add 'up' to. What about syr, stirr, throwin, stickem, giddy, roundem, knees and the ever-popular Prince Phil.

The only human contact I had had in this region was with the woman who wouldn't look at me in Bridgetown. I wasn't going to test our close relationship by asking her about this.

At Nornalup I hit the southern coast, but again if it hadn't been for the map book on my tank bag I'd have been none the wiser. As if on cue, the cloud descended and it got a little parky again. A few spots of wintry rain fell and I chugged into Denmark, 50 kilometres the African side of Albany, to tank up.

I had to ask for the toilet key, but this time the guy actually looked at me so I knew I was among friends. I was desperate for something hot and, here's the surprise, they had fried food for sale. A coffee, a Mrs Mac's meat flesh pie and a sausage roll later, I felt two things: warmer, and like throwing up. The fried food was getting to me, but then again it had to be hot, so what was I expecting? A plate of fajitas? Most of their customers were road workers and logging-truck drivers. Ergo, they sold stuffed cheese sausages and bacon-and-cheese cordon bleus.

At Albany I was faced with a route choice. Get to Jerramungup via the Stirling Ranges and (why wasn't I surprised about these?) Porongurup, Amelup and Ongerup, reputedly a nice bike ride, or direct to Jerramungup via nowhere. The latter route was 12 kilometres shorter. Fine sleet was starting to fall, so I belted out on the South Coast Highway. There was a 110 km/h speed limit.

A third of the way I had to slow for a settlement called Manypeaks. Except there were no houses and it was completely flat. So I had to ride at 60 km/h along a stretch of road that was clearly the Manypeaks central business district as there was a derelict recreation hall and a far-off cement factory or something. Why didn't they use local naming conventions and call it Peakup? The reason is that no-one cares because it's right out in the sticks, and that, my friends, is its new name from now on. Peakup Sticks.

And so I reached a distant Jerramungup, and the haven of warmth and tranquillity that is Cabin No. 8 in the caravan park. There was no cellphone signal, but the cabin had a microwave. I just didn't have anything to cook in it.

I sat by the fan heater reflecting on a day of conflicts. The changing weather, the resignation to eating fried food, but most of all, how it was a day of ups and towns.

BIKE'S FUEL FOR DAY: 47 L, costing $70.
RIDER'S FUEL FOR DAY: Two muesli bars, Mrs Mac's beef pie, chicken dim sim, sausage roll, two coffees and two teas, biscuits, no water.

Chapter 17

Jerramungup–Kalgoorlie

DAY'S RIDE: 697 kilometres.
JOURNEY TO DATE: 11,848 kilometres.

THERE ARE SOME days on the bike where I can't help getting caught up with numbers. Specifically, distances and times. And every possible permutation thereof. Today's ride from Jerramungup to Kalgoorlie was one such day. On days like this, my brain simply goes into some sort of bizarre mathematical state and I can't stop repeatedly calculating things. Firstly, I have the GPS mounted in full view on the handlebars. This device spews out numbers and averages from the highly essential, such as distance travelled since last fuel top-up, to the highly whimsical, such as average time stopped while still idling. The GPS reports that last one in a slightly overly scolding manner — I feel — as if it's important to know how long you were stopped at traffic lights anyway.

You can convert the GPS into a talking GPS by flicking a switch. You then have several choices for voice 'style'. There's American male, British female, German male or Spanish female. The males I find a fraction condescending when giving directions, and, let's face it, what red-blooded male really wants to accept directions from another bloke? The German male voice in particular seems to forget just who's riding the bike. The Spanish female is too sultry and suggestive, especially when giving 'distance to next turn, señor' and all but adds 'perhaps you make turn and come up for — how you say — nightcap, yes?' That's why I have a British female giving me the essential statistics in my helmet speakers. If you imagine Judi Dench bellowing in your ear 'Rider will turn left in zero point four kilometres. Rider will decrease speed by one five kilometres per hour in order to make turn safely. Rider will please do this now. Rider will BLOODY WELL do this now.'

As well as the GPS, there are handy marker posts on the roadside. Say it's 180 kilometres to Esperance. Every 5 kilometres a small green sign will say E-175, then 5 kilometres later another one E-170, and so on. The thing is that whoever put the road markers in must have been pacing it out by foot as they don't match the GPS. It's a head-to-head battle of road markers versus GPS as to which is more accurate. I zoom past a marker for E-150, and suddenly through my helmet speakers I hear Judi say 'Destination is 149 kilometres. Rider will disregard that BLOODY marker.'

So when there isn't a lot else to do on the bike, plunging along a deserted featureless highway, the calculations are all-consuming. I also develop an obsession for round numbers. If my riding average is 103.8 km/h I'm driven to get that up to 105 km/h. If that average was over the last 100 kilometres, then it's a tall order. I try to ride along at a speed that is a multiple of five and see how long I can keep it exactly on that speed. My record is maintaining a speed of precisely 100.00 km/h for eight seconds before my throttle hand twitched and it lurched up to 100.8 km/h. I almost spat in disgust as I was aiming for the symmetrically beautiful 10 seconds.

The time I really understand that I have to stop and seek therapy is when I find myself in a rut of performing an action every kilometre.

Today, for example, between Grass Patch and Salmon Gums — a distance of 29 kilometres — to relieve the boredom I stood up on the pegs every time the GPS clicked over 1 kilometre and shouted 'A for Apple', then 'B for Banana', and so on until I had made up a fruit or vegetable name for each letter of the alphabet. But the shocking revelation happened at kilometre 14, when I was stuffed if I could come up with one for 'N'. I hear you snigger derisively. OK, just put down this book for a second and think of a fruit or vegetable starting with N. See? And you haven't got Judi Dench shouting in your ear 'Rider will think of a fruit for N in zero point three kilometres and will BLOODY WELL hurry up about it.'

It was only 6.30 a.m. in Jerramungup Caravan Park and the dawn had just yielded to a wintry pall of half-light. I peered out of my cabin window and saw mist, wet ground and nobody around. I slumped back into the creaky bed, pulled the sleeping bag around my ears and pretended I was in a five-star hotel about to head down to a breakfast of croissants, poached eggs and coffee, a morning paper and the agony of deciding whether to do half an hour in the gym or a few lengths of the tepid pool on the roof.

This fantasy was interrupted by a scratching on the door. It was either housekeeping with my breakfast tray or a wallaby. I knew it was the marsupial option as I had seen the caravan park's pet wally moping around when I came in last night. I opened the door and two things came in: a blast of wintry air and a wet nose. I gave the wallaby a crème biscuit and it went away. Looking back, I believe this to have been a portent. An hour later I would be a whisker away from killing this wallaby's cousin.

I learned my lesson from the previous day's frigid start and rugged up in padded jacket, padded trousers, double socks, T-shirt and two merino-fleece tops. For added warmth, I sucked on a Smint. I rode away from a slumbering Jerramungup and braced myself for the opening chapter of the day's ride, 300 kilometres to Esperance. On the horizon, the morning mist camped around the trees in the valleys. The sun was a wintry one, pallid and hidden behind thin grey cloud. The road was wet and dewy, the corners looked slippery. There were patches of new seal that had collected puddles of rain overnight and most of the time I rode inches inside the dotted centre line. The road was completely devoid of traffic, except for a couple of utes that passed me coming the other way and no-one, including me, waved. It was that sort of insular morning.

I rode along the empty highway fiddling with the iPod that had jammed on Rod Stewart. I didn't blame it. As I was stabbing the iPod with thickly padded fingers and getting nowhere, I glanced up at the road and saw a kangaroo crossing in front of me. I'm no student of animal behaviour, but if I were a kangaroo in the middle of the road and were in imminent danger of dying, I'd flick off fairly quickish. Skippy didn't. It loped, as if in treacle, across to my side of the road. My brain talked to my throttle hand and automatically I buttoned off. I believe I was an inch away from running over its tail. There was no time to review options such as swerving, braking or profaning. Had the kangaroo decided to stop in the road and watch the harbinger of instant death bear down on it, then it would have been bike *v* animal and . . . who knows which one (if either) would have survived the encounter. However, it sloped off into the undergrowth and I can only hope it filled its pouch, because I certainly filled mine. This was 9.30 a.m. and the books say these li'l fellas are all off the roadsides by then. Looking back on this incident, I blame Rod Stewart.

Still hyperventilating, I rode past a sign that said 'Fitzgerald'. This was a standard green sign that I'd seen used to announce approaching towns or settlements. One kilometre later I passed the same green sign but on the other side of the road. Therefore Fitzgerald, the place, was somewhere in that kilometre. I swear to you there was nothing but scrub and bushes. There were no side roads, 80 km/h signs or evidence of anything whatsoever that might have been man-made. If Fitzgerald had ever been there, it wasn't this morning. It was a *Doctor Who* moment. Where had the town gone? Had I ridden through a time warp?

And then came my second close encounter with Australian wildlife.

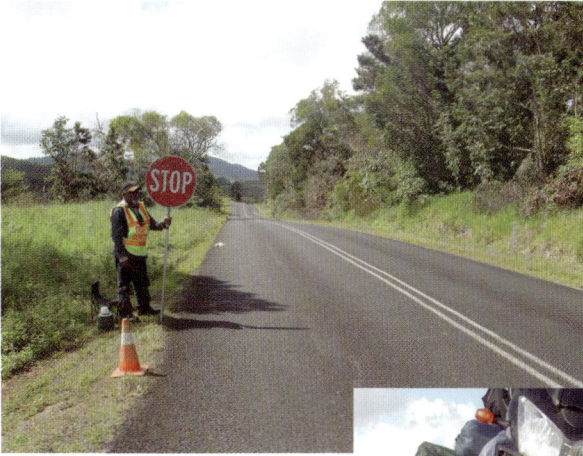

I had a love/hate affair with Stop/Slow men. Two kilometres further down this road there was a grass cutter on the other side. We would nod civilly to each other, but you wouldn't say we became friends.

My first encounter with Australian wildlife was hardly a David Attenborough moment. I was itching to pop it with a screwdriver and see what happened.

In the ocean of road users in Northern Queensland there is an unwritten hierarchy. Here the krill meets the whale.

That blue tube delivered lifesaving water into my mouth from the Camelbak. Something to wash the flies down with.

After 3,000 km the bike and I got on each other's nerves. We needed some time apart and to be in our own space.

This is the stunningly boring Stuart Tree, albeit steeped in heritage. The famous explorer Stuart's initials are said to be carved on the trunk. All I saw was 'Kylie', 'BJ' and 'Gunter from Frankfurt'.

OK, let's run through the risk management plan. Got enough daylight, water, oil, tyre tread, Minties? I feel there's something else, but I can't put my finger on it.

WARNING
NO FUEL
FOR 500km

Tablelands Hwy 228

BIKESTHENICS Exercise #7 'Handlebar Hoists'
See how the long-distance motorcyclist keeps fit on the bike. It is just as effective at 100 km/h, but harder to use the foot brake.

BIKESTHENICS Exercise #11
'Seat Ups'
Put this book down and
try it at home. If you don't
have a bike, your BBQ table
or lawn mower will do.

Remember *Crocodile Dundee*
when the big fella surges out at
Linda Koslowski? Fortunately
I'm holding a can of chain
lube in case of attack.

I had a sudden gripping
obsession about seeing a
snake and overturned some
rocks to see what happened.
Don't worry, kids, see how I'm
wearing my helmet in case
a python lunges at me?

I passed thousands of
these conical 2-metre-high
mounds. Finally I realized
what they were for.

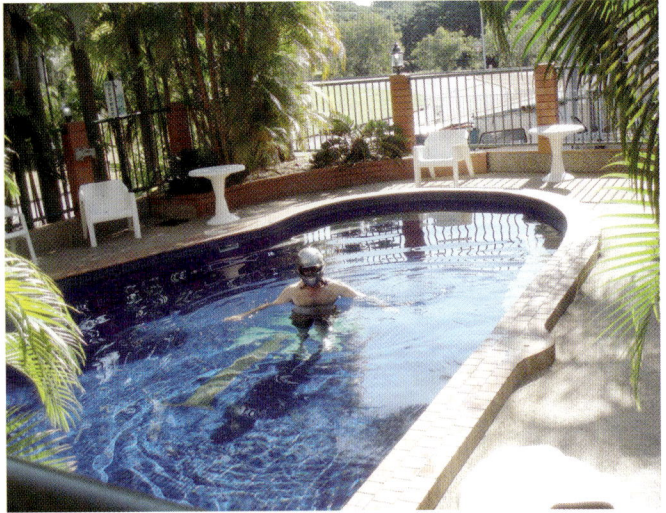

My treat of the trip, a swanky motel in Darwin. Here I am cleaning my boots. Several young children in the pool were quickly ushered inside by their mothers.

The jumping crocs at Adelaide River. Dangle a hunk of meat on a pole off the side of the boat and call the result a jumping croc. Tourists love it.

OK, imagine the receptionist at the local caravan park here in the Kakadu answering the phone and trying not to sound like a chicken: 'Bukbukluk Park, Kakadu.'

Camping in the outback the flies were hell. Lucky for me I had a helmet accessory designed for this very purpose. Regrettably, I got so hungry I ate the corks.

This poignant photo was taken the day Glovey was lost to the Kakadu. Lest we forget.

At the Katherine Caravan Park my cabin neighbour was Hardy, who raked leaves there in return for lodging.

I got so bored in WA I started riding the bike backwards. The only way I knew I had crossed the Tropic of Capricorn was seeing this photo after I got home.

In Western Australia you need to keep your mind alert. Highway T'ai Chi is a good remedy to stave off boredom.

Western Australia's landscape was forever changing. Around each corner was a new and exciting vista. To prove it, I've taken photos over the windscreen at hourly intervals throughout the ride from Broome to Karratha. Here's the view at 9.00 a.m.

10.00 a.m.

11.00 a.m.

12.00 noon

1.00 p.m.

2.00 p.m.

Another day, another border crossing. I declared an apple, bribed the guard with a fridge magnet and rode through. Western Australia is five times the size of Texas.

On the left: road kill. On the right: road dill.

The famous roadhouse all-day breakfasts: baked beans heaped on fried onion and mixed in with grilled tomatoes. Even the birds out here are on daily cholesterol pills.

How well do you know your tyre wear? Name the issue with my rear tyre. Stranded 300 km from the nearest bike shop, I removed the wheel and caught a bus.

Two days and 600 km later, I was returning on the bus with my wheel and its new tyre.

Barry and Kel, the crossword-toting bus drivers who took good care of my 'rubber-clad rotating device': five letters, W-H-something-E-something.

What's this? Hint: I liked to have an aperitif before dinner while out riding. Answer: Double gin and tonic.

This lady is an emu murderess, but her pastry was to die for. Squeeze on plenty of sauce and it tastes like chicken.

This is the starting gate to the Nullarbor at Norseman. What do you think . . . Adelaide for lunch?

In the middle of the Nullarbor I came across an exhausted kangaroo. Using my wildlife rescue training, I applied CPR (cardio pulmonary roo-suscitation). No joy.

What you see here is the first corner after 146.6 km of the longest stretch of straight road in Australia. But look carefully. Why does it have to bend up there? It could have just carried on.

Looking over the cliff at one of the lookouts at the Great Australian Bight. The edge was a bit crumbly, so I put my helmet on just in case.

Here is the yellow ute, which played leapfrog with me all day on the Nullarbor, turning into Nundroo roadhouse. Note it's about to fill up with Saff fuel, not f***ing BP.

SNOOZUKI position #5 'The Horizzzz Ontal' Sleeping on the Suzuki proved very successful thanks to the Snoozuki programme.

SNOOZUKI position #19 'The Napster' You can try this at home using a laundry basket, wheelbarrow or even in a tree. Better than Pilates.

This is the track across the Nullarbor along which thunders the twice-weekly Indian–Pacific Sydney-to-Perth train. Lucky I'm wearing my helmet in case of bad timing.

This is Jason and his Harley Davidson with a police siren mounted on the front guard. This was his 18th country. One day, if I keep riding, I'll have a beard like that.

Here I am in Kingston, SA, with a craving for some seafood, but as I look up and down the main street I can't see any sign of a seafood restaurant. Burger King it is.

Summitting the Victoria Pass between Queenstown and Hobart in Tasmania. The one drawback with riding solo is that you have no-one else to hug.

Despite Dr Throttle's best efforts at resuscitation, Mr W. M. Bat was pronounced dead on the roadside at the 5.25 p.m. on Friday. No leaves or branches at the funeral, please.

Thanks to the Victorian 'take a powernap' campaign, I was able to have a quick snooze in designated areas.

Robert applies graphics to the bike before shipping.

Gavin wires up the comms unit under the seat which manages the iPod, GPS, digital camera and laptop chargers, and my hair dryer.

The welcome home committee and Twisting Throttle support crew complete with Hairgama banner.

The starting line at Sydney on Day 1.

The finishing line at Sydney on Day 35.

A black bird, possibly a crow, lifted off the road surface as I sped towards it. Instead of the usual flight path away from the bike, this bird flew, at my helmet height, in the same direction and of course I was gaining on it. I was sure it would angle off at any time, but it didn't. Flying away from me, it weaved to the left and then back to the right, and then to the left again, all the time right in my path. It was as if it was constrained by some invisible corridor. Then suddenly it lofted like a jet surging into the sky and vanished over my head. The bizarre thing is that if it hadn't done that, I simply would have ridden into it and head-butted its bum. Unlike the kangaroo event, this incident made me laugh out loud for the sheer insanity of it.

I plugged on along the coast road heading to Esperance. Showers came and went and the sum total was that I got wetter and wetter. I now understand that there is a direct link between low temperatures and brain malfunction. How do I know this? Consider what happened in Ravensthorpe.

Ravensthorpe is a tidy town about 200 kilometres west of Esperance. I pulled in and parked the bike under the shelter of a shop verandah. My intention was to turn the page of my map book which was wedged in my tank-bag cover, as the red line I was riding along had reached the right-hand margin. When I went to put my gloves back on I had the usual wet-hands wet-gloves problem. In a flash of inspiration I fired up the bike and held my gloves open over the twin exhausts so the hot fumes quickly dried out the insides of the gloves. I then dried my own hands over the exhausts and congratulated myself on this innovative solution to a nagging wet-weather problem. The inside of my helmet was also damp so I applied the same rationale and held it open over the emissions from the exhaust pipes. The helmet lining was toasty warm within seconds and the visor defogged instantly.

As my hair and face were also damp, it seemed a natural extension to likewise exhaust-dry them using the very successful technique previously employed. In a spectacular act of stupidity I knelt down behind the idling bike in the main street of Ravensthorpe and placed my head inches from the burbling exhaust pipes. Granted it was warm but I involuntarily inhaled and received two lungsful of carbon monoxide. I fell over backwards into the gutter by the bike and lay there like a gasping snapper on the deck of a fishing boat. I sat on the kerb for 10 minutes wheezing like an idiot.

'Y'okay, mate?' It was the shopkeeper standing above me with an expression on his face I took for mild amusement. I wasn't sure how much of the incident he had seen, so I played it cool. 'Yep, just takin' a break.' 'Should clear shortly.' I tossed up whether, by that comment, he meant the weather or my breathing. 'Is it far to Esperance?' I rushed to change the subject even though I knew how far it was to Esperance. 'One ninety kays give or take.' I mentally begged him to leave me alone as I felt sick in the stomach. 'That's a good bike you got there. Honda?' I prayed he wasn't one of those 'had a bike as young man and let me tell you about it' types. I like a good chat and can hold my own by pretending to be interested in motorbikes of the 'seventies, but sitting in a gutter in Ravensthorpe, cold, damp and suffering from carbon monoxide poisoning, I just wanted to throw up and then find a somewhere that sold Smints. It was a low point, no question, and one day I'd like to get back to Ravensthorpe to make it up to the kindly shopkeeper who just wanted a chat with a stranger.

I reached Esperance at lunch-time and rode into the town centre to find an ATM. The harbour was choppy, bleak and freezing cold as the wind off the sea went right through me. On my way back out to the main highway I saw a business called Kar Kare. I kan't stand people who kan't spell and kursed the kompany owners. I headed north on the road to Norseman that was 180 kilometres away. The sun came out in patches and it even got warm. I was crooning away to The Tremeloes and The Drifters. The loneliness of the long-distance rider knows no bounds.

After 80 minutes, Norseman appeared over my screen and I selected Caltex as the petrol station of choice, as it looked clean, inviting and free of trucks — but the clincher was that it was the only garage in

Norseman. I pulled up to the pump, switched off and de-helmeted. Out of a loudspeaker came the sound of a promotional tape that could be heard all over the forecourt, up the main street and probably in most residents' houses. This voice-over extolled the virtues of shopping at the Caltex petrol station and was a brilliant example of up-selling. 'After you fill up, why not top up that jerry can as you may need extra fuel on the Nullarbor?' it suggested. 'Come inside our store and use our electronic facilities, such as fax, ATM and internet. And our special today is wholemeal bread for only $1.20. Feeling peckish? Inside we have many hot items from sausages to dim sims. Our range of hot drinks is ready for you to enjoy. And you can't visit Caltex Norseman without trying Rosie's famous chicken.' Then the tape repeated. 'After you fill up, why not . . . ' This type of barefaced add-on selling I hate. I am a discerning and intelligent customer and I don't need to be 'sold to'. I pulled in here for fuel, not food. I went inside, paid for the fuel and bought a cheese sausage, a hot chocolate and some of Rosie's chicken. It was delicious. I'd be having the $1.20 wholemeal loaf of bread for my afternoon tea.

It was another 200-kilometre sprint from Norseman to the twin towns of Kalgoorlie and Boulder. Norseman is the big junction for the Eyre Highway to Port Augusta and I would be back there the next day, ready to plot a course for the Nullarbor. Meantime I wanted to get to Kalgoorlie for the night and to meet Garth Irvin who was going to show me around. Garth was a mate of Steve and Pete, my Chapter 1 BMW-riding escorts out of Sydney.

At 3.30 p.m. we met up at the BP truck stop outside Boulder and I followed Garth up to the lookout over the Super Pit. This had to be seen to be believed. It is a massive open-cast gold-mine and is basically a huge hole in the earth. Roads spiral down into its bowels, along which Caterpillar dump trucks crawl like ants. Each of these trucks weighs 350 tons loaded, and from a load of boulders, rubble and debris a knob of gold the size of a cellphone is extracted.

Later on in the Federal Hotel public bar we drank handles of Carlton Mid across the bar from fluoro-orange-jacketed mine workers. The soccer World Cup had started, there was an Aussie Rules football game on the pub's big screen, and my tummy was ready to put the memory of Rosie's chicken behind it. I had arrived in paradise.

If only I had the guts to call across the bar 'You blokes think of a fruit or vegetable starting with N?'

BIKE'S FUEL FOR DAY: 54 L, costing $83.

RIDER'S FUEL FOR DAY: Two muesli bars, Rosie's chicken and chips (four pack), one cheese sausage, two cups of tea, one hot chocolate; for tea — roast lamb, French onion soup, five handles of Carlton, three chocolate crackles.

Chapter 18

Kalgoorlie–Madura

DAY'S RIDE: 715 kilometres.
JOURNEY TO DATE: 12,563 kilometres.

Tonight I had a conversation that went on for no less than 15 minutes, during which I had no idea whatsoever what was being talked about. Having said that, I admit I knew it was about Aussie Rules football (also known as AFL, also known as footy), but beyond that I might as well have been brain-dead. I had the conversation with the lady who served me a chicken burger, chips and a beer at this roadhouse in Madura, where I am overnighting.

Playing on a big screen down the end of the café was a game of Aussie Rules. The problem was that she assumed I knew what was happening, who was playing, why the crowd screamed at the ref and why it was an injustice that Johnno got whacked. ('Whacked' is footy talk for getting whacked.) I suppose it was a compliment that she thought

I was a local, or at least not some deadhead tourist. It may have been the stubble, the *odeur d'highway* or the fact that I thanked her for the chicken burger by saying 'beaut'.

She was a rabid fan of one of the teams playing — I suspect it was the West Coast Eagles, as every second sentence contained the phrase 'them Eagles'. The point here is that the conversation was so far advanced I couldn't suddenly call a halt, throw up my arms and say, 'Enough, what's it all about?' So I winged it and I believe I got away with it. There was some guy called Johnno. I might have got the name wrong, but it was something like that. It was Johnno this and Johnno that. 'That Johnno,' I enthused, 'he's a star no worries. How many plays has he had this season?' Bizarrely, that inane question must actually have made sense because she answered it and thus my fate was sealed: she had pegged me as an Eagles devotee. Like I said, it would have been rude to bail out and reveal myself a fraud. It was a long 15 minutes but she was in full flight. I sipped my beer, picked at the rapidly cooling chips, asked closed questions but got open-ended replies, and eventually enjoyed a cold chicken burger when it was, mercifully, all over. All I can say is I hope Brad, another Eagles icon, gets back on the team after his shocking ruptured anterior cruciate ligament has kept him on the bench all season. His discomfort is nothing compared with mine seated at the lone table suffering rising paranoia that my faked support of them Eagles would be exposed.

Madura is part-way along the Eyre Highway that runs 1,500 kilometres from that tiny speck in the desert, Norseman, to Port Augusta. I was a quarter of the way along it and smack in the middle of the famous Nullarbor Plain. The repeat 200-kilometre stretch back to Norseman that morning from Kalgoorlie was, well, a repeat.

The one odd thing I remember about this two-hour ride was a weird sort of forest of trees that had no bark, no leaves and looked dead. So then the question is: why are they there at all? How can they grow with no foliage and what purpose do they serve? Birds can't nest in them, they are too puny to be milled for timber and I can't see squirrels storing nuts in their trunks. Which raises a point about Australian flora in general. The place is so vast that it doesn't matter that millions of acres can be covered in vegetation that is seemingly completely useless for anything and all but dead. That includes the endless scrub and barren bushes that I complained about in Northern Territory. These bleak plains are obviously used as Nature's hospice.

As I rode out on the first 200-kilometre stint of the Nullarbor, it pelted down. Within 10 minutes my worst fears were realized when I felt the first drip of cold water inside my collar. Any motorcyclist knows that when riding in rain it is only a matter of time before moisture worms its way inside the protective clothing. The single cold drop trickled down my back and I waited for the stream to start. The funny thing was, it was only ever one droplet. Then the weather became sunny and warm. Steam curled up from the road. Road trains brought with them swirling vortexes of spray that soaked me as I fought with the compression waves as well as these drenchings. And then the creature hit me. I have no idea what it was. This is what happened.

I was pounding along a drying highway counting down the miles to Balladonia, more petrol and a toasted sandwich. I was preoccupied with going through the choices of fillings in my mind. I like to plan in advance — it saves time, since I don't have to dither around at the counter. Cheese-and-onion was top of the fantasy-filling list when suddenly something thwacked into my helmet visor. It jolted my head back and I flinched in fright. It had the impact of a rubber bullet.

But now for the biology question. What hit my visor had turned into a clear liquid that I saw splattered an inch in front of me. There were no antennae, legs, body, or even the usual red smear that appears when an insect ends its life by visor. Whatever had hit me had morphed into a blob of clear jelly, as if I had ridden into a huge single water droplet. It must have been a creature of the air, but what? What flying insect is made up of water? Bees, moths, dragonflies — they all have semi-solid body parts which take a bit of rubbing off with my little spray bottle of Mr Muscle. The question, like the splodge on my visor, stayed with me until I reached Balladonia. It was unresolved even then, and I didn't want to ask the staff about it in the same breath as ordering a cheese-and-onion toastie. I squirted some Mr Muscle on my visor and wiped away the mystery. I would love to know what I thwacked into, but the secret remains out there on the Nully.

Balladonia has two claims to fame. The first is that it was around this area where NASA's *Skylab* crashed in 1979. The local Shire Council wags faxed off a $400 littering fine to NASA and actually received a phone call from President Jimmy Carter apologizing for the mess.

The *Skylab* incident proves just how far technology has come in 30 years. Consider this. As *Skylab* was plunging to Earth in steadily decreasing orbital circles, NASA tried to predict where it would crash, presumably so you or I could get out of the way. The first NASA expert predicted it would crash in Cornwall. Then India was put on full alert. *Skylab* weighed 77 tons and was expected to break up into 500 pieces. To have it eventually plummet into the sparsely inhabited Nullarbor Plain was probably a relief for NASA. It was certainly pay-day for Balladonia, Esperance and environs.

Also for Stan Thornton. At the time, this 17-year-old beer-truck driver lived with his mother in Esperance, and on the night of *Skylab*'s crash the conversation in the Thornton living room would have gone something like this. 'What the b****y hell was that?' 'Don't know, Mum, want me to check?' 'OK, Stanny, and make sure the chickens are all right.' Ten minutes pass. 'Mum, I found this by the shed.' 'What the b****y hell is that?' 'It's a piece of an American space station Mum. It fell on the chicken shed roof.' 'B****y Yanks. Better take it in to Sheriff Johnson.' And at that point I'll stop, because it's turning into *The Andy Griffith Show*. But the young Stan heard about an offer put out by the *San Francisco Examiner* in terms of which the first person to deliver a piece of genuine *Skylab* to its offices would get $10,000. Stan drove like a madman to Perth where he boarded a flight to San Francisco — arriving without a passport but somehow managing to get to the newspaper's offices with his supermarket bag containing a still sizzling metal panel. The story goes that with his $10,000 he built a new hen house for mum.

Balladonia's second claim to fame is being the starting gate for the longest stretch of straight road in Australia. It runs for 146.6 kilometres before it goes around a bend. And the funny thing is that it didn't have to. Go around the bend, that is. The road could simply have carried on being straight for 150 kilometres — and even further — if it had wanted to. The bend at the end seemed unnecessary, but obviously there was some surveying reason why there had to be a kink in the road.

The long, flat, straight road was . . . well . . . long, flat and straight. I pounded along at 120 km/h but felt a little on edge and kept glancing up into the sky. Why? A truck driver back in Norseman had got chatting as we scoffed our chips at neighbouring tables. He was a Nullarbor pro, regularly plying between Adelaide and Perth. I had overtaken him at speed between Esperance and Norseman, and his revenge was to inform me of the police's method of catching speedsters 'crossing the paddock' (the locals' name for the Nullarbor). Seemingly there are discreet lines painted across the road, like starting and finishing gates. A spotter plane flies up and down the road. The spotter watches you cross one line, clicks a stopwatch and times you until you cross the next line. From that he can calculate your speed. If you're over the limit, he radios to a patrol car down the road — and bingo! It occurred to me vaguely that he might be pulling my chain, but he wasn't smiling like a chain-puller eventually would. As I rode across the Nullarbor at 120 km/h I glanced up occasionally. I never saw any lines across the road, spotter planes or stationary patrol cars. I took it my chain had been duly yanked.

The end of the 146.6-kilometre stretch was at the Caiguna road-house where I topped up. So for the duration of a complete tank of petrol, between Balladonia and Caiguna, I hadn't, apart from stopping to take photos, got out of sixth gear, leant on the handlebars or used the clutch or brakes.

At Caiguna I visited the gents. This may seem like more information than you really want to have at this juncture, but here's my point. In the mirror I looked at the awful visage looking back at me. Long-distance riding is no course of beauty treatment. But the weird thing is, my hair didn't seem to have grown. It seemed — albeit in its plastered-down, oily and tufty state — to be the same length it had been when I started out in Sydney three weeks before. Could this be right? What does hair need in order to grow? Sunlight? Air? Conditioner? A comb? It had had none of these. My head had been encased in a helmet for virtually all of three weeks. Had that somehow retarded hair growth? It was, frankly, a thing to dwell on for the next 25 kilometres before I thought of a more compelling issue to worry about. And that was: were my fingernails suffering the same stunted growth, since they were similarly entombed in gloves all day, every day? It makes you think.

Just after leaving Caiguna I passed a sign that read 'Central Western Time Zone — Advance Clocks 45 minutes'. This is a little-known yet highly interesting time-travel fact. As a bit of background, you cross three time zones in Australia — east, central and west. Going from east to west you go back a total of two hours from one side of Australia to the other. Therefore Perth is two hours behind Sydney. Western Australia is so big it is its own time zone. Then you have daylight saving from October to March, but not every state observes it. For example in the middle of the three time zones, comprising Northern Territory and South Australia, there is a north-to-south half-hour offset. South Australia has daylight saving, Northern Territory doesn't.

I remember being stumped about repeating the same half-hour when I noticed a time difference between my watch and a petrol receipt in Katherine. So in winter take Darwin and Nullarbor, where I was now, which are roughly at the same longitude. There is an hour's difference between them. And to totally confuse the traveller, there were the implications of the sign I'd just ridden past. A small strip of time between Caiguna and the SA border at Eucla is called the Central Western Time Zone. For a stretch 350 kilometres wide, you advance your watch 45 minutes. It's an unofficial time zone, but you wouldn't want to ignore it if you were catching a train. I could imagine the conversation as a tourist enquired about the train at Eucla station.

Tourist: Excuse me, could you tell me the time of the next train to Perth?

Stationmaster: Sure, you'll be wanting the 11.30 from Adelaide. Except it doesn't leave Adelaide until 12.00 due to daylight saving in SA. Once it gets to Border Village and WA it becomes the 11.30 again except it doesn't because it has entered the CWT, so it's technically the 10.45, except, let me see — yes it's over halfway to Perth so it's the 8.45 except it's now December daylight saving, so that makes it the 9.45. It'll be here in 20 minutes.

Tourist: OK, I'll wait.

Stationmaster: Fine, but you've already missed the train. It came through an hour ago. When I said 20 minutes, I meant Australian Central Standard Time, but here in Eucla we're on Australian Western Standard Time with no daylight saving and a 45-minute Central Western Time differential.

Tourist: One more question. Can you pass me that shotgun?

The story would be a little more believable if Eucla actually had a station or was even within 100 kilometres of the railway line, but you get the drift.

Continuing to plug across the Nullarbor beyond Caiguna I saw a large black eagle perched on the bloated carcass of a kangaroo on the verge. I passed within 3 metres of it and the eagle did not flinch. I suspect its talons were already embedded in the flesh of the kangaroo ready to make kebabs. The eagle looked at me challengingly and sullenly. Its mood was, like the sky, brooding. There were huge banks of grey-black clouds with shafts of sunlight bursting through, spotlighting small patches of the barren wasteland that is the Nullarbor Treeless Plain. Occasionally, a sleety squall would descend on the road and within five minutes the sky would be blue again. I knew I was near the southern coastline and assumed these fronts were coming in from the sea. I passed Cocklebiddy too tired to wonder why it was called that and pressed on to Madura to make a nice round 700-kilometre day. In the 140 kilometres from Caiguna, I had passed not one vehicle.

So, all things considered, a good day at the office — but admittedly one that had posed some unanswered questions. Which insects explode in a watery mess, what trees don't have anything treelike about them, is helmet hair a bad thing — and, most important of all, will Johnno get back on his feet and take them Eagles to the finals?

BIKE'S FUEL FOR DAY: 52 L, costing $92.

RIDER'S FUEL FOR DAY: Two muesli bars, bacon and eggs for breakfast, two teas, one flat white, toasted cheese-and-onion sandwich, fresh ham-and-tomato sandwich (meant to be toasted but they stuffed up the order), chicken burger and chips, can of Carlton beer, three cholesterol pills.

Chapter 19

Madura–Ceduna

Day's ride: 681 kilometres.
Journey to date: 13,244 kilometres.

I'M TYPING UP today's log hunched over the laptop in a small cabin in Ceduna. The cabin, known as a basic cabin, costs $21 for the night and its furnishings run to a bed and a chair. I suspect that I might pay the price later tonight for declining the seriously more lavish standard cabin that costs $45, for which you do get a fan heater, TV and pillow.

It's just that last night I had been forced to get an $80 motel room at Madura because I couldn't go any further and that's all there was in Madura. If it'd been the Sheraton Madura at $500 a night, I would have had to cough up. The whole day today I was piqued at having spent so much on accommodation the night before, so I resolved to get the cheapest bed in Ceduna — bar sleeping on their wharf under a dinghy.

157

So, all in all, a humble overnight facility this certainly is but what it lacks in actual furniture it makes up for in its compact use of space in a monastic-motif sort of style. For example, the bed is a single one, measuring 2 metres by 1 metre. The cabin measures 3 metres by 2 metres, so the bed is ingeniously placed lengthways in the cabin, leaving a metre at the side and end of it for miscellaneous leisure pursuits, provided such pursuits involve a chair, as you have to climb over it to get to the door. But it's OK, I can roll up my bike jacket for a pillow, stay in my riding gear for warmth in my sleeping bag, and doss down for a solid night's sleep. Why pay more for luxury?

Now this cavalier attitude stems from having had a good day behind the handlebars. It's all gone right today and, spartan surroundings aside, I am a happy camper here in Ceduna as darkness falls and cats start yowling. Today nothing thwacked into my visor, there wasn't a cloud in the sky, I saw the ocean, crows lifted off the road in plenty of time, road-train drivers waved — one even said 'hair-gama' at a petrol station — the iPod, now playing on shuffle, belted out my favourites from the Eagles to the Mavericks. My mood has been upbeat. The bike surged along the ribbon of tarmac all day with twin cylinders thumping. I had a stunningly delicious cold pie at the WA/SA border. The road was fast, dry, ready to be worked.

Leaving Madura at 7.30 a.m., I rode out onto the Eyre Highway, nose pointing east to the border 200 kilometres yonder. Rounding a wide, sweeping bend, I saw a group of black crows on the road ahead. They were gathered around a heap of fur. Some were on the heap pecking like mad. I leaned on the horn. The crows scattered. I pulled up at the heap. It was a kangaroo that had lost a game of road-train roulette in the early pre-dawn. The red smudge went 10 metres along the white centre line. The roo had half its belly missing, thanks to the crows. The stench was revolting. The crows circled high overhead like vultures waiting for the voyeur to slope off and let them resume their breakfast. I had no idea these birds were this carnivorous. But what did I expect out here on the Nullarbor? That crows exist on juicy worms or slugs?

I rode off, and by the time I was in third gear the crows were back on the roo as I looked back at the grisly scene in my mirror.

Eucla is a dot on the map and its name is in bold font. That theoretically means it is of some size. It isn't. Eucla has a petrol station, campground and lookout. I filled up with fuel there, a little earlier than I would normally have, but the reason I did this will emerge shortly. Perched on the edge of an escarpment, Eucla looked out over the most amazing view I have seen for a long time. Amazing because I was completely ignorant of how close I had been to the ocean. Eucla was up on this ridge and you could look back down the last 20 kilometres or so of highway that had been running no more than 2 kilometres from the coast. This was the Great Australian Bight and it was the fourth and last side of Australia I'd be reaching.

The Tasman Sea at Surfers Paradise, the Timor Sea at Darwin, the Indian Ocean at Broome and now the Southern Ocean at Eucla had been milestones in the journey that I felt were iconic moments. To capture the emotion of such moments, you find a way to mark them with a gesture that will, in future years, rekindle the feeling. I bought a pie. This was no Mrs Mac's hearty beef job. It was a plain-pack mince, and it was cold. I swear to you it was the best pie I had tasted since the last best pie.

I found the lookout that had a big white cross 10 metres high called the Travellers' Cross. The plaque said it was dedicated to those Christian road workers who'd forged the highway from Eucla across the Nullarbor. From that I took it that there hadn't been any Muslims, Buddhists or agnostics on the road gangs. If there had been, they didn't get an acknowledgement on the cross.

I crossed the border into South Australia without incident, probably because the border post was unmanned, and pulled into the roadhouse there called Border Village. The fuel station was a BP one, and why that's important is about to be revealed. I bought a sausage roll and a coffee. No sense in dropping my dietary standards just because I was in a new state. That's when the yellow ute pulled up.

To backtrack first. Before I left Madura, I was fussing around outside the motel unit tightening my chain. At the next-door unit was parked a bright yellow Falcon ute with mags. Out strolled the owner, last night's neighbour. I don't know his name. He was a nice guy, friendly and chatty, but had one conversational feature that bears mentioning. Every second word — and I'm being almost literal here — was f**ing. I use asterisks because this is a family book, but you'll get the gist. And he had a problem with BP stations.

These two strange elements came together like this. 'Hair-gama,' I led off. 'F**g good, mate. Should be f**g warmer today. F**g greasy on that f**g bit after f**g Balladonia. F**g roadworks. Be f**g good when it's f**g done. Where're you heading for? You want to watch f**g fuel prices at the f**g border, mate. Fill up at f**g Eucla. What's the f**g place again? Ah, f***. F***, yes I know. Ampol. Make sure you fuel up at f**g Ampol. Not at Border f**g Village at that f**g BP.' He paused for breath. I said, 'Why not, mate?' 'F*** that BP. F*** 'em. They charge f**g $1.80 a f**g litre for f**g premium. F**g BP. At Eucla it's $1.75. Fuel up there before you cross the f**g border. Not at that f**g BP.'

So I rode off with the advice ringing in my ears and thinking about how, if he trimmed out a lot of his adjectives, he'd have so much more time on his hands as his sentences would be half the length. And what was with these BP issues? But still a friendly enough bloke who I probably wouldn't be seeing again. How wrong I was.

To understand the rest of the story it would help if you have seen that classic 1970s movie *Duel* by Steven Spielberg. That's the one in which Dennis Weaver is driving through the desert in his car, overtakes a sinister smoke-belching black fuel tanker and the rest of the movie is about this fuel tanker, the driver of which you never see, terrorizing Dennis Weaver. He pulls into a diner, the tanker is there on the other side of the road, idling away. He rounds a bend, the tanker is parked up the road waiting for him. And so on. It's quite gripping. The yellow ute became my fuel tanker.

Two hundred kilometres from Madura I fuelled up at Eucla, not at that f**g BP station at Border Village, mind. I rode 13 kilometres on to Border Village, f*** 'em, and went in to buy a sausage roll. When I came out, what should be parked by my bike but the yellow ute. The guy came over. I immediately confirmed I hadn't bought fuel there, just this sausage roll and coffee. 'F**g BP rip-offs,' he said. 'Should've bought that f**g sausage roll at Eucla mate, would've been f**g cheaper than this f**g rip-off place. F***.' It was obvious he had a bad relationship with BP Border Village and I didn't want to ask why. Yet here he was using their toilet. I suppose bladder needs transcend fuel obsessions out on the Nullarbor. We said our 'sludder ma's and I rode off.

I pulled off the road at a lookout over the Bight. There were half a dozen lookouts down side roads and I chose this one at random. I had the place to myself with the exception of a Britz campervan containing four, I guessed, Japanese. I looked back, and down the access road was coming the ute.

I said hello for the third time that day. 'F**g ripper view. It's a better f**g view next turn-off. F*** is it what. Have a good f**g ride, mate. We better f*** off too. Look at these f**g Asians. Taking f**g photos of every-f**g-thing.' I'm sorry to admit this, but I was enjoying this guy. I would have loved to ask him what his job was and where he came from. But I was afraid he'd say something like, 'I'm a f**g kindy teacher, mate,' and that would ruin the warm affection I was developing for this linguistic giant and his yellow ute.

The next fuel-up was Nullarbor roadhouse. I had stopped 50 kilometres before that to have a muesli bar at the side of the road. The yellow ute had sped past, horn blaring. 'Paaaarrp, f**g paaarrrp,' it seemed to go.

And there they were at Nullarbor. I'd never talked to his wife but was itching to know whether she spoke colourfully too. I could imagine them at home. 'F**g tea's ready. Wash your f**g hands.' 'F*** off, they're not dirty.' 'F**g please yourself. Now pass the f**g carrots.' The odd thing was the guy was a regular friendly sort that you'd pick — by looking at him — as the owner of a hardware store or something. But BP wasn't out of the woods yet. 'F**g cops. Got me the other side of Eucla. F***. Lucky it was just a f**g licence check. Right after I pulled away from that f**g BP station. F*** that BP w****r.'

They left Nullarbor first. It was 93 kilometres to Yalata. I pulled in there at the derelict roadhouse, which was all boarded up. Then the yellow ute roared past. I had no idea how it had got behind me as I hadn't overtaken it. I rode on to Nundroo roadhouse.

The ute was tanking up there. I daren't ask about the fuel price as we both poured petrol. 'Going on far?' I had to get the obvious question answered and that was whether, the way this intersecting was panning out, we'd end up being cabin neighbours in Ceduna. I prayed he wouldn't say Ceduna. 'Ceduna,' he said. 'Or maybe Kimba. F*** knows. See what it f**g wants to do at Ceduna.' I didn't know if he was referring to his wife or his ute. This time, as we said our fifth goodbye, he whacked me on the back. 'Take it f**g easy, mate.' We parted, two specks on the vast Nullarbor, but drawn together throughout the day by a bond of passionate hatred of BP. It would be days before I chose to fill up at a BP station again. That was the effect this guy had on me.

Just after Yalata, the Eyre Highway crossed the Dog Fence. This man-made marvel is Australia's answer to the Great Wall of China, but perhaps it's not as imposing and it certainly can't be seen from the moon. The wire fence starts on the cliff top at Wahgunyah, about 30 kilometres away from where I was riding. It ends abruptly, 5,400 kilometres later, up in Queensland in Bunya Mountains National Park.

The fence, previously known as the Dingo Barrier Fence, was built in the late 1950s. In the 1980s it was repaired and extended, and now there's a team of people who do nothing but drive up and down it, fixing holes dug by escapees. On the left of the fence, namely the western side, are cattle and dingoes. On the right of the fence, namely the eastern side, are sheep and no dingoes, because those two don't mix.

I readily admit being a bit taken by the prospect of seeing the world's longest fence and rode slowly up the highway on red alert for any sign of a wire fence across the road. Apparently emus, wombats and kangaroos all break through or tunnel under the fence, and there are so many breaches in its length it's like a leaking sieve. The wildlife resistance movement must be only too happy to see their predators nip over to the other side. I could imagine the dingoes in brown leather flying jackets being assisted through the fence at night by 'friendly' local wildlife in camouflage fatigues and berets. 'Monsieur Dingo. Come zis way if you will. Be very, 'ow you say, quiet.' 'Bloody good show. I say, what do they call you again?' 'We are ze Escaping Marsupials Underground. You may know us as . . . E.M.U.' 'Jolly decent of you all to help. But don't we usually eat you?' 'Not tonight, Monsieur Dingo. You will find juicier, 'ow you say, pickings over ze fence 'ere. Just step through zis 'ole Monsieur. Raoul, 'old ze wire open. *Au revoir*, Monsieur. Good 'unting. I zink you will dine on ze mutton tonight.'

I never did see the Dog Fence. E.M.U. had done its job well. The landscape softened as I rode deeper into South Australia. At Penong I rode past farms that were dotted with windmills operating water bores. There were plenty of irrigated, deep-green paddocks, and tractors ploughed vast tracts of hillside in massive dust clouds. The scrubby Nullarbor vegetation had yielded to arable land. The gnarled, leafless trees I detested so much for their pointlessness were gone, replaced with roadside plantations of leafy trees standing tall and proud, trees being trees for once. The sun was warm on my back and it was preparing to go to sleep in the west as I plugged on eastwards. The shadows lengthened and Ceduna, distant across a bay, was illuminated in the final rays of the departing sun.

And just as night follows day, after 140 kilometres I pulled into Shell Ceduna and tanked up at the pump next to the ute. 'F***. You don't f**g hang around. It's pushing one f**g 50 clicks,' he gushed in admiration, or that was my interpretation. By now it was dusk, chilly, the flies were out and Ceduna was it for me. I could imagine his wife saying to him, as he returned to the ute with chips and Cokes, 'There's that f**g guy on the bike again, hon. Go and tell him to f*** off and stop following us.' I firmly believed I would see them again in Port Augusta the next day.

I recount all this simply because it made me laugh out loud all along the ride today. It added to the mood. The route itself was brilliant. Brilliant in terms of the riding, the scenery and the road. From Nullarbor to Nundroo I rode across what must be the official Nullarbor treeless plain. I know this because there were absolutely no trees from horizon to horizon. There were bits of bushy scrub, but nothing was over a metre high and you felt as if you were an ant crawling across a giant snooker table covered in sackcloth. The vanishing point on the arrow-straight road was a pinprick in the distance. There wasn't any miraging or the illusion of shimmery water on the distant horizon. But the horizon was probably only five kilometres away, and it was impossible to get a feel for distance. The GPS blinked east virtually all day and there were no side roads.

Before setting out, I had set the GPS from Madura to Ceduna, a distance of 680 kilometres. Normally a route this long would have blown the GPS's memory card as there would have been too many directions it would have to give. It would be scrolling for pages as it computed all the route permutations over a distance such as this. Turn left, turn right, proceed straight, do a U-turn you wally. In this case it had two entries. First, depart Madura 0.00 km. Last, arrive Ceduna 680 km. Alpha. Omega. It was a day of straight lines and sixth gear.

Hungry beyond belief I pootled through Ceduna town centre looking for the telltale signs of somewhere to eat. Sure enough, wedged between a bank and a chemist was the lit-up sign advertising 'Bill's Chicken Shop'. Fair enough, chicken for tea it would be. I parked and went inside.

Bill, in my consumer opinion, should rename his shop 'Bill's Wide Range of Fried Food, Including Chicken, Shop'. That's because his menu board was a beauty. It had every possible permutation of essentially the same thing. Here's an example. 'Whole chicken cooked. Half chicken cooked. Quarter chicken cooked. Half chicken with chips, no salad. Half chicken with salad only. Salads on their own. Butterfish and half chips. Butterfish and minimum chips. Flake. Tommy Ruff. Snapper. Chicken burger with pine. Hawaiian burger, no pine.' After reading the menu board for 15 minutes, I ordered a butterfish combo, this being a battered butterfish, tartare sauce, minimum chips, and salad for $8.50. While I was waiting, I tried to figure out why you would have a Hawaiian burger with no pineapple as surely that would strip it of its Hawaiian status.

Bill had branded his Coke fridge as Bill's Refreshment Centre, which I thought a little excessive. Over on the other side of the shop was a fridge labelled Bill's Seafreeze, an ingenious play on the words deep freeze. Everything else was also Bill's something. Bill's specials of the day. Bill's table menu. Bill's fresh fish catch of the day. Frankly I was desperate to see, hear or possibly meet Bill, as in the time it took me to go in, choose my tea, order and wait for it, he'd gained a celebrity status simply because he'd lent his name to everything. There was a guy serving behind the counter. I prayed that he would be wearing a badge saying 'Bill', but he wasn't and may have been called Harry for all I know. I left the shop with my daily ration of saturated fat under my arm yet feeling slightly unfulfilled because I hadn't seen the man himself, in the flesh.

I found the local caravan park in the fading light and negotiated my cabin price. Many people are uncomfortable with negotiating things like accommodation. Here's how you do it. 'How much is your cheapest cabin?' '$21.' 'I'll take it.' So there I was, my legs now wrapped in my sleeping bag for warmth, moths dancing around the flickering light bulb, as I reflected on a good day in the saddle — with the only blemish being ripped off by that f**g BP station for my sausage f**g roll. Good f**g night.

Bike's fuel for day: 48 L, costing $80.

Rider's fuel for day: Two muesli bars, sausage roll, coffee, cold pie; Ceduna Bill's Chicken Shop $8.50 special, being two butterfish, chips and two salads, orange juice.

Chapter 20

Ceduna–Port Wakefield

Day's ride: 681 kilometres.
Journey to date: 13,925 kilometres.

A LL THROUGH THIS journey I have been pleased with my strategic decision-making. Do I buy one or two pottles of sauce to have with my sausage roll? Do I put more air in my tyres at this petrol station or wait until the next one? Do I brush my teeth tonight, meaning a special trip to the ablution block, or wait until tomorrow's shower? On the road there are a thousand decisions to be made and you have to be right on your game to avoid disasters. Put your left glove on *after* starting the engine and you risk upsetting the process. You glove up *before* the bike is running otherwise you risk riding off leaving behind a friend. I still harbour issues about Glovey up there in the Kakadu. But the point is this. The trip is all about making good decisions. The previous night I had not made a good decision. Here's why.

I'd chosen a basic cabin for $21 at Ceduna to save money. Overnight South Australia had recorded its coldest temperatures for 17 years. It was all over the news the next day. Farmers' livestock froze in the fields and cars skidded on icy roads, virtually unheard of in South Australia.

It was about 1.00 a.m. when I first woke up, curled like a foetus in my sleeping bag, shivering uncontrollably. I felt like a cold sausage in a fridge. The cabin was made of wood and the window had frost on the inside. I was wearing a T-shirt, two merino-fleece tops, my padded bike trousers and two pairs of socks. In fact, I was wearing all the clothes I had brought on the trip. Mr Blobby couldn't have been more padded up. I couldn't put on my padded riding jacket because that was my pillow. I hunched far into my sleeping bag so my breath would warm up the inside. I almost suffocated and my back ached. I got up, went outside and listened intently at the door of the next-door cabin for snoring or snuffles that would indicate someone was inside. I heard nothing and tried the door. It opened. I lifted the mattress off the bed and lugged it into my cabin. I went back into my sleeping bag sandwiched between two mattresses like a panini. I seriously considered putting on my helmet to warm up my ears.

To get back to the point, renting this cheap cabin was a strategically bad decision, taken in the interests of saving $20 or so. I spent that, and more, at the first roadhouse in the morning shovelling down a pastie and coffee to apologize to my tummy for last night's refrigeration. And all this is why I am typing this diary entry out in a warm and loving environment at a motel in Port Wakefield. In Unit 8c. The weird thing is that the units here are all numbered 8 something: 8a, 8b, 8c, 8d and so on. Why would that be, I wonder? Why not just number the units — and I'm thinking laterally here — 1, 2, 3, 4 . . . ?

The unit cost $65 a night and it has a TV, fridge with milk pottles, a bin, and — I am not making this up — a toaster. I washed my supporting riding apparel (undies in other words) and socks in the shower, scrubbed my boots with the motel's toilet brush and watched two replays of the Socceroos beating Japan in the World Cup. I strung up my bungee cords across the room to make a washing line to dry everything, except my awful socks. To raise the temperature, I switched on the fan heater, the electric blanket and the kettle. Did I mention the toaster? That's for the socks.

The motel's owner introduced himself as Gaz, presumably short for Gary, from Coober Pedy. Actually he moved here from Coober Pedy in 1987 after opals evaded his serious efforts to mine them. He advised me to get a pub meal at the local, three streets down on the left: that night 'they got a house special of schnitzel and a beer for $8.00'. His wife was down in Adelaide shopping, so he might see me there.

If the barman was fat, I was to say to him, 'Oi Andy, you big fat b******, give us a schnitzel special and by the way Gazza at the motel says f*** you.' I was led to believe, by Gaz, that Andy would then laugh gaily and clip me jauntily on the ear before serving me a beer. Another strategic decision . . . should I risk it? What if it wasn't Andy who was on duty behind the bar tonight, and I said it to the wrong guy? What if Andy and Gaz were actually mortal enemies and it was a set-up? That's why I'm still here in my room on my third cup of tea, to make use of the perpetually boiling jug, and a packet of digestive biscuits that have been with me from Perth.

It took an hour in the saddle after leaving Ceduna that morning to thaw out. And the landscape was struggling to thaw out as well. But when the sun became wintry warm, and then by lunch-time toasty warm, the scenery was stunningly beautiful. From Ceduna there was a little settlement every 40 kilometres. This was riding across the Eyre Peninsula, that triangular wedge which sticks down like a map of India between the Spencer Gulf and the Great Australian Bight. Wirrulla, Poochera, Minnipa, Wudinna, Kyancutta, Kimba, Iron Knob — each one appeared as huge white grain silos and then a small township clustered around them, usually off the road.

There were farms, windmills and vast ploughed paddocks. I saw a flock of sheep, the first I had seen in Australia. I passed an 80 km/h roadwork sign. I slowed to 100. Three kilometres later there were still no roadworks. Eventually I saw four orange cones on the other side of the road, guarding a pothole. Two kilometres further on a sign thanked us for our cooperation and permitted us to go back to 110 km/h.

Approaching the town of Wirrulla I passed a sign saying, 'Welcome To Wirrulla — Town With A Secret'. Wirrulla is one of those towns which seems to have suffered simply because the main highway does not go through it. It is tantalizingly close, though. The Eyre Highway, along which I was speeding at 110 km/h, merely veers away from Wirrulla with only two left-hand turns over the railway line plaintively signposting the town centre, almost begging travellers to brake, have a heart and make the left turn. I assumed this was why the townspeople had come up with their town slogan for the welcome sign. Normally they'd have chosen their slogan as something representative of their town such as 'Wirrulla — Town With An Interesting Cemetery' or 'Wirrulla — Home Of The Big Grain Silo'. But in a superb marketing brainwave, they'd cloaked their town in mystery. What was Wirrulla's secret? Would it be obvious if you went to the effort of making that left-hand turn over the railway line? If the town truly had a secret, a skeleton in the closet or a dark past, why would they want to share it with tourists? I braked hard and turned left over the railway line.

Wirrulla's town secret initially evaded me. The town has a population which fluctuates between 70 and 80, depending on whether the Johnson family is heading away for their holidays to Adelaide. There are a total of seven streets. I rode around them all, looking for a secret. 'Wirrulla' is the Aboriginal word for 'rockhole', which, after having been there, I believe is half correct — and I didn't see any rocks. That's a little churlish, but I felt slightly duped by the whole Town-With-A-Secret thing.

I stopped at a small tearoom and went in. On the counter there were photocopies of a hand-drawn town map. After my tootle around the seven streets, I could have drawn one from memory, but I picked one up anyway. On the map was a numerical key, listing the whereabouts of Wirrulla's attractions. No. 1 was the 'Thunderdome', being the town's public toilet. No. 18 was the weighbridge. No. 13 was impishly listed as 'There is no number 13'. Mysterious? Supernatural?

A curtain parted and from the rear of the store hobbled a hunched and wizened old man. There was only one other customer, a young boy with unnaturally bright blue eyes sitting in the window staring at me. 'Greetings, Stranger,' rasped the old man, 'and what brings ye to Wirrulla?' 'I seek the town secret, Old Man,' I replied. The young boy gasped and fled from the tearooms.

'Nay, the secret is not for you, Stranger.' The man recoiled as if I had struck him a blow. 'You must go now, Stranger, quickly, and not speak of the secret to any person.' 'But Old Man, you people have erected a sign proclaiming the secret and it is that which I seek.' 'I can tell you only this: he who seeks the secret secret of Wirrulla, which is secret, must answer one conundrum.' 'And is this conundrum also secret, Old Man?' I pressed. 'Nay, Stranger. For those who seek the secret, such as Sikh seekers, see it secretively secreted so to speak.' 'I'm off to use the Thunderdome. Sludder ma.' I didn't have time for this fannying about.

'Wait, Stranger. Answer ye this conundrum, and ye shall find the secret. What is it that no sailor may sail from, that no fisherman may fish from and no swimmer may swim from? Thus ye shall find the secret. By the way, that's $4.60 for the sausage roll and Fanta.'

I walked out of the tearooms back into the sunlight and mounted my bike. The old man's words rang in my ears. Sailors, fishermen, swimmers? In Wirrulla? A town 30 kilometres from the coast? But wait, what was that rotting structure just across the road? I looked at the map. No. 7 was marked as Secret Town Jetty. 'What th—?' I gasped. A jetty in an inland town? I rode over. It was a derelict jetty on a patch of waste ground with a marooned boat lying on the sand at an angle. On the boat was painted 'Fishing Charters. Leaving Daily'. I had solved the riddle and found Wirrulla's secret. In doing so, I had been relieved of $4.60, and the town had got rid of a town map, got itself the best part of a whole page in my book, and the old man, who was probably the mayor, could report back at the next town meeting that, had he kept me talking longer, the young boy would have finished siphoning out my petrol. Wirrulla — Town With A Brain.

I fuelled up at Poochera. The premium unleaded bowser didn't work. Apparently the tank was empty. The gents' toilet was locked and no-one could find the key. I ordered a latte coffee and got a mug of instant. I wanted to get a custard pie, but the way Poochera was dealing to me I'd get botulism.

Between Kyancutta and Kimba I saw, ahead, a distant figure on my side of the road. As I got closer it looked like a lady pushing a pram. It was someone pushing a cart and walking like a professional walker, with that special swaggering gait. Remember that walker towing a cart in *Priscilla, Queen of the Desert*? It was like that, except this man or woman was pushing instead of pulling the cart. I felt like stopping and talking. Here's my question. The distance between Kimba and Kyancutta is 60 kilometres. We were halfway along that stretch. It was 11.00 a.m. So where had this walker come from? Had he or she truly covered 30 kilometres pushing that thing? Where had he/she stayed the previous night when the temperatures had been below zero? What possessed the person to travel like that? What was in the cart? A tent? A motor? A baby? I slowed down to 50 km/h but the walker didn't look up. I peeped my horn and he or she threw up an arm without looking up and still plodded on, pushing the cart, head down. I simply couldn't decide if it was a man or a woman. This would be the first of two encounters with fellow long-distance travellers today.

The second happened in Port Augusta. I stopped to refuel at a Shell station and parked up in the car park to tighten my slackening chain. Up motored another biker. I heard him before seeing him. He was riding a Harley. He dismounted and shook my hand.

He was Jason, a Birmingham-accented bloke who lived in Sweden. He worked as a truckie in Sweden, and had built his own bike, which he labelled a Harley Mongrel. It had an Evo engine, a Harley tank and everything else was home-built. Australia was his 18th country. He had been in New Zealand a month previously, got caught in a chilly snap in Twizel and shipped over here for warmth. For 17 countries he'd had his girlfriend riding pillion on the back of his bike — which had no rear springs. She apparently called it a day in New Zealand, but he still carried a spare helmet on the back seat. His tent was wrapped in a Union Jack and he had a police motorbike siren mounted on the front. It seemed so in keeping that I didn't ask why.

He was agonizing about where to go from Port Augusta, which of course is where you make the big decision about whether to go north to Alice Springs up the Stuart Highway, or west to the Nullarbor. He wanted to get to Darwin to ship out to Japan, then to Russia and back to Sweden. When we compared trip notes, I felt like a babe in the woods. He said he'd done 26,000 kilometres since starting. I said I'd done 18,000, inflating my actual total by a third to stay in the credibility loop. I put my jacket over my GPS and iPod so I wouldn't look like a yuppie. We took photos of each other, swapped email addresses and he recommended the motel at Port Wakefield. And that's in fact where I ended up staying and, according to Gaz the owner, I was in the same unit, 8c, Jason had stayed in the night before.

Because of the extra time spent kicking tyres with Jason in Port Augusta, I headed out down the Main North Highway towards Adelaide knowing darkness was only two hours away. It was 2.30 p.m. It got chilly at 3.30, and by 4.30 it was pitch-black. Port Wakefield appeared as a mass of lights on the horizon and I was so cheered by the prospect of imminent warmth that I shouted, more than sang, along to 'My Sharona'. My spirits were high until I found out that the lights were those of a refinery. Port Wakefield was a smudge of dim light further on, and I cursed at the extra 25 kilometres. Not even Tony Christie and 'Amarillo' could pump me up.

And so the day eventually ended within spitting distance from Adelaide and a new chain the next day. I suspected that the nature of the riding would change from there on as the population density increased through the rest of South Australia and into Victoria on the Thursday. There were more police on the road, and I'd even seen one on a motorcycle that day. He'd waved at me and I felt a heart-warming burst of camaraderie. The traffic had thickened noticeably in this populated part of South Australia and I'd had to adjust my riding behaviour accordingly. When I overtook a car now, I had to use my indicators and often had to tuck in behind, waiting for a passing opportunity. This was a bit alien compared with the riding style out in the sticks. So I was readying myself for a bit more focus, road nous and slower days in the saddle.

But that was enough for now; I clicked 'save' and stopped typing. The toaster was burning my drying socks, and I was so hungry that I would risk going down to the pub for a schnitzel special. Wish me luck with Andy.

BIKE'S FUEL FOR DAY: 47 L, costing $69.
RIDER'S FUEL FOR DAY: Two muesli bars, sausage roll,
     Mrs Mac's pastie, Fanta, cheese-and-ham
     sandwich, bottle of juice, coffee and biscuits.

Chapter 21

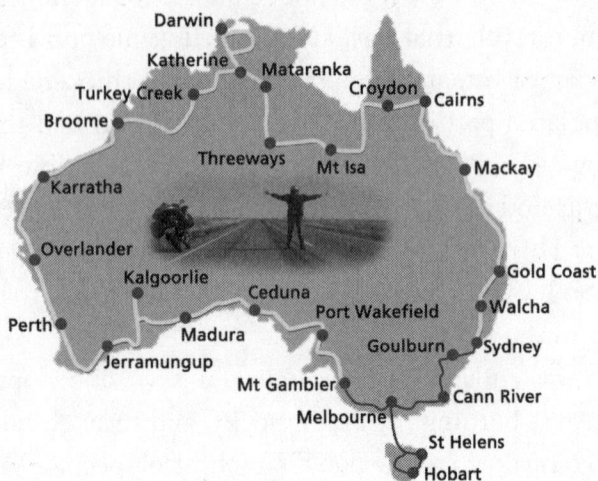

Port Wakefield–Mt Gambier

DAY'S RIDE: 553 kilometres.
JOURNEY TO DATE: 14,478 kilometres.

KALANGADOO, SNUGGERY, KONGORONG. These are names of little settlements I can't get out of my head right now. I've just arrived in Mt Gambier and the last 50 kilometres from Millicent have been like riding through an Australian version of an Enid Blyton story. Firstly the trees in the paddocks have been those stringy bark variety that are all out of shape. I think they're red gums, but I'm guessing. I could make out twisted limbs and tortured faces in their trunks as I whizzed by. I pulled over to take a photo of one of these gnarled trees and saw a ramshackle cottage in the middle of a paddock totally on its own, about 50 metres from the roadside. There was no obvious driveway or track up to this bungalow. At the door stood a lifeless old woman with a headscarf just watching me watching her. In the crook of her arm she cradled either a stick or a shotgun. Normally I'd have waved and called out a cheery 'hair-gama', but for some reason I felt as compelled to be communicative with her as I would have if I had seen Ma Baker flagging me down for a chat.

And then there were the signposts pointing down narrow gravel roads to those oddly-named villages. The one that got my imagination into overdrive was Dismal Swamp and it sort of summed up the whole 50 kilometres. It was an unsettling last half-hour in the saddle and I was glad to pull into this motel in Mt Gambier, lock the door and turn up the TV. Who knows what the residents of Dismal Swamp and Snuggery turn into after sundown?

Port Wakefield. 6.30 a.m. The frost on the bike seat was a bit of a giveaway that the night had been a chilly one. I scraped it off with my Visa card. The day ahead could be described as a functional day. Get to Adelaide, 100 kilometres away, by 9.00 a.m., find the bike dealer downtown, get a new chain fitted and do as many kilometres on the other side of Adelaide as possible by sundown.

It was cold enough to chill bone marrow riding out of Port Wakefield at that crazy time of the morning just before sunrise. The bike pinked and chugged a bit, similarly grumpy about the early start. My visor fogged up at the mere suggestion of cold air and refused to unfog. So I lifted it up and rode visorless. If my name was Amundsen I couldn't have been colder.

It was a dual-lane carriageway all the way into Adelaide, and the morning commuter traffic built up for the last quarter of the 100 kilometres. Since I never get myself fully prepared for riding into a strange city, it always catches me unawares. What I mean by this is that I am taken by surprise, every time, by the extra focus I need to employ. Focus such as looking in my mirrors, actually changing down a gear, indicating before changing lanes, and not looking around like a demented tourist in an information centre. The driving patterns of the vehicles around me were different to those of the vehicles I'd encountered out in the boondocks. What, in fact, was different was that there were vehicles around me. I was not used to this vehicular claustrophobia. The notion of keeping my distance from the car-in-front's rear bumper was foreign after so many miles in isolation. I had become lazy, and having actually to employ road-safety and riding skills was mildly annoying. I was a little resentful of Adelaide for that, but knew it wasn't a fair reaction.

Three lanes of highway approaching a far-off set of lights, which were red, saw cars frantically change lane as they sought to get a few car-lengths further towards the distant city centre. I stayed in my lane like the conventional old-man driver that I am and got there before they did. And this is someone who always picks the wrong line. Woolworths, The Warehouse, Mitre 10, bank or cinema queue, I'll always be lined up behind the person who has something that doesn't scan and the check-out operator needs to ting a bell and hold up the item for the supervisor to come and inspect. Same thing with lane selection. I'll be tucked in behind a white van and it'll want to do a left into a driveway but has to stop on the highway to wait for a car coming out of the driveway first. Pick a lane and it'll be the compulsory right turn I don't want.

And so it was as I wended my way into Adelaide city and left it up to the GPS to find the dealer in Franklin Street. And here — you won't believe this, but it is true — as I was turning into the dealer's driveway (note, driveway, not street), there was a 'Stop/Slow' guy who stopped me. They were resealing the footpath and had reached the driveway. I had to wait for the roller to flatten down the bitumen, a seemingly interminable process. I laughed inwardly at the situation and wondered about a conspiracy. The 'Stop/Slow'-guy network obviously put out a monthly newsletter. In that they document all those road travellers who are picked out as being suitable victims. The word goes out via 'Stop/Slow'-mail and, hey presto! Twisting Throttle is blacklisted and I get stopped by every 'Stop/Slow' guy in the country.

Within an hour at the bike shop the chain had been replaced with a new gold one. I rode away very happy. That happiness paled 2 kilometres down the road. I actually pulled over to think this one out, in case I had to go back. Here is the issue, but I accept the layman may not fully understand it. I'll explain it carefully, as this state of mind goes to the very core of how a long-distance motorcyclist relates to his machine.

The old chain, loose, black, greasy, worn, was back there, in Adelaide city, probably in a skip. On leaving the bike shop I had given no more thought to it than liking the fact that my new chain was a gold one. The old chain, Chainey, had been with the bike since it was new. It had given me 30,000 kilometres of faithful service. How many million revolutions was that? It had performed without complaint. Its last night in service had seen Chainey coated in a vicious frost. That morning I hadn't even sprayed on any lubricant, knowing it would be history in an hour. It was uncoupled by a stranger, slung in a skip and lay there now, waiting for . . . what? Melting down? Landfill?

It was the same callous display as had occurred in Perth, when my front sprocket got replaced. Sprocky was the original cog and again, like the chain, was thrown in an oil drum with rags, cigarette butts and the mechanic's McDonald's wrappers. These bits of the bike were family. They were part of the support crew. And yet I'd given no more thought to saying goodbye to them than I had to farewelling the piece of tissue I'd used to clean my helmet that morning and had then flushed away. I had not thanked them for a job well done, nor given their skips a backward glance. I should have asked for the old bits back, carried them in my top box for the next day or so and then laid them to rest in a better place, perhaps wrapped in toilet paper in a petrol-station litter bin. At the very least, the sprocket and the chain should have been discarded together, as the team that they were. So I had a glove in Kakadu, a rear tyre in Geraldton, a sprocket in Perth, a chain in Adelaide and Lord knows what accessory would be murdered in Tasmania.

I could imagine the other parts of the bike out there in the motel car park at night having a grump session about their owner. 'Look how he flicked old Chainey,' laments the sump. 'Yeah, and after 30 clicks look what thanks Sprocky got,' adds the oil cooler. 'You're next, Sparky,' taunt the front forks. The twin spark plugs shriek in horror until the wise head of the cylinder calms the group down. 'C'mon people, we're just parts,' he intones gravely, 'ain't that right, Tank?' Why do I feel a *Toy Story* moment coming on?

But the fact is this. There is a bond between man and machine which I wouldn't have attached any credibility to before a trip like this. I'm the same with my wardrobe. I can't bear to throw out any old T-shirts or shoes. They simply harbour too many memories to be destroyed wantonly. A box in the attic is the compromise. I will never look at or use them again, but I know they're up there — Shirty, Cappy and Jerseyey.

As I paused for reflection in the mall car park in outer Adelaide, talking myself out of returning to the bike shop for the old chain, I was not a little shocked at my disregard for my accessory friends. It would not be the last time I thought about my support crew.

The three-lane freeway out of Adelaide was a beauty. It curved up and through the Adelaide Hills, surged through the modern Heyser road tunnels, and spurted out into the hinterland. It was like riding on a black mirror, the surface was so smooth. The mid-morning sun was warm and the corners were cambered like those of an Indianapolis racetrack. At Murray Bridge there was a bridge over the Murray. At Tailem Bend there was a bend in the Murray. I turned off down the coast road. It entered the Coorong. I know that because there was a sign that said 'Welcome to the Coorong'. I think the Coorong is the name for the area's wetlands as there were a lot of lagoons, marshes and pelican lookouts.

The road through the Coorong tracked along the coast. Perhaps due to the salt air, I reached a town called Kingston hungry beyond belief. Dominating the main street was a massive orange fibreglass lobster. It stood 17 metres high and was secured by steel cables. Apparently the locals call it Larry and herein lies an amazing fact about Australia.

That is, Australians are fixated on Big Things. I've typed Big Things with initial capitals because this is a genuine collection of structures throughout Australia. To be a Big Thing, the structure must conform to certain loosely defined rules. I don't know which body administers or governs Big Things, and Google does not offer up a Big Thing Society or Council. Number one rule is that the thing must be at least twice as big as the thing it represents. You could not, for example, have an

Ayers Rock Big Thing. Then the Big Thing must be at least twice as big as a human; it must be lifelike and it must be 'enterprising', meaning 'anything goes'. This is a cult phenomenon in Australia and there are tours which simply take groups from Big Thing to Big Thing. There is an underground group trading photos on the internet of its members posing in front of Big Things.

This following started when the Big Banana was put up at Coffs Harbour in 1964, and today every state has a published list of its Big Things. Queensland and New South Wales are fighting to outdo each other and, at the time of writing, Queensland has the edge in terms of Big Thing numbers. The worst-performing state is ACT with only one Big Thing: a 4-metre-high Big Mushroom at Belconnen. Tasmania is almost as lazy, with only two Big Things. One of these is a 3-metre-high Big Penguin at the town of — and, like you, I am stunned by the coincidence — Penguin, near Devonport on the north coast. Northern Territory could do better by improving on its Big Boxing Crocodile at Humpty Doo and the Big Stockwhip at Acacia.

However, all the states have done Australia proud with their Big Things line-up. The official list runs to well over 100 Big Things and I am absolutely stumped to account for having missed them all, since I rode through most of these towns. For example, how could I not have caught sight of the Big Brolga in Townsville, the Big Dugong in Rockhampton, the Big Cane Toad in Sarina or the 8-metre-high Big Gumboot in Tully? What, was I riding through these towns with my eyes shut?

Some of Australia's Big Things are just right for their towns. The Big Rum Bottle in Bundaberg, the Big Golden Guitar in Tamworth, the Big Oyster in Taree, the Big Macadamia Nut in Tambour or the Big Ned Kelly in Glenrowan, which, after all, was where Kello was captured. But then there are the plain stupid Big Things. The Big Paperclip in Brisbane, the Big Mower in Beerwah, the Big Mosquito in Hexham or the Big Chook in Mt Vernon. The ones I liked to hear about, though, were the towns trying to outdo each other. The original Big Banana, in Coffs Harbour, was 11 metres high. Since then Mackay and Carnarvon have built Big Bananas and the Sawtell town council outdid everyone by building a Big Bunch of Bananas. There's a speck of a town in outback Queensland called Sapphire. Its neighbouring towns are called Emerald, Rubyvale and Willows Gemfield, which gives you an idea of their source of income. In Sapphire they have built the Big Spanner and the Big Pick, Shovel and Sieve, yet eight kilometres down the road at Anakie they built a Big Sapphire. Australian culture is plentifully represented with the Big Stubbie in Tewantin, the Big Beer Can in Cobar and the Big Prawn in Ballina.

I could go on about Big Things for pages but you'll be getting a little restless by now, so I'll stop. Suffice it to say that I was very taken with the whole concept and thus it was that I parked in the shadow of the Big Lobster in Kingston, simply grateful I had actually seen one of these elusive Big Things.

Meningie, Kingston, Millicent. These were small towns that all possessed mottos, a police land cruiser parked 15 kilometres each side of the outer limits, a tall water tower, and fuel stops. I could take my pick of BP, Caltex, Mobil or Shell. They were all there. I chose BP in Kingston because it had pea-and-ham soup on the menu. I rode through a *Pinus radiata* forest. It was great. These were trees behaving like trees. Tall, proud and green. I knew the trees were *Pinus radiata* because there was a sign saying 'Radiata Tourist Drive' and a campground called Radiata Park — but the clincher was another sign saying, 'You Are Entering A Pinus Radiata Forest'. Otherwise I'd have been calling them gum trees as usual.

And then, as the sunny afternoon was lulling me into a false sense of *joie de vivre* as the bike and I sped along the empty, dry and sun-dappled coastal road, I decided on the spur of the moment to donate $173 to the South Australian Police Social Club. There's a bit more to it than that, and please bear with me while I tell the story, as it goes to the very heart of my superbly honed negotiation skills. Here's what happened.

I was 20 kilometres the other side of Kingston, near the turn-off to Reedy Creek, still basking in the pleasure of seeing the Big Lobster. I rounded a bend and saw stretching out in front of me a long, deserted straight. There were sheep in the fields, a lone eagle circling high in the blue sky and I was crooning tunelessly to some song on the iPod which may have been by Chris Isaak.

Whoever it was is now deleted as it was the last sound I remember before being intrigued by the lone figure standing in the middle of the road waving me over. With his other arm he was pointing at me what looked like a hair dryer. He wore a hi-viz vest with the word 'Police' stencilled on it. In the shade of some pine trees was parked a Landcruiser, also with the word 'Police' stencilled on it. I decelerated, cursed the Australian law banning radar detectors on bikes and stopped crooning.

He walked over to me, I removed my helmet and waited for the universal chat-up line. Sure enough, 'Going a bit quick there, sir? I've just clocked you at 123 km/h which exceeds the South Australian speed limit of 110 km/h by 13 km/h.' The math was faultless. 'Really? I wouldn't have thought it was that fast.' 'Yes, I clocked you with my radar gun. Look here.' He showed me the LCD readout which had the figures 123 km/h in glowing red digital numbers.

There was no option but to try schmoozing. 'I can't believe I let that creep up. I'm three-quarters of the way round Australia and it'd be the first time I've been over the limit.' 'What do you take me for sir, a dickhead?' He didn't actually say that, but I knew he was thinking it. 'You going far?' is what he really said. This was perfect. Having a chummy conversation would be a great way to deflect him from writing me a ticket. It was on the edge. If I could keep the officer chatting, then maybe we could part friends. 'I'm heading for Mt Gambier. So that turn-off back there was to Reedy Creek?' 'Yes it was. You could take the Reedy Creek road through Lucindale to Naracoorte which would put you on the A60 to Mt Gambier.' 'So this looks an interesting agricultural region.' It was like the condemned man on the guillotine passing the time of day with the hooded executioner merely to stop him cutting the rope holding up the blade. He decided to stop me blethering. 'Just wait there while I check your licence in the cruiser. Won't be long.'

I had five minutes to work out a strategy of damage control, otherwise a $100 hit on today's budget would see me looking for haystacks for tonight's accommodation. I decided the personal approach would work. The officer strolled back to the bike. 'Must be a quiet afternoon for you out here today?' 'Yep, there's not much doing, but we need to police speed as there have been some accidents lately. Mainly locals who get pissed and drive home.' This was an excellent development, as I was clearly not in the target market for ticketing. I was obviously just going to be warned and allowed on my way.

'I'm afraid I'll have to issue you with a speeding infringement notice and here it is.' He handed me a piece of blue paper with my name written on it. Then I saw the fine of $173. '$173. That's a little more than the $100 ticket I got in WA.' I had just contradicted my earlier statement of innocence, but he had me rattled. I heard some magpies start cackling and cawing in the pine trees, and several sheep had stopped eating grass and were watching my strategy to get off the ticket rapidly turn to custard. 'Is it? Perhaps that's because SA takes speeding more seriously.' Not too happy to accept a fine as well as a lecture, I made to buckle up my helmet.

'So you're touring Australia? This is a Suzuki? It's got the TR engine hasn't it? I had a Bandit five years ago. Not a bad sports bike, but it'd get you in the wrists.' And the friendly chat continued. 'I'm stationed up the road in Lucindale but we work in with the guys in Kingston and Robe. You want to get down to Beachport and there's good camping at Southend.' I hate to reveal a negative side to my character here, but I defy anyone to stay upbeat after having been relieved of $173 — totally unnecessarily of course — and then pretend to be friends with the reliever. If he'd had a thermos of tea I'm convinced he would have offered me a cup.

And to finally round off the sheer irony of the incident, I actually thanked him. 'Take it easy Mr . . . (he glanced down at my ticket) . . . Mr Throttle. You have a good day.' 'Thank you. Sludder,' I replied, all but shaking his hand. As I motored away from that damnable clump of pine trees camouflaging his police cruiser, I almost added, 'and kind regards to your family, the lads back at the station and the commissioner'. I felt sick about the fine, the slightly underhand way he'd positioned himself in the shadows, the injustice of being pinged 13 km/h over the limit on such an empty, non-hazardous stretch of road . . . but if coughing up my next two days' accommodation and meals budget would in some small way stop the locals of Reedy Creek driving while pissed, then who am I to be so taciturn?

And taciturn is also a good word to describe my mood as I pulled into Millicent; parked outside the Post Office; queued up at the counter; received the helpful news that fines had to be paid in cash, not by credit card; walked up and down Millicent's main street to find an ATM; queued to withdraw $200 cash and had my card rejected because the machine 'couldn't read card'. I suspect the mag strip might have been damaged when I'd used the card to scrape ice off my bike seat that morning in Port Wakefield. I had also used it to scoop potato salad into my mouth at Karratha, but the card had worked many times since then. I wiped the card a few times under my armpit and, mercifully, it worked and cash came spilling out, together with the morale-boosting little bank-balance docket which included the word 'overdraft' on it.

My criminal record duly expunged, I rode away from Millicent a little more darkly than the pretty town deserved.

I reached Mt Gambier, 20 kilometres from the Victorian border, as dusk was spreading its sultry wings over the countryside and the last half-hour of serene sunlight lulled everything into a false belief that a chilly night wasn't fast approaching. Tomorrow would be the run into Melbourne along that biker's Mecca: the Great Ocean Road. The GOR is an iconic biking route and a must-do. I hoped it wouldn't be icy. I would need the bike to be on its game the next day, but I went to sleep uneasy, hoping the unrest caused by my cold display of heartlessness in Adelaide today was forgotten by the remaining functional bike parts. And, given the number of corners expected tomorrow, at least by Brakey.

BIKE'S FUEL FOR DAY: 26 L, costing $37.
RIDER'S FUEL FOR DAY: Chicken schnitzel roll, coffee, spicy sausage, rice goulash of some sort from a Turkish place in Adelaide, cold pastie, pea-and-ham soup and bread, two teas.

Chapter 22

Mt Gambier–Melbourne

DAY'S RIDE: 585 kilometres.
JOURNEY TO DATE: 15,063 kilometres.

THE GREAT OCEAN ROAD. The name, if you're a motorcycling aficionado, ranks up there with other Down Under iconic biking routes such as New Zealand's Highway 94 into Milford Sound. It's a sort of must-do stretch of 200 kilometres which starts officially in Warrnambool and finishes at Torquay. In between, the road curves around headlands, cliff tops, beaches, forests, valleys and small towns. But it's the stunning coastal formations that are the biggest pull. The road itself is twisty, undulating, and it's almost impossible to overtake anything. It has signs every five kilometres reminding you that you are in Australia and that you should therefore be on the left-hand side of the road. So the Great Ocean Road was true to its name . . . great, by the ocean, and definitely a road.

On leaving Mt Gambier this morning, I said goodbye to South Australia after 10 minutes in the saddle. The border between SA and Victoria was fairly casual. A sign and a dead crow on the verge. Then, within 5 kilometres of being in Victoria, I passed no fewer than 20 signs all about road safety. Apparently Victoria takes its road toll very seriously and clocks up a creditable, if you can call it that, 300 deaths a year. Half of those are people who are busy reading the road signs and run off the road.

Victorian traffic authorities also have a thing about fatigue. Someone in Vicroads has a job dreaming up pithy slogans about taking power-naps. Here are some examples of the powernap signs I passed: 'Got sore eyes? Take a powernap.' 'A micro-nap can kill. Take a powernap.' 'Losing concentration? Take a powernap.' 'Feeling drowsy? Take a powernap.' 'Sick of taking powernaps? Take another one.'

The other road sign issue I dwelt on for much of the day's ride was the odd policy of signs simply slowing you down for nothing. For example, you are beetling along through the countryside at 100 km/h. Around a bend there is an 80 km/h sign. You wonder why, but fair enough, up ahead in the distance is a barn. Then past the barn you get slowed to 60 km/h. Why? You're not sure, but there is a house on each side of the road and a sign saying, 'Welcome to Cockinbool'. After you pass the houses, you beg to speed up, but the 60 km/h zone carries on for another 2 kilometres. Then there's an 80-km/h restriction for no more than 200 metres, and you're back up to 100 km/h. But then you pass yet another fatigue sign and have to pull over for a powernap. It's a little slow-going in Victoria.

At Codrington there were 30 massive wind turbines on a hillside. The blades were twice as big as usual and they rotated inexorably slowly. But it was the eerie noise that was . . . well, eerie. Like a huge swarm of bees whose voices have just broken, in the far-off distance. At Warrnambool I rode the gauntlet of fast-food outlets but had only one goal in mind and it wasn't the McZinger Whopper Combo. Ten kilometres down the road was the turn-off to the Great Ocean Road, technically known as the B100. You can carry on through to Geelong on the A1 that cuts off 100 kilometres, but it's as sacrilegious doing that as it is to fuel up at Caltex and not buy a sausage roll.

As if to welcome me to the great southern coastline and underline the fact that the next landmass over the horizon is Antarctica, the heavens opened and rain persisted down for half an hour. The first pullover lookout place was Bay of Islands. I pulled over and looked out. It was breathtaking in a Shetland Islands sort of way. The sea was in full turmoil, angry and belligerent. There were pinnacles of rock rising from the sea like the fingers of a drowning man. The cliffs were sheer and I memo'ed it as a place to end it all if I didn't want my body to be found. Salt spray got on my visor, camera lens and watch. It was exhilaratingly spectacular. I rode away and within five kilometres pulled off to the right again. This time the sign said 'Grotto and blowholes'. It was a 700-metre walk down a track. I didn't want to leave the bike and gear for a 1.4-kilometre round trip so I flagged the grotto and blowholes.

The next pullover was London Bridge. It is an arch which stands alone while the sea thunders through a gap between it and the mainland cliff, perhaps 100 metres wide. There was no gap before 1990. In that year, while two tourists were admiring the views from the edge of the arch, behind them came a crashing sound followed by a splash. They looked around and noted with concern that the walkway out to where they were standing was a little different to what it had been 10 minutes previously. Namely, it wasn't there. The span had collapsed into the sea after millions of years of wearing away. You'd want to buy a lotto ticket after beating the odds of being on the arch the moment Mother Nature did that karate chop. A helicopter rescued them and they had a brandy or two that night in their hotel before sending home a 'guess-what-happened-to-us-today' postcard. When I was reading the plaque describing all this, the sun came out, blue sky replaced grey, and the sea took on a deep blue, albeit still threatening, hue. It was stunning.

Loch Ard Gorge, Sentinel Rock, The Arch and The Sisters

materialized as right-hand turns into a car park and the usual short track to the viewing platforms. I kept bumping into three other groups as we were all maintaining the same pace along the Great Ocean Road. The white Honda contained two Japanese men who looked miserable and seemed just to be going through the motions. We kept nodding and smiling as we passed in the car parks.

The green people-mover contained a couple who didn't smile at me or at each other. Here is the odd thing that happened. I am walking down a narrow track to a lookout. It is remote and there is no-one else around. Up the track this couple come walking towards me. I have to stand aside to let them pass. They keep their heads down and do not make any sort of acknowledgement, not even a hair-gama. Is that normal human behaviour? Had I been wearing a hockey mask and carrying a chain saw I could have understood their aloofness. It was a small, insignificant incident, but one which rankled with me for its sheer unnecessariness. Why is it that some people simply do not communicate with strangers? Are they so devoid of confidence that they cannot manage a nod of acknowledgement or a non-taxing 'nice day, innit?' You can walk through a crowded mall and not need to greet everyone you pass. But out on a bleak and windswept walkway to a remote viewing platform where the next closest human being is a lighthouse keeper, surely the most basic of social niceties would at least generate a half-smile to a stranger. Maybe if I'd removed my helmet it would have helped.

The third vehicle I kept meeting was a camper. At each lookout it disgorged what looked like two Asian families. Grandma was struggling with the weather, dad kept assembling the group for photos and the rest 'aaahhed' at everything in sight. I liked their style and enthusiasm and ended up 'aahhing' at the views with them. Twice I took their camera and photographed the whole group. I wasn't invited into any pictures. It was probably the hockey mask that put them off.

The iconic feature of the Great Ocean Road is the Twelve Apostles although there are no longer 12 due to their collapsing into the sea one by one. You know you're at an iconic feature when the track to the lookout has a turnstile, an underpass under the road and is two lanes wide. It needed to be. Materializing out of nowhere were coaches, campervans and cyclists. The toilets were signposted in five languages. I ended up on the platform with a family who — I think — were Dutch. They held out their camera and said the Dutch word for please. I took their photo with the Twelve Apostles in the background. I held out my camera and said the English word for please. They said, 'Thank you, one is enough,' and walked off.

I rode onwards along the Great Ocean Road. The turn-offs had come to an end and now the road concentrated on what it did best. Being a great road by the ocean. It was as though someone had laid out a ribbon of tarmac as close as possible to the cliff edge. It reminded me of Cornwall and its coves, except that the landscape was harsher. The road dived inland for 50 kilometres through the Otway National Park. It was twisty, edged by tall eucalypts with white trunks, and had potholes. On one corner I misjudged my speed and lost my line. I ended up on the other side on a blind bend. I laughed in the face of this danger. I could do this as a safe bet because I hadn't passed a car in 20 minutes. I was also out of practice scraping my foot pegs on the roadway.

The road plunged through stands of magnificent trees. There was a sign warning of koalas crossing. Could there be any worse crime than running over a cuddly koala? If that happened to me, I would scoop it off the road and wedge it back in a tree.

The Great Ocean Road eventually wended its way back down to the coast at Apollo Bay. It seemed like one of those English seaside towns where you stroll along the windswept promenade, except there was no promenade. Unless the sun is shining and the sea is blue, a lot of these seaside places can unfortunately seem morose and taciturn. Not so with Lorne, the next coastal settlement along the Great Ocean Road. It was so appealing I awarded it my business, stopping for fuel and a sausage roll.

And then the road decided to get flamboyant, flinging itself around bluffs, careering around headlands and attaching itself to the edge of cliffs as it plunged on towards a conclusion at Anglesea and Torquay. It was as if it had had enough and could not offer any more. The B100 was spent. It reverted to being a benign strip of tarmac, straight and boring, direct to Geelong.

After Geelong the single lane became five lanes. This was the M1 into Melbourne. Approaching cities in Australia had been a chore so far, and I couldn't describe it as anything else. Melbourne was different. It was an experience. The M1 freeway was as straight as an arrow and the sun was setting behind me. The scene ahead was awe-inspiring. The skyscrapers of Melbourne appeared on the horizon 30 kilometres out. The sun glinted off the buildings and a few had twinkling lights. Remember the opening credits of that TV programme *Dallas* where you surged towards the downtown skyline to the music dang dang-dang dang dang dang-dang-dang-dang? It was like that. The freeway was fast, smooth and I was riding on adrenalin, antennae on full alert. Other freeways merged and yet others split off. On an overhead bridge, a computerized indicator told me my speed was 105 km/h and all but added an exclamation mark in reprimand. I laughed out loud at one of the fatigue signs by the side of the freeway. 'Had enough for today? Take a powernap.' And that sign is surrounded by others advising motorists of the penalties they can expect if they stop on the freeway.

The dusk deepened and the skyscrapers came closer. A few had blue rooftop lights. It was both mesmerizing and intimidating. Then, without warning, the freeway, now at least eight lanes wide, careened up and over a massive bridge called Westgate Bridge. To the left were the downtown buildings, so close I could almost see what desktop wallpaper the office workers had on their computers. To the right, way down below, was the port that spilled out into the bay. This was a bridge where you stuck in your lane and too bad if it swept you out to St Kilda. That's where you would be going. To change lanes required a momentary glance in the mirrors to make sure nothing was changing, at the exact same time, into the gap you were eyeing. And then the gap would suddenly close up anyway. You would look back up and see the red brake lights of the semi-trailer in front that was now only 30 metres away from your front tyre. Then the green freeway signs would start appearing in blue. This meant you were on a tollway. Somewhere up ahead will be the City of Melbourne wanting to collect $1.50 off you.

I mentally prepared for the gymnastics of de-gloving, getting out my wallet, ignoring the blaring horns behind me and so on. But there was no toll plaza. All that happened was you swooshed under the human equivalent of a swipe card reader. Locals have a sticker in their windscreen called an e-tag that gets electronically scanned at 110 km/h and charged to their credit card. There must be a whole department devoted to getting photos of those vehicles that swoosh through and don't have an e-tag sticker. Good luck to them. I was tucked in behind an Ingham Chickens articulated truck; bikes don't have front-facing number plates.

So Melbourne it was and there I was. My focal point there was the ferry terminal to Tasmania. But tonight I would sleep the sleep of the dead. I have never leaned over in so many corners so far in Australia and my body was complaining. My eyes were sore, my right (throttle) hand was screaming about overworked tendons. I was losing concentration, feeling drowsy, had had enough for the day and was aware that a micro-nap could kill. I was off for a powerna . . . zzz.

BIKE'S FUEL FOR DAY: 26 L, costing $40.
RIDER'S FUEL FOR DAY: Muesli bar, hot chocolate, sausage roll, beautiful meatballs, egg noodles and fresh veges, apple, orange and pear.

Chapter 23

Melbourne–Hobart

DAY'S RIDE: 526 kilometres.
JOURNEY TO DATE: 15,589 kilometres.

MY KEY TASK yesterday, a rest day off the bike spent in the welcoming company of my Melburnian cousin Diane Fitzmaurice and her partner Brian Parr, had been to book a ferry trip to Tasmania. It wasn't straightforward, but I got there. It seems a lot of weekenders take their cars over on the ferry on Friday night. There was one motorcycle spot left for that night, and I was in full flight with Stephanie from the Tasmanian Travel Office on the other end of the phone. We'd got to the part about credit card details when her screen froze and that was the sign that someone else had just grabbed the bike spot. Why couldn't she have typed faster? She suggested I ring the *Spirit of Tasmania* directly, as they can sometimes fit a few extras in over and above the booked spaces. I had visions of illegally parking in the captain's space.

This time Megan welcomed me to Tasmania, although technically I was in Victoria, but that was simply their way of answering the phone. She informed me that the next day there would be plenty of spaces and that there was also a 40% discount on Saturday fares. She spoke my sort of language and I grabbed it, keen to while away a rest day in Melbourne anyway.

Now to the question of accommodation on the ferry. It is an 11-hour overnight crossing from Melbourne to Devonport across the Bass Strait. You are unlikely to spend much time out on deck and there is no casino. You can book your own cabin, but they start at $300. That buys you a cell with no porthole because it's in the middle of the ship. I asked for other, perhaps more economic, options and the choice was a business-class cruise seat for $108 or a standard cruise seat for half that. 'What's the difference?', I asked Megan. 'Take the business class one, Mr Throttle,' she replied. 'The standard ones don't recline and it's like sitting upright in a cinema for 11 hours.' I asked if I could sleep on my bike, telling her about the Snoozuki Programme I had formulated in Western Australia, and she said passengers weren't allowed down on the vehicle decks during the sailing. The crew didn't want to be interrupted while going through vehicles looking for valuables.

I had to be at the ship's check-in lane at 6.00 p.m. The first part of the trial was run by Tasmanian Biosecurity who asked if I had any firearms, live birds, gas bottles, ammunition, fruit or veges. I had two pears and an orange in my tank bag, so I answered 'no'. That was tea on the boat. To heck with bird flu.

The bike was tied down on the vehicle deck by four shipsmen or whatever they're called. One was very friendly and chatted while his mates did the work. He gets $70,000 per annum and works six weeks on, six off. That means he sails from Melbourne to Tasmania, or the opposite way, every night for 42 consecutive nights. After they dock, in Melbourne or Devonport, at 7.00 a.m. they get everyone off, clean up and by lunch-time knock off for the afternoon. He usually sleeps.

'So you're back on deck, when — 5.00 p.m.?' I almost laughed aloud at my accidental 'deck' pun. 'Yeah, 5.00,' he replied deadpan.

I lugged my tank bag up several floors to the cruise-seat section that was at the stern of the boat, meaning I walked down the entire length past endless cabin doors. I was itching to have a look in a cabin, possibly find an empty one and claim it. Flushed with success from the previous week's pinching of a mattress from the next-door cabin in Ceduna, I rated my chances of pulling it off. However, they all had swipe-card access. I had a swipe card to the cruise-seat area and it didn't work when I tried it in a random cabin door.

I found cruise seat A25 and found that the staff who allocate seats do exactly what staff do in movie theatres when you go to a movie that isn't that popular. The theatre seats, say, 200; there are 20 people in there. They'll all be sitting in one clump. Maybe the cinema staff do that to save on cleaning. So in this cruise-seat section there were about 300 aircraft-style seats in rows. On each seat was a blanket and a pillow. Seats A1–30 were taken, and that was it. The rest remained empty. The 30 people who had bought cruise seats were sitting cheek by jowl next to each other.

An announcement came over the loudspeaker saying three things. What to do if you have to abandon ship, what to do if you have to abandon ship and you've lost your swipe card to the door, and lastly please don't change seats. By 1.00 a.m., five hours into the voyage, 5 of those 30 people had revealed themselves as snorers. I changed seats.

The *Spirit of Tasmania* pulled out at 8.00 p.m. on the dot and docked at Devonport at 7.00 a.m. on the dot. In Melbourne, on the way down to the port, I had stopped at an all-night chemist and asked for seasick pills. The Indian owner said he didn't have any, but then his wife came flying out of the back room, yelled at him in Hindi and he miraculously found a packet of Travacalm under the counter. 'You'll please be taking two of these approximately one half-hour, that is 30 minutes, before sailing. Be aware. They make you very drowsy, but there is caffeine which fights drowsiness,' he instructed. Given the fatigue road signs I'd discovered on the Great Ocean Road the day before, it seemed the whole of Victoria was preoccupied with drowsiness.

On the boat I took three pills and have no idea what took place between changing seats at 1.00 a.m. and a bump at 7.00 a.m. The bump was the ship nudging the wharf at Devonport. I'm sure the Bass Strait is very pretty. I'll have to buy the fridge magnet to pretend I've seen it.

The stream of bleary-eyed vehicle drivers and passengers trooped down to vehicle deck number two, and there began the ritual of 'find your vehicle'. So let's figure this out. I had parked the bike just inside the front of the ship when I rode on at Melbourne. Let's refer to this as 'the bow'. I left the bike and walked almost the length of the ship and up six floors to the cruise seats. These seats were looking out over the back of the ship, hereinafter referred to as 'the stern'. Each floor took two flights of stairs to go up or down to, so, symmetrically speaking, if I walked back the length of the ship, from stern to bow, and went down six floors I should, in theory, be facing the bow, location of my bike. But should I turn left or right when I go out the vehicle deck door? And should I use the left or right, sorry, port or starboard, exit door?

It means nothing that cars are facing a certain way as they may have done a circuit inside the vehicle deck. But surely it is a drive-on, drive-off boat? I stepped off the narrow walkway to allow a family to pass. The father looked vexed. He had also lost his car. Our eyes met briefly and we shared a bond that belonged only in the domain of the eternally damned. It was like forgetting where you parked in a multi-storey, but worse. There was time pressure.

Car doors were slamming and engines starting. The ship's engines had died to a distant throbbing, suggesting it had docked and was starting to unload. You didn't want to get to your car to find that the shipworkers were using a forklift to get it out of the way. There are times when you may be quite happy to look like — and I quote the

Australian term for 'idiot' here — a dickhead, but this was not one of them.

I resorted to trying to work out which was the bow and which the stern. The walls, sorry hull, of the ship seemed to be narrowing behind me. That meant I was walking towards the stern where my bike wasn't. I stepped off the walkway, turned around and walked back, against a stream of people who looked at me knowing I'd gone the wrong way. In their eyes there was sympathy, not mockery. I heard a Harley start up and almost shouted with joy. I reached the bow. All the other bikers were loaded up, helmets on, pillions astride and looking to lane-split their way off the ship first. I purposefully sauntered over to take a photo, giving the impression I was laid-back and the ship could wait for me. In reality, I was making a mental note to bring breadcrumbs for the next time I wanted to find my bike. In three days I would be doing this again.

I rode out into a chilly Tasmanian dawn. It was 7.30 and just getting light. A man in a fluoro jacket worked his way along the line of vehicles queued up in no-man's-land between the ship and the gates which would spill us out onto Tasmania. It was another fruit-and-vege inspection. I still had a pear in my tank bag and an orange in my top box. The way to beat these checks is to declare only one item. I held out the pear as he walked up to me. I felt like a kid offering his teacher an apple. 'That it?' he asked, but his eyes were on a ute behind me. 'Just a chicken with watery eyes and sneezing a lot.' Actually, what I really said was, 'Yep'. I entered Tasmania with an illegal orange and a guilty conscience. At Caltex Devonport where I fuelled up, I threw the orange in a bin. Smuggling fruit across borders simply didn't give me the buzz I had hoped it would.

And then began my own personal 'brass monkey' ride. I chose the B14 to Sheffield as the opening salvo. The road wound through farmland that was white with frost. The sun peeped over the low hills but it made no difference. It was too cold. The night's sub-zero temperatures had been too severe to suddenly wilt at a hint of warmth. Cattle stood stock still in the paddocks. White breath hissed out of their nostrils. A flock of geese waddled down to a pond. As they flopped into the icy water I grimaced on their behalf.

A cloak of mist shrouded the countryside, suffocating trees and veiling the hills. Smoke curled up slowly from farmhouse chimneys and I started to fantasize about hot porridge and hot cakes on the griddle.

The back wheel shimmied briefly and I returned to the now with a small descriptive verbal exhalation. I had ridden over an icy patch but hadn't seen it. The road was black, the ice was clear. I'll bet they call that black ice. And for the rest of the morning, whenever I rode in shadow, under trees or in fact on any part of the road that wasn't basking in sunshine, I convinced myself there was black ice and tensed accordingly. It's funny how the mind works. I saw ice where there wasn't any. I imagined the bike sliding uncontrollably off a bluff. I begged my brain not to use the back brake. It was a patch of edginess that lasted about three hours and I couldn't shake it. Mostly it was unjustified and groundless. Apart for that one slight shimmy there was no other problem. The fact that I was riding at 50 km/h probably helped.

I saw a wombat on the side of the road. It was covered in frost and not moving. I stopped on a one-lane bridge over the Forth River to take a photo. It was a calculated decision as there had been no vehicles for an hour. With helmet and gloves off, I focused the camera. In an incredible quirk of timing, a convoy of army trucks and jeeps braked hard over on the other side. I snapped quickly and rode off the bridge with my helmet still perched on my mirror and gloves tucked into the fairing. To the macho truck drivers I pretended I spurned luxuries such as helmets and gloves. It was one of those men-are-men moments. The convoy stretched back one kilometre. All the drivers waved as I passed. After the last one was out of my mirrors I pulled over. My ears, nose and fingertips were in pain. It would have been warmer climbing Everest in a T-shirt. The price of ego. And the photo of the Forth River was blurred.

The B14 became the C136 that became the C132. At Daisy Bell the road swooshed through open moorland. My anxiety was evaporating, helped by the black road becoming light grey, the warming sun and the blue sky. I rode up to the staggeringly majestic Cradle Mountain along the narrow, but paved, access road. You have to pay a $10 fee to get past the visitor centre. At the Dove Lake car park there were dozens of people rugging up to go tramping.

A Korean couple handed me their camera and I took their photo. The man pointed to the bike and asked me some question. I took it that he was offering to reciprocate by taking a photo of me, and I nodded. He then jumped onto the bike and his wife took a photo of him. There was a lot of 'aahhing' and nodding. I got into the spirit of the thing and put my helmet on his head. That sent them into an 'aahh' frenzy. More photos. Had I switched on the iPod, he would have been there all day.

I rode back to the main road and my ice phobia had all but faded after the uneasy morning. The C132 joined the Murchison Highway and I careered into Rosebery full of *joie de vivre* and bellowing along to 'Run to Paradise'. At the small two-pump BP garage, the lady commented that I must be mad to be out on a bike. She called me 'love' and I knew she was about to force me to down some of her homemade and piping-hot vege soup, while warming my gloves on her potbelly stove and knitting me a helmet warmer. The lapses into fantasy were still occurring. I checked to see I hadn't used the diesel pump by mistake.

The Murchison turned into the Zeehan Highway and wound me down from the upland plateau into Queenstown. This small town was completely overshadowed by a massive opencast copper mine. The mountainside looked like a disastrous rockslide waiting to happen. I was hungry beyond belief and was starting to look twice at road kill.

There was only one eatery open and it served chicken and chips. I ordered two pieces of chicken and two dollars' worth of chips. The guy who served me looked like a miner without the hard hat and light, but he was friendly enough, if a little monosyllabic. There was a display cabinet with pieces of chicken laid out and a tray of chips. He took my money and said it wouldn't be long and did I want chicken salt on the chips. 'Is the Pope a Catholic?' I offered.

But the thing is, he then didn't do anything. Well, he did, but it wasn't to do with chicken or with chips. I think he was washing up. Two teenage girls came in and bought a $3 bag of chips. He served them from the chip tray in the cabinet. I was convinced he had forgotten I was there, so I had to make a noise. I went to the drinks fridge, got out a can of lemon and with excessively heavy footfalls stomped to the counter and set the can down with a light, explosive crack. The guy, without reaction, tea towel over his shoulder, went to the cabinet, got out two pieces of chicken and a bag of chips and handed them to me. No communication passed between us and I walked out with a free can of lemon and a victorious feeling of ascendancy.

Queenstown, to be honest, was a dump. The houses were ramshackle and miserable, but all of them had Sky satellite dishes. There were no bright colours and the Sunday market consisted of three or four trestles under the verandah of the pub. It started to drizzle and the chicken was off. I rode away in a funk.

Within 10 kilometres two things changed that. The Lyell Highway and Mike and The Mechanics. The Lyell slices across the middle of southern Tasmania and ends in Hobart. It's a 266-kilometre treat for motorcyclists and is named as one of Australia's 50 top rides. A quarter of it carves through a World Heritage Area called Franklin–Gordon Wild Rivers National Park. You ride through the Scottish highlands, the English countryside, the American prairies and the Colombian rainforest all on this one route. For three-quarters of the Lyell I passed no more than half a dozen cars.

Cresting the Victoria Pass I stopped to take two things. A photo and a pee. Both actions meant I took my gloves and helmet off. I would have been safer doing that in Antarctica. It was bitterly and inhumanely cold up there on the summit of the pass. Yet within five minutes of riding off again, the sun was beaming through a crack in the brooding cloud cover.

At Derwent Bridge there was amazingly a bridge over the Derwent River. I passed turn-offs to the settlements of Plenty, Hollow Tree and Bagdad. The road descended into a wide valley just as the sun was flexing its last rays of the day. The valley (I think it was called the Ouse) was awash with light and the sun was warm on my back.

I rode through Hamilton and stopped at New Norfolk to fuel up before the final run into Hobart. I went into the BP to pay for my 16 litres of Ultra and decided to pick up a few supplies for tea. Perusing the nutrition section, I selected a combination of dietary products, these being a Pepsi, fruit-and-nut chocolate and a bag of crinkle-cut chips.

I got to the counter and was processed by a chatty guy whose name just had to be Clem or Wal. 'Why didn't you buy the special?' he looked at my three items with what I thought was a little too much incredulity. 'Look, your Pepsi alone is $3.25.' He pointed to a display and I was blowed if I could see anything about a special. Anyway, what if it was half as much again but you got some free shoe polish? Just let me buy these things, Clem, and take my leave. But I was in his territory and wasn't going anywhere. 'See, mate, you've got a Pepsi, 375ml at that, a small bag of chips and a bar of chocolate 150g. Put those chips back, get a 200g bag over there, keep the chocolate as that's the same as the special, put your drink back and get a 1.5 litre from over there by the chips. See, you'll be paying $6.50 for the special and saving money. I buy these things in bulk and can special them.' I walked out with flavours of drink and chips I didn't want, but to refuse his kind-hearted help would have been, well, un-Tasmanian. As I rode off, top box oozing cholesterol, I could imagine him calling to his wife, 'Got rid of another of those avocado chips, honey.'

As dusk lost the battle to encroaching darkness, I felt the chilly fingers of another impending freezing night stroking my gloves. My toes were also stinging, another sign that it was time to dismount at the next hostelry. I found myself crawling along at 65 km/h in a queue of traffic stuck on a narrow part of the Lyell heading into Hobart. The culprit up front was a rubbish truck that quickly got both out of the way and a fair share of drivers' waving fingers when the dual carriageway started. Fifteen minutes later I was cruising into Hobart, twinkling with lights under the shadow of the towering Mt Wellington.

It had been a wonderful riding day and emotions had veered from the morning's ice tension to the afternoon's Lyell euphoria. As I tucked into my 200g bag of avocado-flavoured chips and 1.5-litre bottle of sphagnum moss juice, I reflected on how the day had been full of contrasts. Most of all, I thought about how I now had two days to come up with a solution to finding my bike on the return ferry.

BIKE'S FUEL FOR DAY: 36 L, costing $55.

RIDER'S FUEL FOR DAY: Chicken and chips, bottle of water, four pieces fruit cake, El Scorcho pizza, fruit-and-nut chocolate, Pepsi, avocado chips, can of Solo lemonapple.

Chapter 24

Darwin
Katherine
Turkey Creek • Mataranka
Broome • Croydon
Cairns
Threeways • Mt Isa
Karratha
Overlander
Kalgoorlie
Ceduna
Perth • Port Wakefield • Walcha
Madura
Jerramungup • Goulburn • Sydney
Mt Gambier • Cann River
Melbourne
St Helens
Hobart
Mackay
Gold Coast

Hobart–St Helens

Day's ride: 271 kilometres.
Journey to date: 15,860 kilometres.

L IFE HAS NEVER been better. Why? Here is the situation. I am sitting
here in cabin K5 in the St Helens Caravan Park. I have just found
out that the bed has an electric blanket on it. It is 6.00 p.m., dark
outside and I am sitting up in the bed typing this daily log on my
laptop. Bed is the warmest place in this cabin. I'd be standing under
the shower but my boots are drying in there. I have just washed them
in the basin with the toilet brush. This cabin, although described as
'budget', has everything a traveller could ask for.

Half an hour ago I bought some fish and chips for tea from the
St Helens 'Something's Fishy' fish-and-chip shop. The lady in there
called me 'darl' and recommended the trevalla. Possibly that was
because it cost $5.50 a piece, whereas flake cost $3.50. I asked about

her advertised fish-and-chip special which included a free Coke. She looked pained and said it was just cheap processed fish. I ordered the trevalla. It was OK, but at the end of the day would I really have known the difference between trevalla and flake?

St Helens is on the east coast of Tasmania, near the top. From here the road goes west towards Launceston and it's a quick sprint from there back to Devonport. That's tomorrow's ride and will complete a three-day loop around Tasmania.

The distances here are not great and I'm finding it unusual to think in 40-kilometre increments between places of note rather than the 200-kilometre stretches that I've been used to in other states. I've only covered 270 kilometres today, but it seems longer. It was only 270 kilometres because I pootled a lot.

The day started with an exciting ride across the Tasman Bridge over the Derwent River. Exciting because there's something *Boys' Own*-ish about riding across big bridges three lanes wide. The Tasman Bridge was like every other city's harbour bridge, but without any sides. I remember something about a container ship that ploughed into this bridge back in the 1980s or 1990s, but the facts are hazy.

The dual-lane carriageway out of Hobart as far as Sorell, 20 kilometres north, was fast and empty. The Tasman Highway then upped the ante to 110 km/h but, bizarrely, any vehicle I came up behind was going no more than 95 km/h. I never figured out the relatively slow speeds in this state. Possibly they were due to the fact that the highway doesn't really let you get up to full noise for any decent stretch. There is either a town, a twisty bit, or it just gets too wasteful to blast through stunning coastal scenery faster than you really have to.

The pretty rural towns skipped by in a haze of 60-km/h zones, old pubs and country churches. Buckland, Orford, Triabunna. After Little Swanport, the imposing Freycinet Peninsula dominated the seaside horizon. By lunch-time, the morning frost had evaporated and the countryside had a softer hue to it. The waters of Great Oyster Bay shimmered under a wintry yet tepid sun.

Using an overtaking lane, I passed a petrol tanker. The driver waved and tooted his greeting. Every time this happens, I swell up with gladness of heart. I can't put my finger on the reason for this. It's about some subliminal acknowledgement from a fellow roadie, perhaps. Whatever the underlying emotion is, give me a one-fingered gesture (fingernail away from me, of course) and I'm putty. Bryan Adams filled my helmet with 'Summer of '69' and I knew then that a romantic attachment was forming between me and the right-hand side of Tasmania.

Because the ride that day would be one of the shortest, I had decided to have a little treat. And Swansea, on the coast at Great Oyster Bay, was selected as the location for it. Yes, I am referring to stopping at a café to have a sit-down snack, which was a major departure from scoffing down a Mrs Mac's on a service station forecourt while refuelling. I parked the bike outside the café and went in. And so commenced the worst interaction I had with a local over the whole trip. Here's what happened.

I sat down at a table with four chairs around it. I put my helmet on one of the chairs, my riding jacket over the back of the second, my tank bag rested on the third and I sat on the fourth. There was a small menu resting against the salt shaker. I picked it up and started to look at it.

'It's not table service here.' A woman in a pink smock called this warm greeting to me from behind the counter. 'Why's the menu on the table then?' I lobbed back, possibly a little too barb-like. 'I'm sorry, it's not table service here. Choose what you want and order it at the counter.' 'A flat white and a mince pie with bread, butter and sauce, thanks,' I called back. 'I'm not serving you. You have to tell me your order at the counter.'

I got up and walked up to the counter: 'A flat white, mince pie with bread, butter and sauce, you ugly old crone.' I fantasized about saying that last bit, but that the atmosphere was chilly there was no question. '$6.70 and the sauce is not free. It's another 50 cents.' I handed over my Visa card in silence, wanting to punch something. 'No credit here. Cash only. No travellers' cheques either.'

The thing here is that I don't believe, in hindsight, that she was being purposefully unfriendly or rude. She just possessed an unfortunate manner and lacked the social skill to dish out information in any way other than tartly. But standing there at her counter like a schoolboy being scolded when I was spending my money inside her miserable café, I struggled to keep my temper.

Yet the big question hung in the air like a guillotine blade waiting to claim its victim. And that was whether I had to wait at the counter for my pie, or would she bring it to the table. I hung around the counter pretending to examine a rack of postcards which I thought an excellent compromise. My ego saved and she wouldn't have to fling the pie and sauce the length of the café. I thought afterwards you could make a comedy sketch out of that café in Swansea with its female version of Basil Fawlty.

The thing was that the café incident preyed on my mind as I rode north. It was such a contrast to the otherwise brilliant day here in Eastern Tasmania that I dwelt on it longer than was natural. With nothing else to do on the bike as it pounded along the barren Tasman Highway skirting Moulting Lagoon, I conjured up the image of a Clint Eastwood western. As I dismounted my bike and tied it to a hitching rail in front of the Swansea Saloon, the spurs on my bike boots made a clicking sound as I strode up to the swing doors. Inside a piano player was thumping away at a tuneless piano, and several poker games were in progress as I pushed open the doors and took two paces inside. The piano fell silent, cards were placed face-down on tables, and everyone looked up at the stranger. I removed my helmet, spat on the floor and sauntered up to a table with four chairs. The occupants scuttled away and I sat down placing my boots up on the table. I looked over to the woman bartender. 'Gimme a pie, bread, butter. Make it fast.' You could have heard a pin drop. There was a hiss of indrawn breath. 'We don't do table serv—' 'I said, make it fast.' 'Yessir, and may we offer you sauce with that?' 'Long as it's free.' 'Yessir, to you there's no charge. And of course we take all major credit cards.' 'I ain't buyin' no postcards neither.'

Passing the turn-off to Campbell Town I finally left behind this mental baggage and resolved not to let minor disputes affect me so much. The ride soon brought me back to my previous state of euphoria, and not even riding through the town of Bicheno five times could cloud my enjoyment. Bicheno is nice, but not so nice that you would want to ride the main street more than once.

I passed through the first time, casually noting a Mobil garage and spurted out the other side. I was then racked with indecision about fuel. I had barely half a tankful left. Would there be anywhere to refuel before St Helens? Probably not. But on the other hand, St Helens was only 90 kilometres away. What are you: man or mouse? Whiskers twitching, I turned around and rode back through Bicheno.

At Mobil all their pumps were marked 'Unleaded'. Unleaded in Australia means 91 octane. I had to look for 'premium', 'super', 'ulti-mate', 'ultra', 'bonza' or any other word that infers higher than 91 octane. I rode away from Bicheno for the second time deciding to take a punt that I wouldn't run out of fuel.

And then, passing the 100 km/h sign again, I remembered about the Elephant Pass loop I wanted to do. Suddenly the 90 kilometres to St Helens extended to 140 kilometres and would thus entail a long walk with a jerry can. I had to refuel. Back into Bicheno.

The lady walking her dog on the esplanade gave me a smile this time. After four passes we had become old friends. I saw a BP garage down a side road. I topped up with Ultra. Back through Bicheno for the fifth time, and I wouldn't have been surprised if the townspeople had gathered on the roadside for a send-off. Usually my decision-making is a little more structured. That day was shaping up as being flighty. The fuel-dithering was just part of the inertia.

Elephant Pass is another Australian Top 50 ride. It is a winding, twisty, hairpinny type of narrow road that creeps up a mountainside and dumps out onto a plateau in which nestles the small town of St Marys. The afternoon sun filtered through the trees, making riding up Elephant Pass like an endless zebra crossing. From St Marys the road loops back to the coastal highway, again plummeting down what is probably the same mountainside, this time called St Marys Pass.

I passed two sports bikes coming up. Their riders, hunched down with foot pegs scraping the road, gave me a quick nod of acknowledgement and they were gone. I felt like an old hack in comparison, ambling around the bends, enjoying the dappled sunlight and glimpses of ocean through the tall leafy trees. To toughen up I dropped down a gear, leaned over a bit more and immediately lost the line in the next corner.

Twenty-five kilometres later I idled into St Helens. It had been a lonely sort of day. I had spoken to only four people. The old bag in Swansea, the Bicheno BP garage guy, the owner of the caravan park here in St Helens, and the lady tonight who told me to get the trevalla. To each I would have spoken about three sentences. No-one called me 'mate' today or asked me to take their photo.

So there I was, snuggled up in bed at 6.00 p.m., a time that usually sees me still at my desk back home. My average speed had been 75 km/h and a lady in a fish shop had just called me 'darl'. I couldn't order a pie and sauce in a café without having issues. On the only twisty piece of road requiring more than an ounce of motorcycling skill, I almost ran off at a bend. All day I'd been travelling like a granny. A decision on whether to refuel saw me ride through a small town five times. I'd all but got a Teasmade mounted on my bike, which I feel like naming 'Myrtle'.

But that's Tasmania. It lulls you. Even the road kill look serene and apologetic. I'd have to harden up, though, as there was a way to go yet. Time to get back the hard edge, the privation, the adversities of adventure. But first, if you'll excuse me, I have to flick my electric blanket onto three.

Bike's **fuel for day:**   13 L, costing $20.

Rider's **fuel for day:**   Cold El Scorcho pizza, orange, two free biscuits in cabin, bag of chips, cup of tea, pie, bread, butter, sauce (for an extra 50 cents), flat white, trevalla and chips at St Helens, supposedly home of Tasmania's best fish 'n' chips, Cascade lemon-and-lime drink.

Chapter 25

Darwin
Katherine
Mataranka
Turkey Creek
Croydon
Cairns
Broome
Threeways
Mt Isa
Mackay
Karratha
Overlander
Kalgoorlie
Ceduna
Gold Coast
Perth
Madura
Port Wakefield
Walcha
Jerramungup
Goulburn
Sydney
Mt Gambier
Melbourne
Cann River
St Helens
Hobart

St Helens–Melbourne

DAY'S RIDE: 300 kilometres.
JOURNEY TO DATE: 16,160 kilometres.

JONAGOLD. YOU HAVE no idea what that is, do you? It's a type of apple that you can get in Tasmania. How do I know this? Stewart told me. Stewart is my new friend and I have just retired up on Deck 8 to cruise seat A17 after three Cascade Draughts in the lounge of the *Spirit of Tasmania* where I've been chatting with Stewart since we cast off from Devonport three hours ago.

That tells you two things. My pathetic rate of beer consumption, being 10 ounces per hour, and how desperate I am for human conversation beyond paying for petrol, ordering two pieces of chicken and asking how much a basic cabin costs. I say desperate, but that is a little churlish: Stewart was a friendly guy, just slightly one-sided in his conversational manner. I was the listener, he was the talker. On the other hand, why not? I was in his state, although technically not as we were actually in the Bass Strait, but the clincher was that he bought the beers — so that earned my earnest attention for as long as the Cascades kept coming.

I first met Stewart when we were parked in the queue lines in the corralling yard waiting to be loaded at Devonport. I breezed through the security check. The man in the fluoro vest asked me if I had dangerous weapons, gas stoves or hazardous substances. I said no weapons, no gas stoves. But hazardous substances? I'd ridden around Australia and hadn't yet washed the lining in my padded trousers. He blew a whistle, I was wrestled off the bike by men in white jumpsuits and my trousers went into quarantine. What really happened was that he wasn't that interested, and why should he be? I was leaving Tasmania, not entering it. Let Victoria's biosecurity worry about incoming noxious materials.

So, free to go, I rode up to the few cars parked in darkness, drivers mere silhouettes in their seats, switched off my engine and sat in silence, steeling myself for an hour's wait balancing the bike on tippy toes. Immediately the driver of a Holden on one side of me jumped out, and then the driver of a 4WD did the same on the other side. These Tasmanians were Stewart from Smithton (the Holden), and Greg from Deloraine (the 4WD). They looked at the map book I had in the clear pocket on my tank bag. For the next hour, until waved on board, we talked about long-distance driving and routes. These two were both heading for Queensland and had differing views on the best way to go. This is about how it went:

> Stewart: I'm pickin' up the wife in Williamstown, she flies over because she hates the boat, stays with her brother. We'll get on the ring road and pick up the Hume at Campbellfield. Go Hume up the guts of Vic, pick up the Newell at Albury, through Wagga, have a squiz at the museum at Temora, then pick up the Newell at Wyalong, Dubbo, Moree, at Goondiwindi you're on the Leichhardt to Rocky, Bruce to Mackay.

Me: Wagga? That'll be Wagga Wagga?

Greg: No mate, it's Wagga. Just the one.

Me: Why's it called Wagga Wagga on the map then?

Stewart: 'Cos there's a couple of wogs there.

All: [Light tittering at this intelligent racist pun.]

Greg: I'd give the New England a go, mate. Nice drive and not too heavy. Go off at Conna.

Stewart: Conna? Coonabarabran?

Greg: Yep, Conna.

Stewart: The wife's not keen on the New England, she likes straight and direct.

Greg: It *is* direct. It's more direct than the Newell.

Stewart: No it's not, mate. I've driven it four times. Have a look at this bloke's map. Got NSW, mate?

Me: Yep. Here.

[We struggle to squint at my map book in the darkness.]

Stewart: I'm goin' to Mackay, remember.

Greg: You'll need to go off at Rocky.

Stewart: That's what I said mate. Get on the Leichhardt but watch the Mt Morgan road. What you do is turn off at Dululu, look for Gogango then you're on the Capricorn for 50 kays into Rocky. The wife hates Mt Morgan.

[I'm desperate to contribute something to the discussion as I'm clearly a gooseberry.]

Me: You guys driven Melbourne–Sydney? What'd you suggest, coast or inland? [I was committed to the coast but it was the first thing I could think of to actually hear myself make a noise.]

Stewart: Waste of time the coast, mate. On a bike you want to go through the Snowys.

Greg: In winter, you clown? [This to a stranger he had just met 20 minutes ago.]

Stewart: Fair enough. The coast's nothing special to Bairnsdale, but it's nice up through Bega way. The wife likes Tathra.

Greg: The pub in Tathra does a good seafood chowder.

I enjoyed passing the time like this rather than sitting on my bike in the cool night air for an hour. But I'd pretty much had enough by the time we got waved through. Mine was the only bike on the vehicle deck and I got the special treatment from the shipworkers who were none other than the same four who'd tied me down three nights before, leaving Melbourne. And, of course, the chatty shipworker of last time — whose name, I found out, was Pete — still did no work but told me all about his conditions of work.

He must have been to the same finishing school as the guy in the yellow ute back on the Nullarbor who had a BP complex. (Remember him?) 'You work a f**g AB rating here, mate, f**g top ship, you do a f**g shift down on the roping up then up to the f**g bridge for a f**g . . . f**g . . . how long is it? F**g three-hour watch. Kiwis are the f**g same over there, we're all part of the same f**g system, AB rated, I don't know, f**g great system. You get to do it all. F**g excellent.' I had absolutely no idea what he was talking about, so I said, 'Yeah, I get it. You're all AB. Do the lot.' 'F**g right mate, f**g right,' he said, pleased that I was on his wavelength.

To be honest, after all this I was desperate for a bit of personal space, after having craved human conversation — but I had had my fill for the night. I went up to the bar, got a beer and sat down to see if I could get a cellphone signal.

'You on CDMA or digital?' It was Stewart again. He sat down with his beer. I pretended I knew what CDMA was simply to avoid a lecture on mobile phones. 'Digital, I can't get a signal, though,' I said, hoping that wasn't a stupid comment. 'You'll lose a signal 50 kays out of port,' rambled Stewart while I switched my phone off and on again, as if that would somehow get a signal. 'Ship travels at 25 kays an hour, so you've got two hours.'

'G'day men.' It was Greg. We were now one again. 'You blokes had a look at the buffet? You got to pay extra for it?' 'Yeah, it's $16.90 for all you can eat,' said Stewart. 'Bit different to the Sydney sailing, you get it free on that,' said Greg. Again I found myself completely redundant in the conversation, with the only option that involved opening my mouth being to ask a question and sit back while they competed to answer it.

I thought of a question. 'Do you get any decent apples in Tasmania?' And that's how I learned about Jonagolds. Stewart, or Stu as I now called him because he was buying the beers in return for an audience, happened to be a diesel mechanic and therefore an authority on fruit. We also covered fish batter; acid rain in Queenstown; the punt that crosses the Pieman River; why his wife hates flying, boats and Rockhampton; Aborigines in Tasmania; John Howard; *The World's Fastest Indian*; the chocolate factory in Hobart; and, of course, diesel engines.

Three hours later, at midnight, I was so exhausted and drained that I simply stood up and left them to it, still debating what stabilizers actually do on a boat. And that is where I am now as I write my daily log. On Deck 8 in my cruise seat, waiting for two Travacalm tablets to dope me out with antihistamine, listening to the soft snuffling and snoring coming from my fellow cruise-seat occupiers. It is a tortuous end to an otherwise tremendous day completing the loop of Tasmania.

This morning, the ride from St Helens to Launceston had been 163 kilometres of motorcycling pleasure. It was warm, dry, green, quiet and rustic. I passed signs to Goshen, Cuckoo and Breadalbane. I itched to talk to a cloth-capped local to see if he would call me 'sorr'. The few settlements on the road, defined as anything located between 60 km/h signs, were both quaint and a bit run-down.

The quaintest and run-downiest was Derby. Smoke curled up from chimneys. An old lady swept up leaves outside a church hall. Craft shops had hanging baskets and blackboards advertising cappuccinos. Two small boys were on trikes on their front lawn. They waved and I made a shooting gesture with my hand like a pistol. They jumped off their trikes and pretended to machine-gun me. It was backwoods and I loved it. I passed a driveway to a farm. The closed gate had a sign on it: 'Dunrootin. Keep off the bloody gate.'

I fuelled up in Scottsdale. The guy inside the small Mobil garage insisted I stay in Scottsdale to see what they had to offer. He directed me to the visitor centre that was, in fact, a craft shop. Under his stare

I didn't have the heart not to visit the craft shop. I rode up, walked in, ordered a cappuccino, sipped it slowly and rode away from Scottsdale. I think it is an old mining town, like Derby, but I really don't remember. I idled down a hill into Launceston. I had a lot of time up my sleeve as Devonport was only 100 kilometres away on a direct route.

I branched off up the right-hand bank of the River Tamar as the map showed a red line crossing the river 30 kilometres north. Hoping it was a bridge and not a mapping error, I got to the turn-off. Spanning the river was a huge white suspension bridge called the Batman Bridge. It took me over to the left bank and into Beaconsfield, scene of that infamous mining accident where two miners got trapped underground for 14 days and subsequently made their fortunes on the speaking circuit. Parked at the mine and peering in through the locked gate, I tried to imagine what it would have been like down there. All I could do was commiserate with their underwear hygiene problems.

I set my GPS for the shortest distance to Devonport from Beaconsfield and it chose a delightful country lane, scientific name the C715 via Holwell, which peebled through fields and woodland and across twinkling streams. It was as English as England. In that part of Tasmania you will find Exeter, Sidmouth, Windermere and Bridgenorth.

I pulled into the BP garage in Devonport. A lady wandered out, greeted me like I was her university son returning for the holidays and handed me the nozzle. She tweaked the lever slightly and a little bit of petrol spurted out over my tank bag. I pretended I didn't see it, as she was so friendly.

I then made a spectacular error of judgement. Simply to make conversation, I blurted out a question: Was there anywhere in Devonport with a 'Welcome to Tasmania' sign so that I could get a photo of it with the bike, to go with the ones I'd got in the other states? She took this to heart, summoned the mechanic — I think he was her husband — and they discussed the question. A customer came in. That made three of them trying to recall if there was a sign like that in Devonport. The lady picked up the phone and rang the tourist information centre. If there'd been a crack under the door I would gladly have walked out under it. I was desperate to just pay for the fuel and leave. The lady laughed at something the tourist centre person must have said, and I assumed it involved the words 'tourist' and 'dopey' in the same sentence. Then, to compound the agony, another customer came in and joined the quest, suggesting I get a photo of a 'Welcome to Devonport' sign that they knew was by the motorway on-ramp. We were one phone call away from getting an emergency meeting of the city council summoned.

Then the husband clicked his fingers, ran out of the office and called us all out to the forecourt. He pointed up to the top of the forecourt roof where the BP logo was. Next to it was signwritten 'E. Tusker Motors welcomes you to Tasmania' in small letters. Given the circus I had created trying to be magnanimous, I couldn't ride off without positioning the bike under the forecourt, setting up my camera and taking a photo. I all but got a thumbs-up from the gathering. That was my last contact with Tasmanians and while I spent a lot of time looking for a stone to crawl under while it was all happening, it was nonetheless heart-warming.

The photo itself was blurred and useless because I rushed it. I do that a lot with this camera. If only someone knew about digital camera depth-of-field settings. Where's Stu when I need him?

BIKE'S FUEL FOR DAY:　22 L, costing $33.
RIDER'S FUEL FOR DAY:　Two cups of tea; lunch — chicken burger, chips, Fanta in Launceston; pumpkin soup, two rolls, flat white, three beers on the boat.

Chapter 26

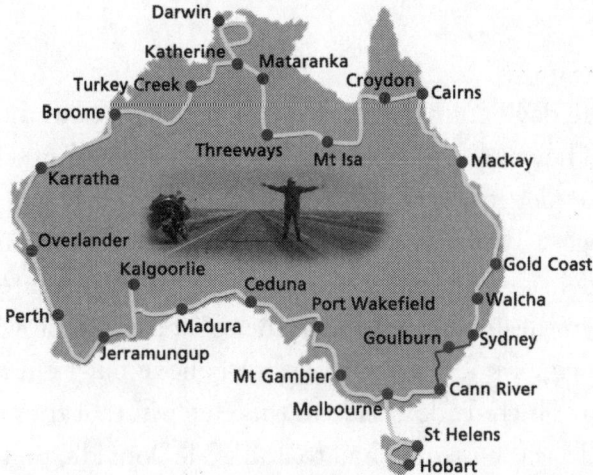

Melbourne–Cann River

TODAY'S RIDE: 483 kilometres.
JOURNEY TO DATE: 16,643 kilometres.

TOMORROW WILL BE my final full day in the saddle as the gap between Twisting Throttle and the finishing line in Sydney closes. I'll try to do 500 or so kilometres, which will see me cross into New South Wales, take a brief foray into ACT (just to get the fridge magnet, of course), and bunk down somewhere near Goulburn. That'll leave a two-hour sprint into Sydney on Friday morning.

Up until now, sitting here in a small cabin in Cann River, Victoria, I haven't really dwelt on finishing, as it's been a matter of taking each day, and each 500-kilometre increment, at a time. Now the vanishing point is not so vanishing, the horizon is not so horizing. The first time I see a road sign mentioning 'Sydney' it'll be a moment to remember. It is hard to believe that the circle is almost joined. But

215

emotion and sentiment will be pillion riders tomorrow, as there is still a state or two between this humble lodging in Cann River and the chequered flag over the Sydney Harbour Bridge. But enough of the big-picture stuff. Back to what the trip's all about — and that, of course, is sausages.

I started the day's culinary intake with six sausages in a town called Warragul. They were stubby beef chipolatas with hardish skins, slightly spicy and tender inside. They were nice and hot and came with two poached eggs. The yokes were runny and there was none of that uncooked gelo stuff around the whites. The toast was white bread, and the person in the kitchen didn't put the eggs on the toast, which meant it wasn't soggy. I know: this is hard to believe but I am not making any of it up. The only downside to this café was that they didn't have a toilet and I was busting. I had to find a McDonald's, pretend I was a customer, use the toilet and creep back out to the original café where my wonderful breakfast was cooling. Over a mug of tea I read the sports pages of the local paper which were all about the World Cup and the Socceroos' chances of beating Croatia.

I'm describing all this because Warragul stands out as a highlight and was worth the three-kilometre detour off the freeway. That breakfast hit the spot so perfectly that it rendered the previous 100 kilometres out of Melbourne a little hazy. And therein lies the joy of the long-distance motorcyclist. An hour of gritty, chilly and unrewarding slog on a busy, featureless and boring road suddenly transforms into a heavenly morning thanks to six small spicy sausages and two poached eggs. I guess you have to be there.

But back, pre-sausages, to the ferry crossing. The Bass Strait was so calm that the ferry's captain upped the ante and shaved half an hour off the crossing time. At 6.30 a.m. the sombre line of vehicles, with bleary-eyed drivers and snoozing passengers, drove out into darkness of a downtown Melbourne that was slowly coming to life.

I set my GPS for all points east and it led me past Flemington Racecourse, towards the freeway called Westgate which turns into a tollway in a tunnel under the city centre. I knew I was getting close to Westgate because my pulse quickened and a droplet of sweat appeared on my visor. This was the 10-lane-wide monster that had got my adrenalin pumping when I had been riding into Melbourne the week before. As if on cue, I missed the off-ramp, being too many lanes in towards the middle, and so was committed to crossing the towering Westgate Bridge heading west, the wrong way, back to Geelong. It was a navigational blunder, but thrilling. The bridge is so high you imagine you are lifting off. I glanced quickly left and right but the lanes were jam-packed with commuters and very fast-moving.

At the first off-ramp over the bridge I exited and circled around back onto the bridge, this time heading east. My iPod cooperated with 'Midnight Oil', so the scene was set for a weaving, high-speed run back under Melbourne's CBD. The GPS was annoyed at the U-turn and a forced route recalculation, however. It purposely — and a little sulkily, I might add — stated it couldn't find satellites. That was because we were plunging under the city in the Burnley Tunnel, cars swapping lanes, trucks using engine brakes, street bikes zig-zagging through the slow patches. All I had to do was stay pointed eastwards and let the motorway expectorate me out into the Melbourne hinterland.

At Warragul I needed caffeine following this high-pressure dash, and stumbled on that café from heaven and its sausages.

The Princes Highway tracks the southern coast of Victoria and around the bend into New South Wales. Trafalgar, Moe, Morwell, Traralgon, Rosedale, Sale, Stratford and Bairnsdale came and went as the highway either bypassed the town centres or stuttered through them with traffic lights, roundabouts and school crossings. Signs for Nar Nar Goon, Loy Yang, Poowong and Koo Wee Rup convinced me I was in Thailand, but then the old favourite Aussie crazies appeared. Toongabbie, Goon Nure, Budgeree, and the essential Bunyip. At Lakes Entrance, so called because it nestles on a spit of land at the sea entrance to four sea-fed lakes, there were fishing boats and crowds of people walking around the town centre.

Bairnsdale is where you turn off for the Great Alpine Road, another of Australia's icon motorcycling routes — but not in winter. I had jotted down in my notebook, back on the ferry crossing, some possible things to do on the way through to New South Wales. Under Bairnsdale the internet offered up the following. The Jolly Jumbuk Country Craft Centre, Egg Shell Dell, the Bairnsdale Antique Clock Museum, Krowathunkooloong Keeping Place or the Canoe Tree. This tree is in a local park and has an unusual trunk growth caused by Aborigines cutting bark off it for a canoe 170 years ago. Under the heading 'Funparks', Bairnsdale offered two minigolfs, a children's playground and a flying fox. I rode through.

At Orbost I fuelled up and tootled up the main street following a police cruiser. It drove along at no more than 25 km/h, possibly unaware I was behind it. I moved towards the centre line, into the line of sight of the driver's mirror. It kept pootling. Should I overtake it, a police vehicle in the main street of a small town that the cop probably treats as his personal kingdom? I stayed behind it. My track record of talking my way out of tickets so far in Australia was 0 to 2.

Through the Bemm River Forest the road cascaded around sweeping bends under a canopy of eucalypt monoliths. A logging truck and I competed for the rapidly approaching single lane as I'd left my overtaking run in dual lanes a little late. I waved in acknowledgement as I won the race. He flashed his lights in obvious humility and supplication, although that may have been my charitable interpretation.

At Cann River, where the Monaro Highway perpendiculates off towards Canberra, I had had enough for the day, after little sleep the previous night, almost 500 kilometres of riding, and with the sun setting rapidly. The cabin there is part of the local café, and the hook to get you to stay is the offer of a free breakfast — continental, of course. So I paid for my cabin and selected cornflakes. I was given a breakfast tray and the room key. On the tray was a small carton of cornflakes, a jug of milk, four slices of bread in cling-film, a saucer with pats of butter and Vegemite. I had to walk 100 metres down the main street of Cann River, from the café to the cabin, carrying the tray. I then went back and got the bike. This probably wouldn't happen if you were checking in to the Sydney Hilton. I had the toast and cornflakes for supper and it was wonderful. I just couldn't face any more fried food on this trip.

It was a trifle early to turn in and I was desperate for a cold beer. After my cornflakes and toast at 6.00 p.m., I didn't want to remember Cann River as a night-time breakfast stop. The fact was, I was also missing my interaction with heartland Aussies and, with a couple of days left, I had a hankering to seek out some local flavour. My last in-depth conversation (if you don't count the listening role I played back on the boat with Stu and Greg) was my stoush with the 'we-don't-do-table-service' lady back in Tasmania.

Which is why I found myself standing at the bar in the Cann River Hotel. 'Yes, mate?' the publican asked. 'Victorian Bitter, mate,' I said, choosing the local brew also known as 'VB'. 'Pot?' he replied. 'Yeah, OK, but let me have the beer first.' All right, I made that up. 'Pot' is the term for a 285-ml glass in this state. If I were in a pub over the border in New South Wales, I'd be asking for a 'middie'. In Northern Territory it's a 'handle'. In South Australia a 'schooner'. And back in Tasmania I'd be ordering a '10-ounce' — but obviously up at the bar, not expecting table service.

The VB was, in a word, paradisiacal. Ice cold, no froth, not too gassy and not too much of a deep taste. VB is brewed by the Foster's Group and is sometimes quite maligned as being a touch like — and I lapse into Australian beer reviewers' jargon here — camel's piss. Put it this way, you'd tend to drink VB on the terraces at a cricket match rather than, say, on the lawn at Government House.

I was on my second pot when the barman brought out a plate of mini spring rolls and a bowl of tomato sauce. He walked over and put it on a table by the window where two guys were nursing their beers. They saw me looking and signalled me over. 'Come over here, pal. Get stuck in.' I pulled up a chair and the three of us hogged into the spring rolls as if we hadn't eaten for a week.

'Hair-gama.' 'Hair-gama.' The pleasantries dispensed with, they shouted me my third pot of VB. Their names were Owen and Steve. I deduced they had been there in the pub from about the time I was riding past the Jolly Jumbuk in Bairnsdale four hours earlier. I concluded this from the topic of conversation. They had moved on from Aussie Rules, politics and interest rates to dissecting the nuances of Australian culture. They resumed talking to each other and Owen was clearly the brains of the partnership. He was telling a joke, and Steve, who was a shade under the IQ radar and had been in the pub most of the afternoon, simply didn't get it.

> Owen: This bloke walks into the bedroom with a sheep under his arm, and he says, 'Darling, this is the pig that I have sex with when you have a headache.' His missus is lyin' on the bed, looks up and says to the bloke, 'I think you'll find that's a sheep, you idiot.' And the bloke replies, 'I think you'll find I wasn't talkin' to you.'
>
> Me: [laughing] Excellent.
>
> Steve: Why's a pig lyin' on the bed?
>
> Owen: No mate, there's no pig on the bed.
>
> Steve: But he has sex with a pig, you said.
>
> Owen: Mate. His missus is on the bed. The bloke's got a sheep under his arm. The bloke talks to the sheep and says 'Darling, this is the pig I have sex with—'
>
> Me: '— when you have a headache.'
>
> Owen: Yeah. And the missus says, 'I think you'll find that's a pig—'
>
> Me: '— you idiot.'
>
> Owen: And the bloke replies, 'I think you'll find I wasn't talkin' to you.'
>
> Steve: Who *was* he talkin' to? The pig?
>
> Owen: Stevo, mate. Bloke, sheep, missus, no pig. He was actually callin' his missus a pig, and talkin' to the sheep under his arm.
>
> Steve: OK, mate, that was pretty funny. G'day, Viv.

A young lady wearing a fluoro vest comes over and plants herself at the table with the three of us. 'G'day, Viv,' Owen said. Viv put her glass down. 'Owen, Stevo, g'day mate.' That last reference was to me and I beamed. 'Spring roll?' I offered her the rapidly emptying plate. 'Cheers, mate.'

> Steve: Viv, a bloke walks into his bedroom and sees his missus with a sheep under her arm—
> Owen: You're a dickhead, Stevo. Drink up, it's your shout.
> Me: I'll get them. VB?
> Viv: This bloke is stranded on a desert island for over 10 years. He sees a speck on the horizon and as it gets closer he realizes it's not a ship or a raft. Out of the surf walks this drop-dead gorgeous blonde bit in a black wetsuit. She strips off her mask and scuba tanks and says to the bloke, 'Tell me, mate, how long is it since you've had a cigarette?' 'Ten years,' says this bloke, starting to tremble. The gorgeous blonde then pulls out a packet of ciggies from her wetsuit's left pocket and hands it over. 'F*** me,' he says, 'I'd forgotten how good a smoke can be.' Then the blonde says, 'How long's it been since you've had a cold beer?' and she pulls out a tinnie from her wetsuit's right pocket and hands it over. 'F*** me,' says the bloke taking a long swig, 'I'd forgotten how good a beer can be.' 'And how long's it been . . .' says the blonde as she slowly undoes the zip down the front of her wetsuit ' . . . since you played around?' 'Strewth,' said the trembling bloke, 'don't tell me ya got golf clubs in there too!'

All four of us pounded the table, creased in laughter. Stevo got it first time. It wasn't so much the joke, which I'd heard before, but how Viv told it. I guessed she worked for a road gang or some such, and she was the complete opposite, if I may be so awful, to what I imagined the wetsuited blonde to be.

I was desperate to make a contribution but it's a rare gift to be able to trot out jokes, funny ones, on tap. I bought a round of four pots of VB and went back to the table. The spring rolls were all cleaned up and the three of them gulped down half of their full glasses of beer without pausing for breath. I took a couple of big mouthfuls, rapidly reaching that point where bloating commences. This beer was 4.9% proof and, while it didn't taste overly alcoholic, my head was entering that slight spin-cycle phase where too much beer in a stomach clad only with cornflakes quickens the stupor. It was embarrassing not to be able to keep up with their consumption. And here's the staggering thing. In the hour and a half I had been in the pub, none of these three had got up and gone to the toilet. Their bladders must be iron-cast. When I got back to the table after my third visit in an hour, Owen was in full cry again.

> Owen: Two drovers standin' in a bar. One asked 'What are you up to?' 'Ahh. I'm takin' a mob of 6,000 from Goondiwindi to Gympie.' 'Oh yeah . . . and what route are you takin'?' 'Ah, prob'ly the missus. After all, she stuck by me durin' the drought.'
> Viv: Which Aussie animal most resembles an Aussie male?
> Steve: A pig?
> Viv: Nope, a wombat. 'Cause he eats roots and leaves.

I left them there in the pub bent double in laughter. I had enjoyed their company for two hours, and in that time I found out nothing about who they were or what they did. They never asked my name or what I was doing in Cann River. They drank beer at double my rate. I went to the toilet at three times their rate. We parted with 'sludders' all round. It was a wonderful evening.

Back at the cabin, lying on my bed in a semi-stupor, I turned my thoughts to the implications of the ride in the morning: the first stage of the last full day in the saddle. I would need an early getaway to avoid the logging trucks, and, of course, due to my rash consumption of tomorrow's breakfast this evening, I would ride away from Cann River on an empty stomach. As creeping unconsciousness rapidly engulfed me, I went through the mental checklist of what to do in the morning. This is the safety and risk management process which has thus far kept me on the road with minimal problems (the rear tyre and Glovey being notable exceptions). Fuel up bike, check tyre pressures, look at oil level, top up Scottoiler, clean bugs off windscreen and visor, fill Camelbak, fast-forward iPod past Billy Ray Cyrus, zero GPS stats, see if anything in cabin is worth pinching, and so on. But the unresolved question still hung in the air like the Sword of Damocles. Where could I get another six sausages without going back to Warragul?

BIKE'S FUEL FOR DAY: 24 L, costing $35.

RIDER'S FUEL FOR DAY: Flat white, hamburger and chips, lemon fizzy, breakfast chipolatas, eggs, tomato and toast, cornflakes and toast for tea, numerous spring rolls and pots of VB at the pub.

Chapter 27

Darwin
Katherine
Turkey Creek   Mataranka
Broome   Croydon   Cairns
                Threeways   Mt Isa
Karratha   Mackay
Overlander
        Kalgoorlie   Gold Coast
                    Ceduna
Perth   Port Wakefield   Walcha
        Madura   Goulburn   Sydney
Jerramungup
        Mt Gambier   Cann River
        Melbourne
                        St Helens
                        Hobart

Cann River–Goulburn

DAY'S RIDE: 487 kilometres.
JOURNEY TO DATE: 17,130 kilometres.

'YOU MOVE,' BARKED the Chinese tourist, pointing to my helmet and
tank bag. 'They stay,' I said, trying to bark as well. This was the
opening salvo of a minor altercation I had with an Asiatic gentleman
wearing a cream jacket and an expression that was dour, to say the least.
If a young child had been passing by, they would have burst into tears.

The brief background to this clash of cultures was this. I was at
the Australian War Memorial in Canberra admiring the view down
Anzac Parade towards Parliament. I had set up my tripod and was in
the middle of posing like a grinning idiot as the camera ticked down
10 seconds.

It was always going to be a close-run thing as a bus had just pulled
up and ejected a load of 'aahhing' Chinese. They swarmed over the

lookout area and one walked in front of the camera as it flashed. The photo was of a jacket pocket. There were, for the purposes of making my point, 20 couples on the bus. Therefore there were 10 cameras. The husbands stood ramrod stiff, completely hard-faced, while the wives snapped them. Then she did the ramrodding while he snapped her in exactly the same position, with the identical background.

A few observations. Why not vary their positions? Their photo albums back home must be twice as thick as they need to be. They take two photos of everything. One with him. One with her. And the bored relatives being shown the holiday snaps must wonder why they are so grim in the photos. And another suggestion. Every 10 photos, why not moon the camera? Anything but look like Mao eating a lemon.

The group chattered and 'aahhed', seemingly happy with life, but the moment they got in front of a camera the shoulders went back and the expression soured. There was only one permanently contented member of the tour party. He was the blue-shirted tour guide and was grinning because this was a free attraction; that is, there was no admission fee because it is a war memorial, yet he had probably charged his group $25 each for 'enter fee'. That last unfounded accusation is pure angst on my part as the whole spoil-my-photo thing had gotten under my skin.

But back to the spat. Prickled because my iconic photo had been knackered by the herd, I put down my tank bag and helmet. This destroyed the ambience of the cream-jacketed one's photo, but the items weren't exactly in the way. And so what if they were? I'd been there first. Move two metres to the left and the helmet wouldn't be in the way. Also, and here's the incredible thing, Anzac Parade would probably remain in the same position, so why not wait until I'd gone? It's called 'queuing', 'waiting your turn', even 'courtesy'. So after my brief rebuff, they took their photo and in a masterful show of one-upmanship, I took a photo of them taking a photo. Now they are in my book and known throughout the Western world as those bolshy Chinese who had a problem with my helmet. They may be a superpower and used to getting their way, but Twisting Throttle moves his helmet for no-one.

Perhaps it was because the journey was nearing its end that I made such a meal of this chance encounter. I would not normally have been so rebellious; usually I would have just let this crowd do their tour-party thing and move on. On any other day I would have stood back, rolled my eyes, tut-tutted and moved my helmet. Perhaps it was their method of seeing Australia that rankled. The tightly scheduled, on-the-bus-off-the-bus system was so at odds with a solo bike ride that we represented two opposing tourist types. Possibly we were, if you really analysed it, visitor enemies.

That was a minor blip in a day relatively free of blips. There were drips but not blips. It was wet that day, and I suppose I had to get one down my back. New South Wales delivered a front that in turn delivered rain, mist and skiddy roads. Cann River to Eden was a solitary ride of 110 kilometres under skies threatening to dump water on me.

At Narrabarba, just across the border between Victoria and New South Wales, it delivered on its promise. It was not torrential rain, just the misty, drizzly stuff that worms its way into the neck of your jacket and makes you wince as that first cold drip delays its decision whether to go for back or crotch. The following drips queue up at the neck and patiently wait for their single-file march towards skin. I had four layers on. How is it possible that the innermost one, a T-shirt, is damp? Or was that a sweaty result of a couple of rear-tyre shimmies on corners?

This was a day when a corner speed recommendation sign, for example 35 km/h, should actually be taken seriously. Logging trucks use the Princes Highway around Mt Imlay as a training ground for wet-weather driving. I know this because I faced no fewer than several thousand of them on this stretch. They hurtle along the sodden highway, creating a vortex of swirling spray across the whole road. It blasts your helmet and you are blinded. Avert your head to protect your visor and you are riding through the maelstrom looking sideways, which is not a totally suitable option.

This comes on top of existing visor issues. When it is cold outside my breath, passing across a warm heart, fogs the visor up. I then have to lift it an inch to clear the fogging. This lets the rain in, which spots on my tinted inner visor. So the tinted inner visor is splattered, the clear outer visor is splattered, and both are fogged. A logging truck rounds a bend and I'm in a momentary state of vulnerability. My brain is trying to remember how close the bend is and whether it curved left or right. I stop to clean my visors. I take off my gloves and my hands get damp. Ever tried to put on padded gloves on a ski field when your hands are wet from the snow? I end up with one floppy glove finger and try to work out which two of my fingers are in the same hole. I ride for 10 kilometres before I discover my helmet isn't done up. I stop, de-glove and the whole circus starts over again. I don't like rain riding.

The opening stretch of the Snowy Mountains Highway from Bega to Cooma climbed up from sea level to about 1,200 metres as I crested the Great Dividing Range that runs up Australia's eastern seaboard. The piece of hillside it chooses to do this on is called Brown Mountain. The Brown Mountain climb is one of Australia's Top 50 rides, according to the atlas I had in my tank bag. They seem to define a 'top ride' as one where there are twisting corners and a few pubs. In the dry, the Brown Mountain corkscrew would satisfy both of those criteria. I rode up like a nervous granny, as it was wet, skiddy, foggy and there were leaves on the road. At Bemboka the pub was closed. At Nimmitabel the pub was closed — and had no roof on it. Up on the tops it was like riding across a bleak and forbidding moor, a bit tussocky and with a side wind like a battering ram.

Thirty-four years ago when I was in high school, I got to visit Cooma on a student exchange. One of the side trips was to a farm at Rock Flat on the highway I now rode along. I have a vivid memory of the farmer on an old tractor ploughing a paddock right by the road and of the local newspaper taking a photo of us standing in the paddock with the farmer on his tractor. The by-line was 'Exchange student learns about crop cultivation at Rock Flat'.

But what sticks in my mind in particular is being invited for lunch in the farmhouse. As if it was yesterday, I remember a silent meal in a very dark kitchen where three adult daughters and the farmer were on the opposite side of a long table to us two students. There was no conversation that I can recall, and the lunch was a plate of boiled potatoes. There were probably other things, but it was the potatoes that I can see in my mind. We had a plateful each and they were only half-cooked. We were too polite to leave them, so we slogged our way through. At the end they were cold and hard. After 34 years I remember cold, hard potatoes in a dark, dingy kitchen with the Addams family.

That's a terrible thing to say, but it spooked me when I saw the freshly-ploughed paddock and then the house this day at Rock Flat. And then the questions tumbled through my mind. Where were those people now? Has it been the same guy who has been ploughing that paddock over the past 34 years? What if I stopped at the house to see if anyone was home? Maybe they'd remember me? What if they invited me in for lunch? I rode on.

Cooma dished up a ham-and-cheese toasted sandwich and a fresh chicken roll. While I was eating this and thawing my hands on a mug of flat white, the two ladies behind the counter had what seemed to be a domestic. 'Can you turn the grill off?' asked one. The other lady walked the length of the servery to turn the grill off. Then she decided she had a problem with that. 'Did you hear that, Dawn?' This to a third lady. 'I walk all the way up there for this. Where is she?' 'Outside doing the tables.' It was riveting stuff and other customers looked up from their papers to eavesdrop on the exchange, anticipating a full-on brawl between the café staff. Another customer came in and stood waiting to be served. 'Yours, Dawn.' 'Did you hear that? Cheeky madam.' 'Go and tell her she's got to do the counter.' 'I will. Can you get this one first?' 'Yes, dear? What'll it be today?'

I rode out of Cooma thinking that the tearooms argument was what I'd remember it for. Perhaps in 34 years' time when I'm back, I'll go back to that place and it will be my new Rock Flat.

Half an hour up the Monaro Highway heading towards Canberra I rounded a sweeping bend and saw a small settlement up ahead called

Bredbo. Just past the 60 km/h sign I was flagged down by a man in a bright yellow hi-viz jerkin who waved his arms at me. I pulled over and he just stood there making no further contact. 'How's it going?' I said. 'Good, mate,' he replied. Nothing else happened. A rooster crowed in the distance. 'Did you flag me down?' I asked. 'No.' 'Why did you wave at me?' 'There's been an accident.' 'Where?' 'There.' He pointed to a van parked in the car park of the pub. It had a dented side. 'See you round,' I said. 'Yep.' I rode off, mulling over the question of why this dill was slowing down traffic, which was already crawling through town at 60 km/h, for a damaged vehicle which was 20 metres off the road. Had I careered into the car park it might have been a hazard, but not while I was on the Monaro. Give someone a hi-viz jerkin and the authority goes to their head. I suspect he was actually the mayor of Bredbo.

I reached Canberra in a dry spell and my GPS took me to the Houses of Parliament for a photo. There was a single tent pitched on the lawn there with some hard-to-read sign about Aboriginal rights. I rode around State Circle, down King Avenue and up to the Australian War Memorial and its stunningly regal view down Anzac Parade back to Parliament. And this was where I had my cultural intercourse with those Chinese rays of sunshine.

The Federal Highway from Canberra to Goulburn was 100 kilo-metres of throttle overload. It was at last sunny and dry. The road was a dual-lane with almost nothing on it. A cop in the shadow of some trees pointed a radar gun at me. I was beetling along at the time, doing 107 km/h in a 110-zone. Nothing could touch me. My visor was bone dry and everything was good with the world. Israel Kamakawiwo's 'Somewhere Over the Rainbow' with impeccable timing seemed to sum up the final hour of the day's ride. I rewound it twice.

The fuel light was blinking on 'empty' as I chugged into Goulburn. I had to think about what amount to put in as tomorrow would be the final 200 kilometres to the finishing line in Sydney. I would have to crate up the bike with an empty fuel tank. I put in $20 worth.

The finishing line. It was hard to believe that the chequered flag was just over the horizon. From Goulburn it was the Hume Highway right into Sydney. It would be dual-lane all the way. I was not sure what it would feel like, riding over the Harbour Bridge. I had to select which song, out of the 492 I was now completely sick of, would be awarded the honour of crooning through my helmet speakers for the last five minutes of glory. I was favouring something nostalgically Australian, perhaps Cold Chisel, to keep it relevant, but we'd see. Tonight I was nuggeting my boots and scooping out a petrified wasp carcass that'd been wedged in my helmet vent for the last 7,000 kilometres. His free ride was over. The mayor of Sydney might make it down to the Opera House to officially welcome me back but he might have a clash of dates with Nicole Kidman's wedding. She'd have washed more than I have in the past five weeks, her right hand would not be permanently gnarled as if clutching a broom handle, and she wouldn't have Mrs Mac's breath. It'd be a tough choice for him. Maybe I'd just have to find a friendly Chinese tourist to take my photo instead.

BIKE'S FUEL FOR DAY: 29 L, costing $44.

RIDER'S FUEL FOR DAY: Fresh chicken-lettuce-tomato-cucumber bread roll, ham-and-cheese toastie, chicken teriyaki Subway, blueberry muffin, two coffees, sausage roll, lime Fanta.

Chapter 28

Darwin
Katherine
Mataranka
Turkey Creek
Croydon
Broome
Cairns
Threeways
Mt Isa
Mackay
Karratha
Overlander
Kalgoorlie
Ceduna
Gold Coast
Perth
Port Wakefield
Walcha
Madura
Goulburn
Sydney
Jerramungup
Mt Gambier
Cann River
Melbourne
St Helens
Hobart

Goulburn–Sydney

DAY'S RIDE: 220 kilometres.
JOURNEY TO DATE: 17,350 kilometres.

THERE WAS SOMETHING unsettling about packing up the bike for the
last time. I couldn't put my finger on it. It wasn't just the forlorn
and slightly overwhelming realization that this impending short ride
would be the final chapter. I mean, who can really be too despondent
about tying on a bungee cord for the last time? I was racked by a sense
of unease and was uneasy about being uneasy. As I rode down the
on-ramp onto the Hume Highway at Goulburn that would fire me
like a missile into Sydney, I couldn't shake the feeling that the next
200 kilometres to the finishing line wouldn't be without problems. I
mentally ticked off the 'what could possibly happen'. A puncture on
the freeway, a nose-to-tail in the swirling fog which sat over the road
like a dirty blanket, a chance encounter with a diesel spill, a speeding

ticket, a bird plastered on my visor . . . I remembered that back at the outset I had had the same moroseness descend on me the day I rode out of Sydney. It had lasted for 50 kilometres before I had snapped out of the funk.

It was irrational and was spoiling what should have been a two-hour victory ride. I should have been imagining ticker tape, cheering schoolchildren and the Lord Mayor with an outstretched hand holding the key to the city in it. Instead, I was mired in a stupor of self-doubt. In reality, I was tensing with anxiety about not dropping the ball when closure was so imminent. I talked myself through the next two hours. Nice and easy, sit in the middle lane, over-indicate, take no chances, focus and think about what song you want to crash over the finishing line to.

Through the gloomy and suffocating fog, the outer suburbs of Sydney gradually appeared, but only as off-ramp signs. Traffic on the freeway trebled, the number of lanes doubled and my gloomy doldrums evaporated as the bike and I were swept along in a tide of commuter-herd mentality. It was wonderful. At last adrenalin was kicking in and the excitement swamped me as I surged under freeway overpasses and weaved through slowing traffic.

The fog had lifted and in the distance I glimpsed the Sydney CBD high-rises. Centrepoint tower glinted like a beacon as the freeway tunnelled under the airport runways, spitting us all out onto what seemed like the true home straight. A taxi driver cut me off and returned my one-fingered acknowledgement, but there was no malice in it. I was over dwelling on the hierarchies of the road. This town may have been the taxi driver's castle, but I was the knight charging across the drawbridge about to conquer it.

Suddenly, without fanfare, the freeway split off to the Sydney Harbour Tunnel. I was caught four lanes over from where I should have been and couldn't believe the sheer lack of planning which saw me about to go under, not over, my finishing line. Surfing the 100-km/h wave of commuter traffic heading to the North Shore, I had no choice but to plunge across the entire freeway like a maniac to just make the exit to the on-ramp to the harbour bridge. This was not my finest road-safety moment, but I believe I completed this — the hairiest manoeuvre in 35 days — without a single honk. Sydney was understanding.

The iPod had been on pause for the past half an hour because I wanted exactly the right song to be playing in my ears as I crossed the finish line. For my arrival anthem I had chosen 'Glove Hurts' by Roy Orbison, in memory of my five-fingered friend who should have been twisting the throttle at the end but instead was lying up there in the Kakadu bush. I stabbed the 'play' button and, in the middle lane, with a lump in my throat and a Holden Commodore right up my backside, I crested the Sydney Harbour Bridge — and thus started a second lap of Australia. Had I kept going past the North Sydney off-ramp, that is.

I could indicate left, cross two lanes and stop in Milson Point, which is where I had started from 35 days before. Or I could indicate right and blast on up the freeway to Newcastle. Left would take me to a world of fresh fruit, Voltarin, human conversation not involving the words 'mate' or 'worries', risk-free beer consumption, soft sheets, a family who, in all probability, had forgotten what I look like, and my own pillow. Right would lead to a continuation of my relationship with sausage rolls, premium unleaded petrol-pump nozzles, looking for twitching index fingers in oncoming trucks, and avoiding looking Aboriginals in the eyes. I indicated left.

And so ended a lap of Australia around the outside. The bike had soldiered on for 17,350 kilometres. Had I ridden in a straight line from Sydney, that would have seen me get to Moscow. Australia, it has to be said, is a fair-sized landmass. It might have been better to tackle Austria first-up.

I chose to ride counter-clockwise around Australia and I'm not sure why. Had I gone the other way, I would have ridden further and you need to figure that one out, but it has to do with the side of the road one drives on. I'd learned a lot on the bike as I'd had a lot of time to dwell on things and just mull. There was some unfinished business that I hadn't managed to sort out. For example, what exactly is Roger

Whittaker's 'I Don't Believe In If Anymore' all about? How can you actually believe in 'if'? Do you also believe in 'of', 'so', 'whether', 'but' or . . . 'or'? But the biggest question is this. Why did I download Roger Whittaker to my iPod in the first place? This and other unanswered vexatious issues I had to leave out there on the highway, but it would take a day or two to do so.

I had learned a lot about myself and my relationship to the bike and my riding gear. All I can hope is that some passing rider found Glovey, took him in and that he's twisting the throttle of a Moto Guzzi. In other words, that he's gone to a better home. And the contributions of the chain, front sprocket, front and rear tyres and the old dirty oil have to be remembered and revered. Had I taken a jar with me, I'd have brought the oil back home and put it on the mantelpiece. Instead, it's gone into a drum somewhere in Perth. It's that callousness which shocked me and I believe I'm now more respectful to motorcycle parts as a result.

So the Suzuki V-Strom is cleaned and crated up. My socks, underwear and toothbrush are in the rubbish bin of this motel I'm staying in tonight. I have to consider the real possibility of being searched at Customs, who would be happier finding a tube of Semtex than coming across these hazardous items. Essential they have certainly been, and out of respect I gently placed — rather than tossed — them in the bin, but you can't cross international borders with a suitcase full of weapons like my possum merino riding socks that have been on my feet 9 hours a day for 35 consecutive days. I have met some wonderful people on my trip — from the generous hosts who gave me some real food and conversation to the roadhouse-counter girls who knew what an all-day breakfast really was. None of that parsley, garnishy rubbish. Just pile on more beans and mix in some fried onions to bind it together. I go home with a crumpled map book, a fridge doorful of cheap souvenir magnets, two speeding tickets, a helmet whose lining badly needs sterilizing and an iPod which is about to have 492 songs immediately erased.

Thank you for coming on my Australian ride. You may now have some time to recover, return to reading fiction books and get back to normal . . . but not for long.

They tell me that the breakfasts, road kill and freeways are bigger in America. Their sausage rolls have more than 25% meat, they have federal laws against listening to Julio Inglesias, and their traffic cops can be bribed. The questions are forming in my helmeted head already. What's the American equivalent of 'hair-gama'? Do their Greyhound drivers do crosswords or actually drive the bus? Are there any f**g BP stations over there? But the most serious question looming in my mind is: Is it possible to plot a route through all 48 continental states of the US without dipping into any state more than once . . . and get around in under six weeks?

That noise you hear as you quietly close this book? That's my throttle hand twitching in anticipation of Twisting Throttle America. I'm game if you are.

Sludder ma.

Acknowledgements

ANY SOLO JOURNEY is, of course, not really solo. There's the up-front guy, the figurehead, the stooge — and that'll be me. But back home at Twisting Throttle HQ I left a support crew without whom the lap of Australia would have been that much harder.

I wish I could devote a page or two here to the many company sponsors who gave me free things, like a bike, riding gear, insurance, satellite phone, laptop, camping gear, servicing on the way around, a courier backup for any parts, or even a T-shirt would have been great. But apart from the global movie deals this book will undoubtedly bring (and I'm thinking Cruise to play Twisting Throttle, and a Ducati to play my Suzuki), I am a fairly anonymous person who likes being self-sufficient and wouldn't have the gall to ask for handouts. That said, I'm interested in any corporate out there who would like to put their logo on my helmet in return for a swag of cash to finance my next trip so I can stay in places which have rooms with mini-bars, heating, white satin sheets and broadband. And you'd think Mrs Mac's, after the extensive airing they've had in this book, would at least send me some free samples.

But back to my support team. A motley bunch, to be true, but if I mention them here, that should buy me their help for the next adventure. So here goes.

Preparing and kitting out the bike needed someone with motorcycle knowledge and mechanical savvy, and who could be palmed off with a crate of beer in return for tens of hours of free labour. That someone was Gavin Sargent. 'Sarge' wired up the Suzuki so that the GPS, iPod, radar detector and helmet speakers worked — except when the radar detector picked up a signal and the iPod consequently started playing John Denver. That forced me to veer off the road, so I guess Sarge knew his stuff after all. He punctured both my tyres in his garage and set about repairing them, with me making notes, mentally calculating the odds (with a titter of concern) of successfully breaking a tyre bead in the outback. He installed a Scottoiler chain lube system and hard-wired the Baehr comms unit under the seat. He mounted a radiator guard and bash plate to protect the oil cooler and sump. But it wasn't all him doing the work. I made the cups of tea and swept up. When I bent the pannier rack after dropping the bike on a pre-trip run, he thwacked it with a large piece of wood. It lined up perfectly. If it wasn't for his habit of wearing his underpants outside his trousers, I'd have asked him along. Sorry, Gav, that last sentence was harsh, but thanks for your DIY genius. It was almost disappointing not to get a flat just to test how good your instructions were.

Mike Mahon, whose unique day job comprises sometimes managing a base in Antarctica, hard-wired up my top box with a power inverter which kept my laptop, cellphone, camera and hair dryer charged. He finally found a way of getting a dial-up connection working with roaming, so I could upload logs and photos to my website via cellphone. I suspect that if I had asked him he could have also manoeuvred a satellite over Australia to help with the signal.

Arthur, Chris and the team at Digitise set me up with a website which allowed followers to log in and see the progress and the day's photos, and read the scratchy logs. Thanks, Digies, that was a great service.

My mate Tim Coleman pirated the 492 iPod songs off the net. He included a Bucks Fizz track and renamed it 'Riding In The Outback' so I wouldn't delete it. As I said, the Twisting Throttle support crew were not selected on their integrity.

Over in Sydney, just over the harbour bridge, lives Le Compte de Monte Carlow, Steve Darwen, Comptesse Kay and tennis-ball-aholic dog, Scruff. Without the help of Steve, shipping the bike to and from Sydney would have been logistically nightmarish. He converted that into a dream by being my Australian minder. But he also had his other uses. Only a local knows how to properly eat a Harry's pie at Woolloomooloo. Steve and Kay's hospitality at both ends of the lap was wonderful. It was Steve and his mate Pete Windemeyer who decided that I needed a hand to navigate out of Sydney. Kay and Shelley rolled their eyes, knowing the familiar agenda that was developing. 'But what if I just turn north and follow the signs to Brisbane, lads?' 'No, mate, you need us to escort you. Tell you what, we'll quickly saddle up our beemers and get you clear of the suburbs.' Two days later I said goodbye to them just south of the Queensland border. These guys make an annual pilgrimage down to Philip Island on their bikes. They don't need much excuse. Thanks for the hand, Steve. No hard feelings about Scruff and my rear tyre, too. It needed a bit of a clean anyway.

In some places around Australia I enjoyed the luxury of staying in peoples' homes. There were Allen, Rona, Chris, James and Megan Larder in Mudgeeraba, Graeme and Diane Raymond in Surfers,

John and Geraldine McLean in Perth, Mal and Kathy Rayner in Rockingham, and Garth Irvin and Maxine Thornton in Boulder. I enjoyed the contents of their fridges and soft pillows. Thanks for the tour of Kal, Garth. Liked the red-light area and that miners' pub with those girls serving the middies. Don't you think they'd have been a bit cold? Strangely, all these families, soon after my arrival, asked me to remove my riding boots off their property. A unique Australian foot-wear custom, perhaps. Diane Fitzmaurice and Brian Parr in Melbourne were wonderful hosts who showed me around and wouldn't let me pay for anything.

The morale-boosting duties fell into several camps. First, there were the Dust Devils, a rag-tag mob of over-40s motorcyclists who can't decide if dark-side KTMs or BMWs are the number-one adventure bike. Gavin, Carol, Donald, Annette, Phil, Sharlane, Bill, Rosalie, Brent, Cheryl, Rob, Bridget, Sam, Mandy, John and Dorothy were with me in spirit and sometimes in body at the airport departing and arriving home. They all suffered my photo albums full of 800 photos and didn't complain. They gave me a handy helmet accessory which comprised an elastic band off which hung 20 corks. Good on you, Devils, thanks to you I didn't have a single fly problem.

At HarperCollins*Publishers* my sincere thanks to Lorain Day and her team for seeing an opportunity in what was originally a rookie's rambling manuscript and taking me on board. My fantastic managing editor is Kate Stone who must have thought she drew the short straw when she saw the photos. I believe Kate has been seen recently brows-ing around bike shops in Auckland.

My family were always checking the net for Twisting Throttle's progress and sent me emails of support. Mum, Alison and Raymond, Nikki and Lisa, Geoff, Maree, Sarah, Andrew and Matthew, Stephen, Lesley and Rachel, Joe, Mike and Bren, Steve and Emma. Sarah made a stunning hair-gama banner for the airport greeting party. Dad, who passed away in 2000, would have been on the edge of his armchair following progress, such was his interest in travel. At times I felt he was somewhere up there with an atlas tracing the route.

But the most important members of my support crew were back home here, paying the bills, watering the plants, going to work and school and quietly indulging their husband and father in his mid-life crisis. Robert, my son, is a signwriter. He designed and applied the stunning graphics to the bike's tank and fairing. Sophie, my daughter, missed me a bit judging by the strength of the hug I got on my return home. Robert, partner Elyse, and Sophie kitted me out with some Lonely Planet guides for Christmas. But the anchor person in the support crew was my wife, Sandy, who was the driving force behind this book making it to press. 'See if you can fund the next ride, Mike' were her poignant yet disquieting words. Always eager to pillion on the back of the Suzuki, Sandy drew the line at Australia. I must admit that posing with road kill, enjoying the company of blowflies, and living on Mrs Mac's meat-challenged products might well have tested our marriage. 'And,' as she said as we drove home from the airport, resigned to the fact that I couldn't carry too much duty-free on my bike, 'you can never have too many fridge magnets.'

That's what I call a support-crew team leader.